Ulrich Lossen

Portfolio Strategies of Private Equity Firms

GABLER EDITION WISSENSCHAFT

Innovation und Entrepreneurship

Herausgegeben von
Professor Dr. Nikolaus Franke,
Wirtschaftsuniversität Wien, und
Professor Dietmar Harhoff, Ph.D.,
Universität München

Innovative Konzepte und unternehmerische Leistungen sind für Wohlstand und Fortschritt von entscheidender Bedeutung. Diese Schriftenreihe vereint wissenschaftliche Arbeiten zu diesem Themenbereich. Sie beschreiben substanzielle Erkenntnisse auf hohem methodischen Niveau.

Ulrich Lossen

Portfolio Strategies of Private Equity Firms

Theory and Evidence

With a foreword by Prof. Dietmar Harhoff, Ph. D.

Deutscher Universitäts-Verlag

Bibliografische Information Der Deutschen Nationalbibliothek
Die Deutsche Nationbalbibliothek verzeichnet diese Publikation in der Deutschen Nationalbibliografie; detaillierte bibliografische Daten sind im Internet über <http://dnb.d-nb.de> abrufbar.

Dissertation Universität München, 2006

1. Auflage Juli 2007

Lektorat: Frauke Schindler / Stefanie Brich

Der Deutsche Universitäts-Verlag ist ein Unternehmen von Springer Science+Business Media.
www.duv.de

Umschlaggestaltung: Regine Zimmer, Dipl.-Designerin, Frankfurt/Main
Gedruckt auf säurefreiem und chlorfrei gebleichtem Papier

ISBN 978-3-8350-0577-8

Foreword

Driven by the convergence of international financial public markets, investors around the globe are searching for alternative asset classes which provide diversification of their portfolios while earning attractive returns. Private equity, denominating equity investments in privately held companies, promises to fulfill both criteria. Over the last three decades, the global private equity industry has experienced an enormous growth. Private equity has become an important ingredient in the portfolios of institutional investors, such as banks, insurance companies and pension funds.

Despite its increasing importance, relatively few are known about the characteristics and specialities of private equity. Therefore, practitioners are turning to researchers for systematic information in order to take sound investment decisions.

In his dissertation, Ulrich Lossen contributes to this need of information. Lossen applies advanced econometric methods to a unique data set which he assembled specifically for the purpose of this thesis. His analysis focuses on the choice of portfolio strategies by private equity firms and the impact of this choice on funds' performance. His research proceeds in three steps. First, Lossen models the trade-off between diversification and specialization in private equity funds theoretically. Secondly, he analyzes the influence of external factors on the choice of private equity firms to diversify their portfolios across different dimensions, such as financing stages, industries, and geographic regions. Finally, he examines the impact of such diversification on private equity funds' performance.

This book is the product of more than three years of intensive research which earned the author a doctoral degree at the Ludwig-Maximilian-University of Munich. Ulrich Lossen's studies of private equity funds are a remarkable contribution to the field. I am sure that these results will find the attention of practitioners and researchers alike.

Prof. Dietmar Harhoff, Ph. D.

Acknowledgements

"La cumbre no es más que una excusa para recorrer un bello camino."

Cristián García-Huidobro
(after the first Chilean ascent
of Mount Everest in 1992)

Though the ascent of a high mountain and the writing of a doctoral thesis appear unlike, they share many things in common. They are both exciting, joyful, yet delicate and demanding challenges. Along the quest, one's entire energy is focused on reaching the ultimate objective. Yet, it is the journey which reveals extraordinary experiences and genuine enrichment. It is on the path one overcomes throwbacks, achieves knowledge, and receives the support necessary to reach the top. Without the encouragement, critics, and support of many people I would not have been able to complete my thesis. I am deeply indebted to all of them.

First, and foremost, I wish to thank Dietmar Harhoff, my doctoral advisor for his support, encouragement and guidance throughout the past three and a half years. His enthusiasm and passion to empirical research has been a true inspiration to me. He has granted me a remarkable degree of freedom and has been a constant and reliable source of advice for my thesis. In particular, I wish to thank him for enabling me to stay at the MIT Sloan School of Management in Cambridge during my dissertation project.

Moreover, I would like to thank Christoph Kaserer, my thesis referee and scientific advisor, for his outstanding support and valuable advice.

I am grateful to Hans-Ulrich Küpper and Hubert Job, who have been my advisors during MBR studies.

For inviting me to Cambridge and for his advice during my stay at the MIT Sloan School of Management I wish to thank Eric von Hippel. Research and financial support from the German Academic Exchange Service DAAD for this stay is gratefully acknowledged.

My dissertation critically depended on the access to confidential data on private equity funds. I wish to thank the managing partners of the fund-of-funds investor for their trust and willingness to support my quest for information.

I am grateful to my past and current fellow doctoral students at INNO-tec and the Munich School of Management for maintaining an atmosphere of high spirits and their joint support.

In particular, I thank Karin Hoisl and Christian Tausend, who have become friends for the countless and fruitful discussions during past years. I am also grateful to Alexander Susanek for repeatedly reminding me about true importance in life. For turning my German-flavored English into a language trying not to give away the author's nationality, I am indebted to Melinda Lyman and Rosemarie Wilcox.

I especially wish to thank Mirka Wilderer for her continuous encouragement and support over the past three years, in particular in difficult times. It was her enthusiasm which motivated me to pursuit with my doctorate.

Anne Schröter has been a faithful support and source of energy for me in the past year. I deeply thank her for her long breath and understanding. She granted me an immense degree of freedom.

Finally, I cannot but express my deepest gratitude to my family, who supported me during the long way through higher education. They kept faith in my decisions and supported my activities. In particular, I highly acknowledge that only due to their warm support and understanding the many experiences of my numerous stays abroad became possible. It is their continuous encouragement and loving affection which accompanied my personal development. Thank you very much!

Ulrich Lossen

Table of Contents

List of Figures

List of Tables

List of Abbreviations

BO	buyout
CEPRES	Center for Private Equity Research
e.g.	for example
HHI	Herfindahl-Hirschman-Index
i.e.	that is
IPO	initial public offering
IRR	internal rate of return
MIRR	modified internal rate of return
NAV	net asset value
NBRM	negative binomial regression model
OLS	ordinary least squares
PE	private equity
PME	public market equivalent
Q-IRR	quasi-internal rate of return
Q-MIRR	quasi-modified internal rate of return
Q-PME	quasi-public market equivalent
TVE	Thomson Venture Economics
VC	venture capital
VIF	variance inflation factor

Chapter 1

Introduction

1.1 Portfolio strategies of private equity firms

Over the last three decades, the global private equity (PE) industry has experienced an enormous growth. According to the statistics of Thomson Venture Economics new funds raised worldwide by PE firms have grown from USD 1.7 billion in 1976 to USD 192.3 billion in 2005, with a peak of USD 260.6 billion in 2000.[1] PE firms are financial intermediaries providing investors with investments in privately owned companies, which offer the potential of extraordinary returns, but whose outcomes are highly uncertain and develop over a long period of time (Chan 1983, Amit, Brander & Zott 1998). Consequently, PE firms need to manage the performance of their funds. In order to do so, they have two complementary options. At the level of a single portfolio company, PE firms have developed various instruments to solve the selection and agency problems they face. Among the most important are: a detailed selection process (Tyebjee & Bruno 1984, Birley, Muzyka & Hay 1999), the staging of capital infusions (Gompers 1995), extensive control rights (Sahlman 1990), and the use of convertible securities (Gompers 1999, Schmidt 2003). In addition, PE firms are active investors who aim to increase the value of their investments (Gorman & Sahlman 1989, Wright, Hoskisson, Busenitz & Dial 2001). By means of these activities, a PE firm tries to optimize the return-risk characteristics of each single portfolio company. Over the last 20 years, these instruments have been analyzed in a large number of theoretical and empirical papers.

At the fund level, a PE firm can apply different portfolio strategies to manage the performance of its funds. On the one hand, it can focus on certain financing stages, industries, or countries in order to gain and benefit from specialized knowledge. On the other hand, it can invest in a variety of companies with different characteristics in order to diversify unsystematic risk. The decision determining portfolio composition plays a crucial role in the formation of a

[1] Thomson Venture Economics is a commercial provider of PE information. It runs one of the largest databases on PE: VentureXpert. For more information, go to www.ventureeconomics.com. The numbers are taken from a report listing commitments to PE funds by vintage years including TVE fund focus categories: Seed Stage, Development, Early Stage, Balanced Stage, Expansion, Later Stage, Buyouts, Recap, Turnaround, Generalist, and Other Private Equity. The report was generated on April 3, 2006.

PE fund. It is a long term strategic decision that is difficult to change. The maximum amount a PE fund is allowed to invest in a single company as well as in certain financing stages, industries, or countries is fixed in the partnership agreement with the limited partners, i.e., the investors. A deviation from this agreement is only possible if all limited partners approve. Furthermore, because of the private nature of portfolio companies the decision to fund companies in a certain financing stage, industry, or country involves investments in specialized assets (e.g. human capital and network ties). This fact becomes more and more important as economies globalize and technology cycles decrease. Together with the return-risk characteristics of the portfolio companies, the portfolio composition determines the return and risk of a PE fund.

In this thesis, the expression *portfolio strategy* denominates the level of diversification of a PE fund across five dimensions: (1) 'naive' diversification across the number of portfolio companies, (2) 'dynamic' diversification across time, 'systematic' diversification across (3) financing stages, (4) industries, and (5) countries.

The relationship between the choice of a portfolio strategy by a PE firm and its impact on PE funds' performance is outlined in Figure 1.1. Before a PE firm is able to start fundraising activities, the characteristics of the new fund have to be set including the portfolio strategy. Whether the PE firm will offer investors a widely diversified fund or a highly specialized fund depends mainly on two aspects. On the one hand, the PE firm has certain expectations regarding future investment opportunities. On the other hand, the PE firm has preferences concerning return and risk. Both aspects are influenced by a variety of external factors, which can be described by the following four groups: (1) the prediction of future economic development at the time of fund formation, (2) the conditions of the PE industry at the time of fund formation, (3) the characteristics of the PE firm and its management team, and (4) the characteristics of the fund itself.

Based on the expectations on future investments and its return-risk preferences, the PE firm chooses the portfolio strategy which maximizes its expected utility. The diversification level across the number of portfolio companies, time, financing stages, industries, and countries is set and fixed in due diligence documents.[2] Potential investors use this information in order to select funds suiting their investment strategy.

When the PE firm has reached its fundraising target, the new fund is legally formed. During the lifetime of usually ten to twelve years of a PE fund the PE firm searches for, invests in, manages, and exits attractive portfolio companies fitting into the fund's portfolio strategy. At the end of a fund's lifetime, the performance of the fund is realized and can be measured.

[2] It is assumed that PE funds can make take-it-or-leave-it offers to potential investors. This assumption is true for high quality PE firms with a good reputation and track record. These PE firms are frequently offered more capital than their fundraising target. Nonetheless, the assumption might not always be true for young PE firms or PE firms with a less successful track record.

Figure 1.1: Framework of thesis

The figure displays the relationship between the choice of portfolio strategies by PE firms and its impact on PE funds' performance

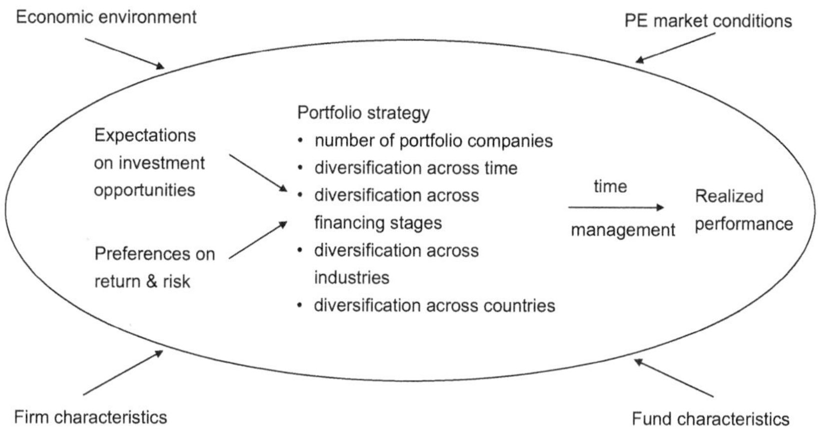

1.2 Objective of thesis

Despite its importance, little is known about portfolio strategies applied by PE firms, or about its impact on PE funds' performance. There are few empirical and theoretical articles dealing with aspects of the choice of portfolio strategies by venture capital (VC) firms (Gupta & Sapienza 1992, Norton & Tenebaum 1993, Cumming 2004, Kanniainen & Keuschnigg 2003, Bernile & Lyandres 2003). These studies generally agree that VC firms predominantly involved in seed and early stage financing prefer less industry diversity and a narrower geographic scope in their portfolio than VC firms focused on later stage financing, while bigger VC funds tend to have larger portfolios than smaller VC firms. Furthermore, little is known on the impact of diversification on PE funds' performance thus far. The empirical studies of Weidig & Mathonet (2004) and Schmidt (2004) shed some light on this important issue and report that shortfall probabilities and return variation across PE portfolios decrease with the number of companies in the portfolios. The first attempt to evaluate the impact of diversification across industries on the rate of return of PE funds presents no return penalty for diversified PE funds (Ljungqvist & Richardson 2003*a*).

The cited studies reveal interesting insights. Nevertheless, there is a lack of systematic information on the choice of portfolio strategies by PE firms and the impact of this choice on funds' performance. This thesis contributes in three steps to this research gap following the framework depicted in Figure 1.1. At first, a theoretical model is developed evaluating the trade-off between diversification and specialization in PE funds. The model is based on modern portfolio theory (Markowitz 1952, 1959) and provides a basis for the derivation of hypotheses for the empirical studies conducted in this thesis. Secondly, the external factors influencing the expectations and preferences of PE firms during the formation process of a new fund are empirically evaluated. The driving question is, what determines the choice of portfolio strategies by PE firms? Finally, the impact of diversification on PE funds' performance is empirically examined.

One limitation of this thesis should be acknowledged. It neither aims to discuss the efficiency of diversification at the level of a PE fund nor the right level for diversification within the vertical chain of portfolio company, fund, fund-of-funds, and investor. The thesis responds to the fact that very different portfolio strategies can be observed across PE funds. Hence, specialization or diversification at the fund level are viewed as rational, utility maximizing behaviors of PE firms. The objective of this thesis is to examine the economics underlying these decisions.

To conduct the empirical analysis, a unique and manually collected data set on PE funds is utilized. The information includes for each portfolio company a set of descriptive variables as well as the exact cash flows between the company and its fund. For the first time, the data allows, the exact evaluation of portfolio strategies applied by PE funds. The entire data set contains information about 6,758 investments made by 227 PE funds from 51 PE firms. To the best of my knowledge, it is one of the most comprehensive data sets on PE funds available to research.

To summarize, the thesis presents the first comprehensive evaluation of portfolio strategies applied by PE firms and the impact of these strategies on PE funds' performance. Hence, the results should prove to be important for both the research community as well as practitioners.

1.3 Basics of private equity financing

This section provides some basics of PE financing. First, the terms private equity, venture capital, and buyout capital are defined. Secondly, the dominant organization of PE funds – the private limited partnership – is explained. Finally, the management process of PE is briefly described.

With reference to Gompers & Lerner (2004, p. 17) *private equity* is defined as dedicated pools of capital which are managed by independent PE firms and focus on equity or equity-linked investments in privately held companies. PE is further categorized according to the development stage of the company funded:

Venture capital: The term VC is used to describe the provision of equity or equity linked capital to young, high growth companies which have a limited history of operation (Gompers & Lerner 2004). According to the status of operation, VC is divided into (AltAssets 2005, Thomson Venture Economics 2005):

- *Seed / early stage venture capital*: Seed capital refers to the provision of very early stage finance to a company which has not yet been established. Seed capital is often provided before institutional PE firms become involved. Early stage VC is provided to companies which have been recently established. It is used for product development, as well as initial marketing, manufacturing and sales activities.

- *Expansion / second stage venture capital*: It is provided for the first expansion of a company, which is already in production and shipment. The company is experiencing growth in inventory and accounts receivable. However, usually it is still not profitable.

- *Later / third stage venture capital*: The term denominates funding of a company, which has stable operations and is breaking even or profitable. The capital is used for further growth of the company.[3]

Buyout capital: A BO is the purchase of a company or a controlling interest of a corporation's shares or some part of business (AltAssets 2005). The focus of BO capital are mature companies with a proven track record. Various types of BOs can be divided, emphasizing each type one important element of the transaction. The most important are: leveraged BO (LBO), management BO (MBO), management buyin (MBI), recapitalization, and turnaround. The majority of classifications also assign mezzanine financing to BO capital because it is mostly used in BO transactions.

PE pools of capital are mostly arranged in closed funds with a definite lifetime of ten years, plus two years of potential prolongation. The dominant organizational form for PE funds is a *private limited partnership* (Fenn, Liang & Prowse 1995, Gompers & Lerner 2004). The senior managers of the PE firm serve as general partners and run the funds' activities. The investors are limited partners and provide the balance of the PE funds.[4] Limited partners monitor activities of general partners, but do not interfere in the daily management of funds.

The process of PE financing can be divided into four stages: (Bygrave & Timmons 1992, Gompers & Lerner 2004). (1) The *fund formation stage* contains the structuring, raising, and formation of a new fund. In this stage, the strategy of a fund and the compensation of the general partners is fixed in the partnership agreement. (2) The *investment stage* includes the generation of deal flow, the selection of attractive companies, and the structuring of transactions. (3) In the *management stage* a PE firm monitors the development of its portfolio companies and aims at adding value to them. (4) In the *exit stage* the PE firm sells successful companies either to the stock market (initial public offering) or other investors (strategic or financial) and returns capital to the limited partners. The process can be viewed as a cycle,

[3] Sometimes VC is also classified according to the financing round of a company. The first financing round in which a institutionalized PE firm gets involved is called 'A' round (Center for Private Equity and Entrepreneurship 2006). Accordingly, subsequent financing rounds are named 'B', 'C', etc. As a rule of thumb, 'A' and 'B' rounds are roughly equivalent to seed / early stage VC, 'C' and 'D' rounds to expansion / second stage VC, and 'E' and later rounds to later / third stage VC. However, an exact correspondence can only be reached by looking at the status of operation of a young company when a financing round happens.

[4] The general partners usually contribute a very small proportion of the fund's capital (commonly between 1% to 2%) in order to align the interests of both parties.

because PE firms typically raise an additional fund at about the time the investment stage for an existing fund has been completed.

1.4 Structure of thesis

The thesis is structured into seven chapters. Following the introduction, *chapter 2* gives an overview of related literature and previous research of interest for the conducted analysis. Studies on the return and risk of PE financing are summarized before the results of articles dealing with portfolio strategies of PE firms are discussed. Finally, research gaps are identified and the contribution of this thesis is highlighted.

Chapter 3 examines the trade-off between specialization and diversification in PE funds in a theoretical model. An extension of modern portfolio theory allows to deduct the optimal level of diversification in a PE fund. The chapter starts with a review of modern portfolio theory, proceeds with the development and discussion of the optimum, and ends with implications for the empirical analysis.

The data used throughout this thesis is outlined in *chapter 4*. The first part of the chapter describes the composition of the data set and discusses potential selection biases. The entire sample consists of 227 PE funds covering the whole spectrum of PE financing from small seed/early stage VC funds to large BO funds. In the second part of the chapter, the variables used in the empirical analysis are described.

Chapter 5 aims at evaluating factors influencing the expectations and preferences of PE firms during fund formation. Since the expectations and preferences of a PE firm are unobservable, determinants of portfolio strategies applied by PE firms are examined. For each dimension of diversification, hypotheses are derived and comprehensive empirical analyses are carried out. In particular, 'naive' diversification across the number of portfolio companies, 'systematic' diversification across financing stages, industries, and countries as well as 'dynamic' diversification across time are explained by a variety of factors. A consolidation of the results concludes the chapter.

The focus of *chapter 6* is the impact of diversification on the performance of PE funds. After the description of the subsample used in this chapter, the underlying hypotheses are derived. Next, descriptive analysis provides initial insights into research questions, before multivariate regression analysis tests the hypotheses. The impact of diversification on the performance of a PE fund is examined, utilizing three measures: (1) rate of return, (2) intra-fund variation of return, and (3) shortfall probability.[5] Finally, the influence of intra-fund variation of return and shortfall probability on the rate of return of PE funds is studied.

A summary in *chapter 7* concludes the thesis. It recapitulates the main results and highlights implications for the management of PE funds.

---

[5] The measures are explained in detail in chapter 4.

Chapter 2

Related literature and previous research

2.1 Introduction

The institutionalization of PE began only after World War II (Pratt 1988). The first research papers on PE were published in the late seventies. However, systematic research did not accelerate until the mid-nineties when larger data sets became available to researchers. Most of the articles can be classified into two broad groups. The first tries to answer the question how PE firms choose, structure, and manage their investments. A special focus in this field has been drawn on the various types of information asymmetries and principal agent problems which are inherent in PE investing, and on the potential solutions the different parties can use to solve these conflicts. The second group of articles aims at quantifying and explaining the performance of PE investments. One major objective of this stream of literature is to compare the performance of PE investments to the performance of public markets.

As there are no public markets for PE investments, data on private equity investments' rates of return are difficult to obtain. Two early articles analyzing the return and risk of PE investing were published in 1989. Chiampou & Kallett (1989) calculated annual average time-weighted returns for 55 funds of US based independent VC firms using quarterly net asset values over the holding period of 1978 to 1987. Bygrave, Fast, Khoylian, Vincent & Yue (1989) were the first study based on data from Thomson Venture Economics (TVE) founded in 1985. The analysis contains 140 US VC funds which were started between 1971 to 1984. Since 2000, the number of articles on the return of PE investments has grown steadily due to the availability of larger data sets and an increasing interest in PE, provoked by the boom of the PE industry in the late nineties.

The aim of this chapter is to summarize previous research and related literature. Chapter two is organized as follows: *Section 2.2* summarizes studies analyzing the return and risk of PE investments. Among these, two different groups of studies can be identified according to their unit of analysis. The first group of articles investigates the performance of single PE investments. The second group's computations are based on PE funds.[6] Theoretical and empirical research on diversification within PE funds is reviewed in *section 2.3*. First, studies are summarized which analyze the choice of portfolio strategies by PE firms. Afterwards, the results of articles which give an initial view of the impact of diversification on PE funds' performance are reviewed. An examination of existing research gaps and the contribution of this thesis to meet those gaps in *section 2.4* concludes this chapter. Each section contains the most important articles relevant to the thesis. In each section, the cited articles are presented in chronological order of their first publication.

2.2 Return and risk of private equity investing

2.2.1 Return and risk of single private equity investments

A large study on the return and risk of single VC projects was published by Cochrane (2001) based on a data set of 7,765 investments accounting for 16,613 financing rounds.[7] The information on VC financed companies was taken from the Dowjones VentureOne database.[8] To calculate returns for companies which had resulted in an initial public offering (IPO) or a trade sale, the data was augmented with information from the SDC Platinum Corporate New Issues and Mergers and Acquisitions (M&A) databases. Accordingly, Cochrane had no returns for companies, which were still privately held or liquidated. Therefore, he applied sample selection correction by calculating the probability of going public or having a trade sale dependent on the age of a company. Cochrane finds that the return distribution of VC investments is right skewed and is best represented by means of a lognormal distribution. With correction of sample selection, he reports a mean arithmetic return of 59% and a standard deviation of arithmetic returns of 107%. The estimation of a capital asset pricing model using the S&P500 index as market parameter returns an arithmetic beta (slope) of 1.9. However, this large systematic risk does not entirely explain the high mean return, resulting in an arithmetic alpha (intercept) of 32%. The large mean arithmetic return and alpha result from the right skewness of the return distribution. VC investments are like options: "they have a small chance of a huge payoff" (Cochrane 2001, p. 2).

In their study of the investment behavior of PE managers, Ljungqvist & Richardson (2003*b*) analyzed the rate of return of single portfolio companies. The sample consists of 2,744 investments between 1981 and 1998, provided by one of the largest PE investors in the USA, which covers all investments made by PE funds sponsored by the investor. The study reveals that

[6] A third group of articles studies the returns of publicly traded PE vehicles, which will not be further discussed in the scope of this thesis. For a recent study on publicly traded PE vehicles compare Zimmerman, Bilo, Christiophers & Degosciu (2005).

[7] The study of Cochrane was again published in 2005 in the Journal of Financial Economics (Cochrane 2005).

[8] Dowjones VentureOne is a commercial provider of VC information. It is marketing one of the largest databases on VC backed companies. For more information, go to www.ventureone.com.

improvements in investment opportunities have a positive effect on portfolio companies' rates of return, whereas the amount of capital competing in an industry for deals reduces rates of return. The latter result links the 'money chasing deals phenomena' reported by Gompers & Lerner (2000) to portfolio company returns. Furthermore, they report BO transactions to outperform VC investments.

Cumming & Walz (2004) studied the impact of a large range of variables on the rate of return of 2,498 fully realized and 2,619 partially realized or unrealized investments. Their data set was provided by the CEPRES Center of Private Equity Research.[9] To correct for potential bias in the reporting of unrealized investments, a Heckman sample selection procedure was estimated. For fully realized investments, an average IRR of 68,7% is reported.[10] Explaining the heterogeneity of returns, Cumming & Walz identify a positive relationship of investments' return with the quality of legal systems, syndication, and the use of convertible securities. In contrast, portfolio companies' returns correlate negatively with the amount of new funds raised in the portfolio companies' country in the year of investment, the number of portfolio companies managed by one partner, and the holding of a board seat.

An additional study of return and risk of single PE projects calculated a variety of return and risk measures for a sample of 2,380 PE investments between 1975 and 2003, comparing the measures to various public market indices (Ick 2005). The calculations were based on cash flows provided by the CEPRES Center of Private Equity Research. According to the study, later stage investments generate large positive excess returns, whereas early stage investments underperform in relation to the NASDAQ Composite index. Using risk adjusted performance measures, the major finding holds that early stage investments substantially underperform against public markets. Later stage investments do somewhat better and match public market performance.

2.2.2 Return and risk of private equity funds

An initial attempt to quantify the success of European and US VC funds was undertaken by Hege, Palomino & Schwienbacher (2003). They defined success as the proportion of all exits in a VC fund which were realized either through an initial public offering or a trade sale. The sample of 82 funds was derived from a questionnaire sent to VC firms in Europe and USA in 2001. According to the authors, European VC funds were less successful than their US counterparts and early stage VC funds were less successful than later stage VC funds. However, the authors do not explain to what extent the 82 funds included in the analysis were mature, nor do they discuss potential sample selection bias. In the second part of their analysis Hege et al. estimate returns of a subsample of portfolio companies in the TVE databases. As the procedure used to

[9] The CEPRES Center of Private Equity Research is a joint research initiative between VCM VC Management, a German PE fund-of-funds, and the Department of Finance of the Johann Wolfgang Goethe-University of Frankfurt/Main. For further information, see www.cepres.de.

[10] IRR is the discount rate that yields a net present value of zero for the cash flow history of an investment. A mathematical definition of IRR is given in subsection 4.4.2.

calculate the returns of the portfolio companies appears questionable, the results of the article will not be discussed further in this chapter.

A more comprehensive study on the performance of PE funds is presented by Ljungqvist & Richardson (2003*a*), who studied the return and risk pattern of 73 mature PE funds, which are provided from one of the largest PE investors in the USA. The sample is skewed towards large BO funds and seems to slightly outperform the TVE population. The authors report a mean IRR of 19.8% and a standard deviation across funds' IRR of 22.3 percentage points net of fees and carried interest. The mean IRR of mature BO funds in the sample is higher than the mean IRR of mature VC funds, 21.8% compared to 14.1%, respectively. Matching the cash flow streams to public market indices, the average PE fund generates excess returns of five percent relative to public markets. Ljungqvist & Richardson also tried to evaluate the systematic risk of PE funds by assigning portfolio companies to the 48 industry betas provided by Fama & French (1997) and calculating value-weighted betas for each fund. BO funds average a portfolio beta of 1.08 whereas VC funds reveal an average beta of 1.12. This suggests that investments in PE funds are slightly riskier than in public markets. However, the procedure might misstate the risk of private companies, as for instance, portfolio companies of VC funds are young firms with high technical and market risk, which still need to provide proof of their business concept. Similar arguments can be applied to BO companies, although the effect will be smaller as most BO firms are established companies with a proven history. Lastly, Ljungqvist & Richardson estimated determinants of the PE funds' excess returns. They report a non-linear relationship between fund size and excess return, and a negative influence of the total amount committed to BO (VC) funds in the year the sample BO (VC) fund was raised. Finally, the authors find neither a significant effect on the excess return of portfolio betas nor of some basic measures representing portfolio diversification.

Using a sample of 1,245 PE funds provided by TVE, Jones & Rhodes-Kropf (2003) investigated the relationship between idiosyncratic risk and rate of return of PE funds. The authors claim that PE firms are unable to diversify the unsystematic risk in its portfolio companies because of the limited partnership contract design. As a result, equilibrium competitive fund returns should increase in the amount of idiosyncratic risk rather than unsystematic risk. Using quarterly take downs, distributions and NAVs, they report equal-weighted mean IRR's net of fees and carried interests of 19.25% and 9.67% for VC funds and BO funds, respectively. The funds' returns are extremely volatile with cross-sectional standard deviations of annualized IRR's of 51 percentage points for VC funds and 31 percentage points for BO funds. Running quarterly time-series regressions of value weighted portfolios, the quartile of funds with the greatest idiosyncratic risk earns the highest alpha, while the quartile of funds with the lowest idiosyncratic risk earns the smallest alpha. This result holds for VC funds as well as for BO funds.

Studying returns across subsequent funds of PE firms, Kaplan & Schoar (2003) report a strong persistence: "General partners (GPs) whose funds outperform the industry in one fund are likely to outperform the industry in the next fund vice versa."[11] They also find a concave relationship between fund size and the rate of return of a PE fund. The number of first time funds entering the industry in the vintage year of a PE fund lowers its rate of return. Funds with lower sequence numbers are more affected by this effect than funds with higher sequence numbers. VC funds outperformed BO funds, ceteris paribus. Furthermore, the article studies the relationship between fund performance and fundraising success. The size of PE funds increases with the rate of return of previous funds and the sequence number of funds managed by the same PE firm. The results are based on a sample of 746 largely liquidated PE funds which were provided by TVE.

Kaserer & Diller (2004*c*) provided a comprehensive study on the rate of return of European PE funds. Their data also originates from TVE and consists of 190 mature VC and BO funds which were managed by European PE firms. The rate of return in the sample varies substantially with average IRRs net of fees and carried interests of 12.0% and 13.4%, and standard deviations of IRR of 22.1 percentage points and 16.2 percentage points for VC funds and BO funds, respectively. Using the MSCI Europe Index net of costs, they calculate public market equivalents which are slightly lower than one, suggesting that European PE has underperformed European public markets. In their multivariate analysis the authors are able to verify the persistence of returns across subsequent funds of a PE firm. They also find a positive relationship between absolute inflows in European PE markets in the vintage year of a fund and its rate of return, whereas the opposite relationship holds true between relative inflows in European PE market segments (VC or BO) in the vintage year of a fund and its rate of return. In addition, the rate of return of the MSCI Europe Index in the vintage year of a fund has a negative impact on its rate of return. Using the same sample of European PE funds in another study, the authors calculated Sharpe ratios of 35.9% for VC funds and 35.7% for BO funds (Kaserer & Diller 2004*b*).

The comparison between NAV and present value of future cash flows of liquidated funds at the end of each year after the eighth birthday of a PE fund shows, that NAV in the last part of a fund's lifetime is a good proxy of future cash flows (Gottschalg, Phalippou & Zollo 2004). Accounting of PE firms appears to be conservative with an average ratio of present value of future cash flows to NAV of 1.03. Similar to prior studies a high heterogeneity between individual fund performance is reported. Gottschalg et al. also calculate average betas of 1.7 for BO funds and 1.6 for VC funds, documenting a large level of systematic risk relative to public markets. In multivariate regression analysis, betas are positively related to the rates of return of PE funds. Additionally, there is a concave relationship between fund size and rate of return of BO funds, whereas VC funds show a positive linear relation between fund size and rate of return. A higher proportion of European investments is associated with a lower rate of return. First time funds perform worse than later time funds, whereas funds of PE firms which often take a lead position in their portfolio companies perform better than funds of PE firms which seldom take a lead position in their portfolio companies. According to Kaserer & Diller (2004*c*), the total capital committed to PE in the vintage year of a fund is positively related to

[11] The paper was again published in 2005 in The Journal of Finance (Kaplan & Schoar 2005).

its rate of return. Finally, the study indicates that fund performance co-varies positively with business cycles as well as stock market cycles. The data set consists of 642 PE funds derived from the records of TVE.

2.2.3 Comparison of previous results

The various analyses on the rate of return and risk of PE investing can be summarized as follows. Generally authors agree that returns on PE investing are highly volatile and right skewed. There is a nonlinear relationship between the size of a fund and its rate of return. The quantity of investment opportunities available to PE firms (either measured through the number of portfolio companies funded by PE in a year or through the total amount of money flowing in the PE industry) has a positive impact on the rate of return of a PE fund. In contrast, the amount of competing money flowing into a segment of the PE market (measured as the relative amount of capital flowing into one industry, country, or financing stage) has a negative impact on the rate of return of a fund investing in that segment. Likewise, PE funds started in 'hot' public markets (measured by the return of public market indices) seem to perform worse than PE funds started in 'cold' public markets. There is a persistence of PE returns across subsequent funds of PE firms. Finally, US investments outperformed European investments in the past.

However, there is no agreement on whether PE outperformed or underperformed public markets in the past. The same holds true for the comparison of VC investments and BO transactions. While Kaplan & Schoar (2005) as well as Kaserer & Diller (2004*c*) report superior returns of VC funds compared to BO funds, many other studies indicate the opposite (Ljungqvist & Richardson 2003*a*, Ljungqvist & Richardson 2003*b*, Hege et al. 2003, Ick 2005). The different result may be explained by the use of different data sets in these studies. Another unanswered question is how much systematic risk PE investments carry. The different authors state betas ranging from 0.5 to 1.9 for VC and from 1.1 to 1.7 for BO (Cochrane 2005, Ljungqvist & Richardson 2003*a*, Gottschalg et al. 2004). The large heterogeneity between the results derives from the difficulties in calculating betas due to the lack of time series of market valuations for PE funds. Finally, there are differing results on wether the return of PE funds is driven by their systematic and/or unsystematic risk. Ljungqvist & Richardson (2003*a*) find no significant effect of weighted portfolio betas on the rate of return of PE funds. In contrast, Gottschalg et al. (2004) report a positive relationship between funds' betas and rates of return. Following a different approach, Jones & Rhodes-Kropf (2003) document a positive relationship between the idiosyncratic risk of a PE fund and its rate of return.

The conformity of many results has to be treated with some reservation. Four out of the six studies on the performance of PE funds work with mainly equal data sets provided by TVE (Kaplan & Schoar 2005, Jones & Rhodes-Kropf 2003, Kaserer & Diller 2004*c*, Gottschalg et al. 2004). As a consequence, further empirical research on the performance of PE is needed to verify the presented results.

2.3 Portfolio strategies and optimal structure of private equity funds

2.3.1 Choice of portfolio strategies

In the past, only scant research focused on portfolio strategies applied by PE firms. Gupta & Sapienza (1992) analyzed the preferences of 169 US VC firms in regard to industry diversity and geographic scope of their investments. The study is based on the information published in the 1987 issue of Pratt's Guide to Venture Capital Sources (Pratt & Morris 1987).[12] Results show that (1) VC firms specialized in early stage ventures prefer less industry diversity and narrower geographic scope relative to other VC firms, (2) corporate VC firms prefer less industry diversity but broader geographic scope relative to non-corporate VC firms, (3) larger VC firms prefer greater industry diversity and broader geographic scope relative to smaller VC firms, and (4) older VC firms prefer more industry diversity relative to younger VC firms.

In order to analyze how VC firms manage their risks – either via diversification of their investments or via specialization in certain areas – Norton & Tenebaum (1993) carried out a survey of 98 US VC firms. Their main result is that VC firms predominantly involved in seed financing are diversified across a smaller number of industries and portfolio companies than VC firms less involved in seed financing. In addition, the authors calculated the correlations between the percentages of a VC fund invested in different financing stage across their sample. They find the percentages of two successive financing stages (e.g. first and second stage VC) to be positively correlated with each other, while the percentages of capital invested in non-consecutive financing stages (e.g. first and third stage VC) are negatively correlated with each other. Norton & Tenebaum interpret both results as evidence for their specialization hypothesis and reject the diversification hypothesis.

Kanniainen & Keuschnigg (2003) and Bernile & Lyandres (2003) presented theoretical research on the optimal size of VC funds. In a double-sided moral hazard framework, Kanniainen & Keuschnigg (2003) emphasize the trade-off between the number of portfolio companies of a VC fund and the advisory effort allocated to each company leading to an unique optimal number of portfolio companies. In comparative statics the optimal number of investments in a VC fund grows greater with increasing returns of portfolio companies. In contrast, the optimum declines with the acquisition price the VC fund needs to pay for a given stake in the portfolio companies as well as with the entrepreneur's effort cost. Bernile & Lyandres (2003) generalize the results by relaxing some of the assumptions made by Kanniainen & Keuschnigg. Yet, the effect of exogenous variables on the optimal number of portfolio companies in a VC fund are equal.

[12] Pratt's Guide to Venture Capital Sources is an industry guide book. At present, it contains information on more than 1,400 sources of institutional VC. It is regularly published by TVE. For further information see www.ventureeconomics.com.

A more recent article empirically studies the determinants of VC portfolio size identifying the following relations (Cumming 2004): (1) the number of portfolio companies tends to be smaller for independent limited partnerships and corporate VC funds than for government funds, (2) funds that belong to VC firms with two or more VC funds have fewer investments in their portfolio, (3) bigger funds (measured by total commitments) invest in a larger number of portfolio companies than smaller funds, (4) a positive relationship exists between the number of managers and quantity of portfolio companies, (5) the higher the proportion of early stage investments the larger is the number of portfolio companies, and finally, (6) the larger the proportion of investees who reside in provinces, in which the VC firm had no offices, the lower is the quantity of portfolio companies. Moreover, characteristics of deal structure influence portfolio size of VC funds. The number of portfolio companies in a VC fund is smaller when the proportion of staged investments, of syndicated investments, or the percentage of ownership is higher. The sample consists of 104 private independent limited partnerships, 18 corporate funds, 15 government funds, 29 Labour-Sponsored VC Companies[13] and 48 institutional funds started between 1991 and 2000. It was provided by the Canadian VC Association (CVCA).

2.3.2 Portfolio diversification and performance

So far, a systematic study evaluating the impact of diversification on the return and risk of PE funds is missing. Nonetheless, some studies on the performance of PE funds shed some light on this issue.

In their study of the return and risk pattern of 73 mature PE funds Ljungqvist & Richardson (2003*a*) included four measures of portfolio diversification: (1) the number of portfolio companies, (2) the fraction of portfolio companies in the dominant industry, (3) the proportion of invested capital in the dominant industry, and (4) a Herfindahl-Hirschman-Index of the portfolio weights of each company. The authors discover a negative impact of the number of portfolio companies, whereas the other three measures have a positive effect on the rate of return of PE funds. However, none of these effects are statistically significant. Moreover, the results might suffer from a drawback of the data set. The authors do not have a complete listing of all portfolio companies of the analyzed PE funds. The reconstruction of the portfolio composition of each fund relies on various external sources of information. Because of this procedure, portfolio listings are very likely to be incomplete.

An examination of the return distribution of direct VC investments, investments in VC funds, and investments in VC fund-of-funds indicates diversification benefits on the shortfall probability of VC investing (Weidig & Mathonet 2004). Analyzing 5,000 direct investments in US ventures, the probability of loss and probability of total loss for direct VC investments

[13] Labour-Sponsored Venture Capital Companies (LSVCC) are unique to the Canadian VC industry. Ayayi (2002) provides the following definition for LSVCC: "Labour sponsored VC corporations are special corporations designed primarily to provide VC to and promote investment in Canadian SMEs whose shares are not publicly traded. The funds are capitalized by a large number of individual shareholders whose incentive to invest is encouraged by the provision of Canadian federal and provincial tax credits in exchange for committing their capital for eight years to inherently risky SMEs."

are 42% and 30%.[14] According to the returns of 282 European VC funds provided by TVE corresponding values for VC funds are 30% and 1%. The figures decrease to 1% and 0% in a simulation of 50,000 fund-of-funds of 20 randomly chosen European VC funds. Additionally, the authors report average losses to drop from -85% for direct VC investments to -29% for VC funds and to -4% for the simulated fund-of-funds in those cases in which a negative return is achieved.

Studying the return of 642 US direct PE investments, Schmidt (2004) reported comparable results. In a bootstrapping approach, PE portfolios of different sizes were simulated, reducing the average variation in returns by 80% through building portfolios of 20 PE investments.

2.3.3 Comparison of previous results

Comparing the results, VC firms predominantly involved in seed and early stage financing seem to prefer less industry diversity and a narrower geographic scope in their portfolio than VC firms predominantly involved in later stage financing. Bigger VC funds have larger portfolios than smaller VC funds. In periods with high acquisition prices, VC firms fund a smaller number of companies. Moreover, the results suggest a risk reducing effect of 'naive' diversification in PE funds. With an increasing number of portfolio companies, shortfall probability and variation across the rates of return of PE funds decreases.

However, doubts remain whether VC firms specialized in seed and early stage ventures invest in more (Cumming 2004) or fewer companies (Norton & Tenebaum 1993) than VC firms predominantly involved in later stage financing. Furthermore, comprehensive results are presently missing on whether diversification has a systematic effect on the rate of return and risk of PE funds. The studies of Weidig & Mathonet (2004) and Schmidt (2004) only document the effects of 'naive' diversification by increasing the number of portfolio companies in PE portfolios, but do not consider the composition of PE funds or the specific characteristics of portfolio companies. Furthermore, these analyses are mainly based on simulation. The authors do not study whether their simulated portfolios can be observed in reality.

2.4 Summary: research gaps and contribution of thesis

The existing literature reveals several research gaps. First, a theoretical model explaining the effect of diversification on the return and risk of PE portfolios is missing. The work of Kanniainen & Keuschnigg (2003) and Bernile & Lyandres (2003) focuses uniquely on the optimal number of investments in a PE fund. Other dimensions of portfolio composition such as financing stages, industry, or geographic scope are not considered. Since PE funds – despite all differences to public equity (Wright & Robbie 1998) – are portfolios of risky assets, *chapter 3* extends modern portfolio theory into a simple, yet novel direction evaluating the trade-off

[14] The data set was constructed and first used by Cochrane (2001).

between diversification and specialization in PE funds. The model enables the analysis of the impact of different diversification levels on the expected rate of return and risk of a PE fund. The results are consistent with the empirical findings of Gupta & Sapienza (1992) and Norton & Tenebaum (1993), as well as Weidig & Mathonet (2004) and Schmidt (2004).

So far, only the number of investments in a PE fund has been analyzed in a multivariate analysis using information on actual PE transactions (Cumming 2004). Gupta & Sapienza (1992) based their calculations on preferences published in the 1987 issue of Pratt's Guide to VC Sources. Norton & Tenebaum (1993) used data from a survey to US VC firms. As a result, there is a lack of understanding concerning the level of diversification in PE funds. Can different degrees of diversification be solely explained by characteristics of PE firms or do market conditions equally matter? *Chapter 5* offers answers to this question. In order to do so, a comprehensive analysis is conducted on the choice of portfolio strategies by PE firms. The number of portfolio companies, diversification across time, financing stages, industries, and countries are explained through a variety of factors.

Thirdly, the impact of diversification on the performance of PE funds is mainly unknown. Weidig & Mathonet (2004) and Schmidt (2004) only addresses 'naive' diversification through increasing the number of investments in a PE fund, but they do not consider the composition of funds nor the specific characteristics of portfolio companies. In addition, as their analyses were mainly based on simulation the authors do not verify whether their results can be observed in reality. Ljungqvist & Richardson (2003*a*) go a step further calculating two ratios for the concentration of their portfolios across industry. However, as they only studied the effect of these measures on the rate of return, they neglect other performance characteristics of PE funds in their sample. As a response, *chapter 6* will analyze the impact of diversification across various dimensions on rate of return, intra-fund variation of return and shortfall probability of PE funds.

Finally, ambiguity presently exists in the relationship between the rate of return and risk of a PE fund. On the one hand, many authors do not include a measure of risk in their regressions explaining the rate of return of PE funds. On the other hand, studies which include measures of risk reveal diverging results. In order to contribute to that research question, *chapter 6* will also examine the influence of intra-fund variation of return and shortfall probability as proxies for risk on the rate of return of PE funds.

Chapter 3

Optimal level of diversification in private equity funds

3.1 Introduction

The studies of Gupta & Sapienza (1992) and Norton & Tenebaum (1993) have provided interesting insights into the choice of portfolio strategies by PE firms. However, their argumentation leads to conclusions which need to be scrutinized. The main result of their analysis is that VC firms predominantly involved in seed and early stage financing prefer less industry diversity and a narrower geographic scope in comparison to VC firms focusing on later stage financing. Assuming that seed and early stage investments are riskier than later stage investments, the four authors identified specialization as a strategy to lower the risk of a VC fund. They argue that concentration in particular areas leads to specialized knowledge which allows the PE firm to make superior selection decisions and to provide more value-adding services. If that holds true, specialization should also increase the expected rate of return of a VC fund. Thus, a VC firm could lower its risk and enhance its expected rate of return at the same time by specializing in particular areas. Such a negative risk-return-relationship is at odds with the usual assumption in financial theory that a lower level of risk is related to a lower expected rate of return, and vice versa. Second, if specialization is the dominant strategy for VC firms to lower their risk and concurrently to alter their expected rate of return, why do VC firms still spread their funds across different areas? According to the survey of Norton & Tenebaum (1993), more than half of the respondents' VC funds had investments in seven or more industries. One third of their sample invested even in ten or more industries. Lastly, gaining specialized knowledge for a certain area is not for free. In order to do so, a PE firm has to invest in specialized assets (e.g. human capital and network ties).[15] Moreover, the arguments of Gupta & Sapienza (1992) and Norton & Tenebaum (1993) seem to be contradicted by the results of Weidig & Mathonet (2004) and Schmidt (2004). These studies report risk reduction through 'naive' diversification.

[15] I will refer to that point later in detail, when I introduce the concept of set-up costs a PE firm has to pay before it is able to invest successfully in a financing stage, industry, or country.

Augmenting the number of portfolio companies in (simulated) PE portfolios reduces both the probability of loss and the average variation in returns.

The objective of this chapter is to model the trade-off between diversification and specialization in PE funds. In order to do so, the portfolio model presented by Markowitz (1952, 1959) is extended by set-up costs a PE firm has to pay before investing in a cluster of companies. Such an *investment cluster* can be a financing stage, industry, or country. This structure allows the analysis of the impact of different diversification levels on the rate of return and risk of a PE fund. The results obtained from this model are consistent with the empirical findings of Gupta & Sapienza (1992) and Norton & Tenebaum (1993) as well as Weidig & Mathonet (2004) and Schmidt (2004).

In particular, this chapter aims at (1) modeling the trade-off between diversification and specialization in PE funds, (2) giving a rationale for the behavior of early stage venture capitalists reported by Gupta & Sapienza (1992) and Norton & Tenebaum (1993), (3) exploring the impact of diversification on PE funds' risk and return, and (4) providing a theoretical framework that serves as a basis for the derivation of hypotheses for the empirical work of this thesis. Therefore, specific economic aspects are pronounced without trying to rebuild reality completely. The model does not intend to give normative advice to PE firms in which technologies, geographic areas, or financing stages they should invest. Nor does it discuss whether a PE fund is the right vehicle to diversify within the vertical chain of portfolio company, fund, fund-of-funds, and investor.

The remainder of this chapter is organized as follows: *section 3.2* briefly summarizes modern portfolio theory. In *section 3.3* the development of the model is described, key findings are interpreted, and possible extensions are discussed. Implications for the empirical research in this thesis conclude the chapter in *section 3.4*.

3.2 Modern portfolio theory

Modern portfolio theory is used as a modeling framework because PE funds, despite their differences to public equity (Wright & Robbie 1998), are portfolios of several risky assets similar to mutual funds. Sharpe (1964) postulated that the Capital Asset Pricing Model - and therefore modern portfolio theory - applies to all capital assets.[16] Modern portfolio theory was first introduced by Markowitz (1952, 1959) and further developed by Sharpe (1964) and Lintner (1965) to the Capital Asset Pricing Model. Markowitz aimed at providing an adequate theory of investment that covered the effects of diversification when risks are correlated (Markowitz 1999).

According to modern portfolio theory, the investor is assumed to commit a given amount W_0 of his present wealth to one or more risky assets. The terminal wealth of any risky investment is a probabilistic term. Letting W_t be the terminal wealth, the rate of return of the investment is

[16] Also compare Markowitz (1999).

$$R = \frac{W_t - W_0}{W_0} \tag{3.1}$$

This relationship allows to express the investor's utility in terms of R, since terminal wealth is directly related to the rate of return and vice versa (Sharpe 1964). It is further assumed that the investor is acting on the basis of the expected value $\mu = E(R)$ representing the expected rate of return of an asset and on the standard deviation $\sigma = \sqrt{V(R)}$ representing the risk of an asset (Tobin 1958). Assuming the investor is risk-averse, she prefers a higher expected rate of return to a lower, ceteris paribus, and a lower value of risk to a higher, ceteris paribus (Sharpe 1964). Additional assumptions of modern portfolio theory are frictionless market conditions of no taxes, no transaction costs, perfect divisibility of assets, and complete information (Merton 1987). Under these assumptions, the expected return and risk of a portfolio of $i = 1, 2, \ldots, N$ risky assets is calculated as follows:

$$\mu_P = E(R_P) = \sum_{i=1}^{N} X_i \mu_i \tag{3.2}$$

$$\sigma_P = \sqrt{V(R_P)} = \sqrt{\sum_{i=1}^{N} X_i^2 \sigma_i^2 + \sum_{i=1}^{N} \sum_{\substack{j=1 \\ j \neq i}}^{N} X_i X_j \sigma_{ij}} \tag{3.3}$$

where μ_i is the expected rate of return of risky asset i, σ_i is the standard deviation of the expected rate of return of risky asset i, and σ_{ij} is the covariance between the rate of return of risky asset i and the rate of return of risky asset j. X_i is the fraction of the amount W_0 invested in risky asset i. It is assumed that the investor spends her entire initial wealth:

$$\sum_{i=1}^{N} X_i = 1. \tag{3.4}$$

In the case that short sales are not possible, the following equality holds: $0 \leq X_i \leq 1$. In the case with unlimited short sales, the constraint is $-\infty < X_i < \infty$.

The investor maximizes her utility by choosing the portfolio which optimally fits her individual preferences according to the expected rate of return and risk. The optimal portfolio will always be an efficient portfolio. A portfolio is said to be efficient if (and only if) no alternative exists with either (1) the same μ and a lower σ, (2) the same σ and a higher μ, and (3) a higher μ and a lower σ (Sharpe 1964).

Consequently, the combination of several risky assets enables a risk-averse investor to achieve a level of utility which she could not achieve through investing in only one risky asset. Equation (3.3) shows that the risk of a portfolio depends not only on the variance of its assets, but also on the covariances between these assets. Accordingly, a risk-averse investor can increase her utility through diversification as long as there is no perfect correlation between the assets' rates of return. In the context of a portfolio, the risk of an asset can be divided into systematic and unsystematic risk. Systematic risk derives from a common factor and is represented by the covariances with the other assets.[17] Unsystematic risk corresponds to the residual variance of an asset's return which cannot be explained by the common factor. Only unsystematic risk can be diversified.

3.3 Optimal number of investment clusters

3.3.1 Assumptions

In the following, I propose a set of assumptions which allow the analysis of the choice of portfolio strategies by PE firms and its impact on PE funds' rate of return and risk. The presented model takes the view of a single PE firm as sole decision maker. The PE firm does not take into account the decisions taken or strategies applied by other PE firms. Therefore, a specific set of parameter values holds for one specific PE firm. For other PE firms different sets of parameter values are valid according to the characteristics of each PE firm.

The PE firm faces a global investment scope which consists of $i = 1, 2, \ldots, N$ potential portfolio companies. The investment scope can be divided in $k = 1, 2, \ldots, M$ investment clusters. An investment cluster is defined as a group of companies which are connected by a common factor. This can either be a financing stage, industry, country, or a combination of these. Figure 3.1 illustrates the European investment scope with respect to various Western European countries and three different industries (biotechnology, software, and consumer goods). For instance, a PE fund can focus only on German speaking countries but can spread its money across all three industries. In contrast, it may specialize in biotechnology but may fund companies all over Europe. This simple example shows the variety of feasible portfolio strategies a PE firm can choose from.

To keep calculations simple, I assume the following distribution of companies' returns. A priori all companies have the same expected rate of return μ and the same risk σ:

$$E(R_i) = \mu_i = \mu \qquad \text{for all } i = 1, 2, \ldots, N \tag{3.5}$$

$$V(R_i) = \sigma_i^2 = \sigma^2 \qquad \text{for all } i = 1, 2, \ldots, N \tag{3.6}$$

The correlation of companies' returns which belong to the same investment cluster r_{ij}^{w} is perfect, resulting in:

[17] In the Capital Asset Pricing Model the common factor is the global economy. Thus, systematic risk of an asset is represented by the covariance between the return of the global market portfolio and the return of the asset (Sharpe 1964).

Figure 3.1: Illustration of European investment scope - industries versus countries
The figure shows the number of portfolios companies which were funded by PE between 1995 and 2005 in the software, biotechnology, and consumer goods industries across Western European countries. Source: Thomson Venture Economics.

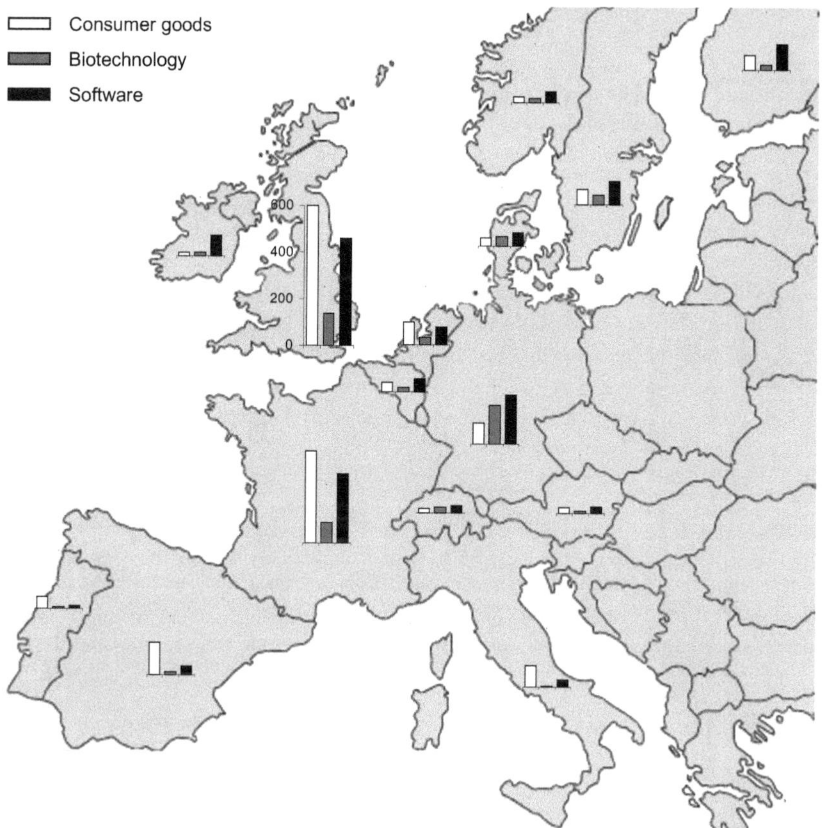

$$Cov(R_i; R_j) = \sigma_{ij}^w = \sigma_i \sigma_j = \sigma^2 \qquad \text{for all } i, j \in IC_k \tag{3.7}$$

In contrast, the correlation of companies' returns which belong to different investment clusters r_{ij}^b is assumed to be 0:

$$Cov(R_i; R_j) = \sigma_{ij}^b = r_{ij}^b \sigma_i \sigma_j = 0 \qquad \text{for all } i \in IC_k, j \in IC_l, k \neq l \tag{3.8}$$

Companies that have different economic characteristics, i.e., that do not belong to the same investment cluster, are more likely to have lower covariances than companies which show similar economic characteristics, i.e., which belong to the same investment cluster. The economic development of companies within one investment cluster is connected by the common factor of the cluster. Examples for events which affect all companies in one specific investment cluster, but which influence companies in other investment clusters to a much lesser extent, can be technology shifts, consumer trends, or changes in legislation.

To account for the private nature of potential portfolio companies, the PE firm has to pay a certain amount of set-up costs C to gain specialized knowledge in each investment cluster it acts in. Without this knowledge the PE firm is not able to successfully make transactions in the investment cluster. The costs emerge from hiring an investment manager, building up and maintaining an investment cluster specific network, initial trial and error processes, gaining reputation, operating an office in a new country, etc.[18] The set-up costs are supposed to be fixed costs (Sahlman 1990), which are independent of the number of portfolio companies the PE firm finances in an investment cluster. Furthermore, for simplicity set-up costs are assumed to be constant across investment clusters:

$$C_k = C \qquad \text{for all } k = 1, 2, \ldots, M \tag{3.9}$$

It is important to note that this assumption does not mean that set-up costs are equal across different PE firms. Equation (3.9) only proposes that set-up costs are constant for one PE firm across all investment clusters. Different PE firms have different abilities and therefore may face different set-up costs.

The PE firm has a fixed budget to invest, i.e., the size of its fund, which represents its initial wealth W_0. I assume that the PE firm spreads its budget symmetrically across K investment clusters. Thus, the fraction of the PE firm's budget in the kth investment cluster is $1/K$ with:

[18] The terminus set-up costs might be interpreted in the sense that these costs have to be paid only the first time a PE firm interacts in a new investment cluster, and a second, follow-up fund of the same PE firm does not have to pay these costs. But this is false. Most of the set-up costs have to be paid during the whole period of time a PE firm funds companies in the specific investment cluster: for instance the costs for rental and administrative personnel running an office in a country, the salary of an investment manager specialized in a technology, the information costs for following the technological progress in an industry, or the costs for maintenance of a cluster specific network.

$$\sum_{k=1}^{K} \frac{1}{K} = 1 \tag{3.10}$$

Within each investment cluster, the PE firm invests in a finite number of companies $i = 1, 2, \ldots, I_k$. This can be justified by the fact that the share a PE firm can buy from a company is not perfectly divisible. The fraction of the budget of an investment cluster k in company i is represented by X_{ki}. In addition, the PE firm has to reimburse the set-up costs from the investment cluster's budget. Consequently, the fraction of an investment cluster's budget used for the set-up costs is $\frac{C}{W_0/K}$. It is assumed that the PE firm is able to invest its entire fund. This assumption is formally represented by (3.10) and:

$$\sum_{i=1}^{I_k} X_{ki} + \frac{C}{W_0/K} = 1 \qquad \text{for all } k = 1, 2, \ldots, K \tag{3.11}$$

PE firms usually do not invest in government bonds. Neither are they able to sell a company's shares in advance, i.e., before they have invested in the company. Consequently, it is assumed that no riskless asset exists and that short sales are not possible.

Another important assumption of the model is that the PE firm chooses the number of investment clusters according to its preferences. An alternative view would be that the limited partners decide on the level of diversification. However, this assumption would be less realistic as the amount a PE fund plans to invest in certain financing stages, industries, and countries usually is written down in the offer memorandum sent to potential investors in the fund raising process of a fund. Investors face a take-it-or-leave-it offer. This is especially true for PE firms with a good track record.

3.3.2 Efficient combinations of companies

Under the assumptions of the previous section the expected rate of return and risk of a single investment cluster are calculated as follows:[19]

$$\mu_k = E(R_k) = \mu - K(1+\mu)\frac{C}{W_0} \tag{3.12}$$

$$\sigma_k = \left(1 - \frac{C}{W_0/K}\right)\sigma \tag{3.13}$$

As mentioned above, a fund consists of $k = 1, 2, \ldots, K$ investment clusters with equal fractions $(1/K)$. Using (3.12), the expected rate of return of a fund is:

[19] The complete mathematical calculations are given in the appendix.

$$\begin{aligned}\mu_F &= E(R_F) = \sum_{k=1}^{K}\left(\frac{1}{K}\mu_k\right) \\ &= \mu_k \\ &= \mu - K(1+\mu)\frac{C}{W_0}\end{aligned} \tag{3.14}$$

Attention must be drawn to two aspects of this result. First, due to the assumed equality of companies' rates of return, the expected rate of return of a fund is equal to the expected rate of return of investment clusters. Second and more important, the expected rate of return of a fund depends not only on the expected rate of return μ of its companies, but also on the number of investment clusters K and the set-up costs C. All else being equal, the expected rate of return of a fund declines linearly with the number of investment clusters it contains (see Figure 3.2). The magnitude of the decline is determined by the set-up costs C.

Figure 3.2: Expected rate of return of a private equity fund

The expected rate of return of a PE fund decreases linearly with the number of investment clusters. The slope is determined by the extent of set-up costs.

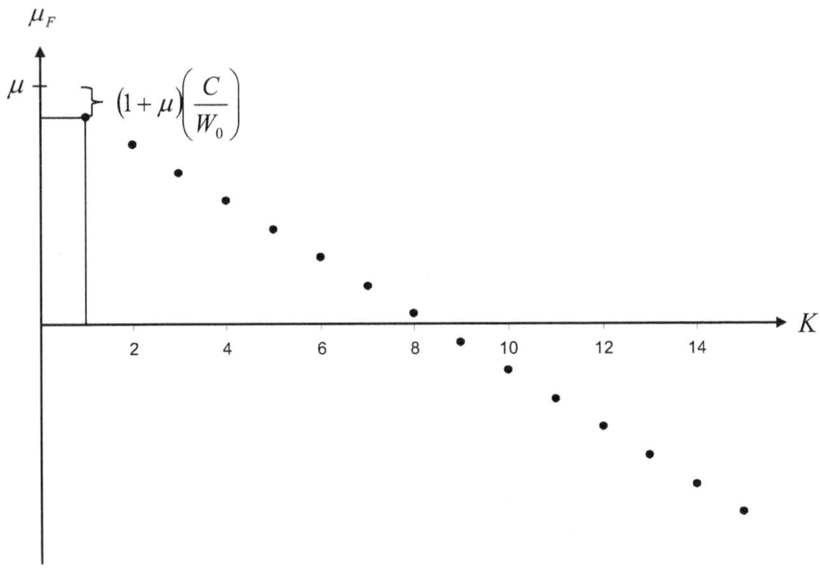

In addition to (3.13), the covariance between investment clusters is needed in order to calculate the expected risk of a fund. As the returns of companies of different investment clusters are uncorrelated, the covariance between investment clusters is 0.[20] Consequently, the expected risk of a fund is:[21]

$$\sigma_F = \left(1 - \frac{C}{W_0/K}\right)\sqrt{\frac{1}{K}}\sigma \tag{3.15}$$

The risk of a fund depends on the number K of investment clusters as well as the set-up costs C. The first and second derivative of (3.15) with respect to K show that with an increasing number of investment clusters risk of a fund diminishes at a decreasing marginal rate.[22] In case, the PE firm only invests in one investment cluster, risk assumed its maximum of $(1 - C/W_0)\sigma$. As the PE firm invests in more clusters risk declines. It becomes 0 in the extreme and unrealistic case that the PE firm spends its whole budget on set-up costs, i.e., $CK = W_0$. Figure 3.3 shows the risk of a fund as a function of the number of investment clusters it contains.

Figure 3.3: Risk of a private equity fund

The risk of PE funds diminishes at a marginal rate with the number of investment clusters.

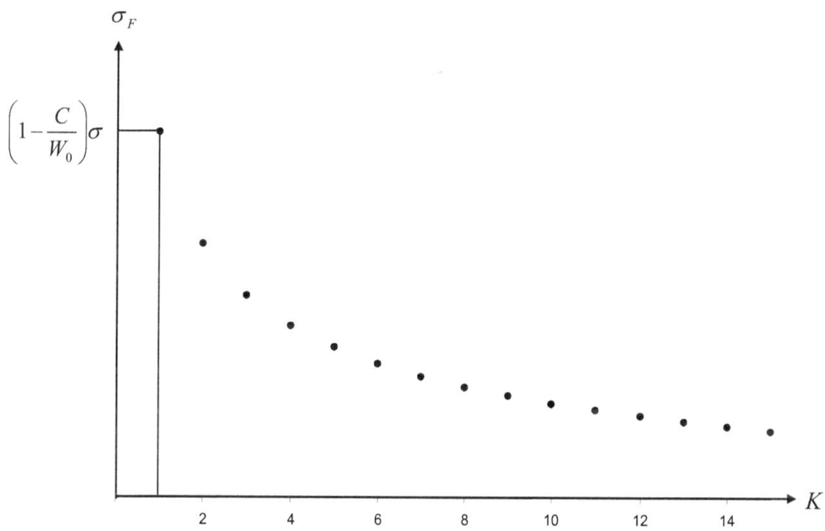

Finally, the set of efficient μ-σ-combinations is obtained by drawing the expected rate of return of a fund μ_F against the risk of a fund σ_F. For $K = 1$ the fund has a maximum expected

[20] Subsection 3.3.5 discusses the consequence of a more realistic correlation structure between companies and investment clusters.

[21] The complete mathematical calculations are given in the appendix.

[22] For the complete mathematical calculations see equations (A.13) and (A.14) in the appendix.

rate of return of $\mu - (1+\mu)(C/W_0)$ and a maximum risk of $(1 - C/W_0)\sigma$. With the increasing number of K of investment clusters, the expected rate of return and the risk are decreasing. In sum, the result represents a positive relationship between expected rate of return and risk (Figure 3.4).

Figure 3.4: Efficient set of return-risk combinations

The efficient set of return-risk combinations displays a positive relationship between the expected rate of return and risk of a PE fund.

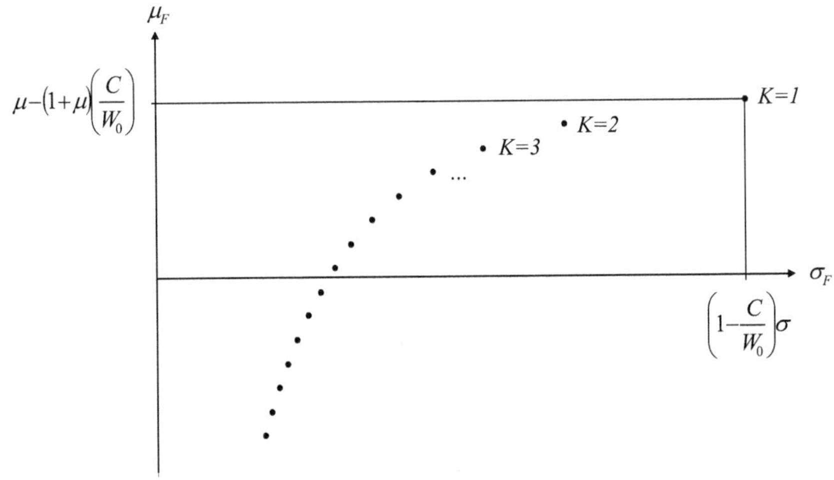

3.3.3 Choice of the optimal portfolio

The PE firm chooses the portfolio, i.e., the number of investment clusters, which maximizes its utility. I assume that the PE firm acts as a risk-averse decision maker. Its risk-aversion stems from the fact that the PE firm's ability to raise new funds depends highly on the performance of its past funds (Kaplan & Schoar 2005). A PE firm whose fund is performing below average will have difficulties raising capital for its following fund or even will not be able to raise any new funds. The negative relationship between prior fund performance and fundraising ability is smaller for older PE firms with a larger number of prior funds. These PE firms are better able to survive the poor performance of one particular fund because of their past track record.

According to modern portfolio theory, I assume that the PE firm's preferences can be represented by a utility function based on the expected rate of return and risk of a fund: $U = u(\mu_F, \sigma_F)$ (Tobin 1958). For a risk-averse decision maker the utility function has the following properties:

$$\frac{\partial U}{\partial \mu_F} > 0 \tag{3.16}$$

$$\frac{\partial U}{\partial \sigma_F} < 0 \tag{3.17}$$

The indifference curves are convex upwards, i.e., the rise in expected rate of return, at which the PE firm is willing to take one unit of additional risk, enhances with the increasing level of risk. In the following calculations, I assume the specific utility function:

$$U = u(\mu_F, \sigma_F) = \mu_F - \frac{\alpha}{2}\sigma_F^2 \tag{3.18}$$

First, it fulfills the above described characteristics. Second, for $\alpha > 0$ it is equivalent to the class of exponential Bernoulli-utility functions $u(x) = 1 - e^{-\alpha x}$ (Schneeweiss 1967). This utility function assumes constant absolute risk aversion. For $\alpha > 0$ the PE firm is risk-averse. The larger α is, the more risk-averse the PE firm. The PE firm maximizes its utility by choosing among all possible μ_F-σ_F-combinations, the combination placing it on the indifference curve representing the highest level of utility.[23] Figure 3.5 shows an example for an optimum containing four investment clusters.[24]

Using (3.14), (3.15), and (3.18) the optimal number of investment clusters can be calculated by maximizing the utility with respect to K:

$$\max_K u(\mu_F, \sigma_F) = \mu - K(1+\mu)\frac{C}{W_0} - \frac{\alpha}{2}\left(1 - \frac{C}{W_0/K}\right)^2 \frac{1}{K}\sigma^2 \tag{3.19}$$

Solving (3.19), the optimal number of investment clusters K^* is:[25]

$$K^* = \frac{\sqrt{(\alpha C\,(\alpha\sigma^2 C + 2W_0 + 2\mu W_0))}\sigma W_0}{2CW_0 + 2\mu C W_0 + \alpha\sigma^2 C^2} \tag{3.20}$$

Comparative statics reveal the following characteristics. First, an increase in the set-up costs C leads to a decrease in the optimal number of investment clusters K^*, ceteris paribus. Second, an extension of the fund size W_0 results in a rise in the optimal number of investment clusters K^*. Third, the more risk-averse the PE firm is, i.e., the larger α is, the higher the optimal number of investment clusters K^* becomes. Fourth, growth in the expected rate of return of portfolio companies μ induces a reduction in the optimal number of investment clusters K^*.

---

[23] Would K be continues the optimal portfolio would be the osculation point between the indifference curve and the efficient set of μ_F-σ_F-combinations, i.e., the point where the marginal personal 'preference-rate' of substitution between expected rate of return and risk would equal the marginal rate of substitution offered by the efficient set of μ_F-σ_F-combinations.

[24] Figure 3.5 is based on the following parameter values: $\mu = 0.2$, $\sigma^2 = 0.6$, $W_0 = 1$, $C = 0.02$, and $\alpha = 1,29$.

[25] The proof is given in the appendix.

Last, the bigger the risk of portfolio companies σ is, the higher turns out to be the optimal number of investment clusters K^*.

Figure 3.5: Choice of the optimal portfolio

A PE firm chooses the number of investment clusters placing it on the indifference curve representing the highest level of utility.

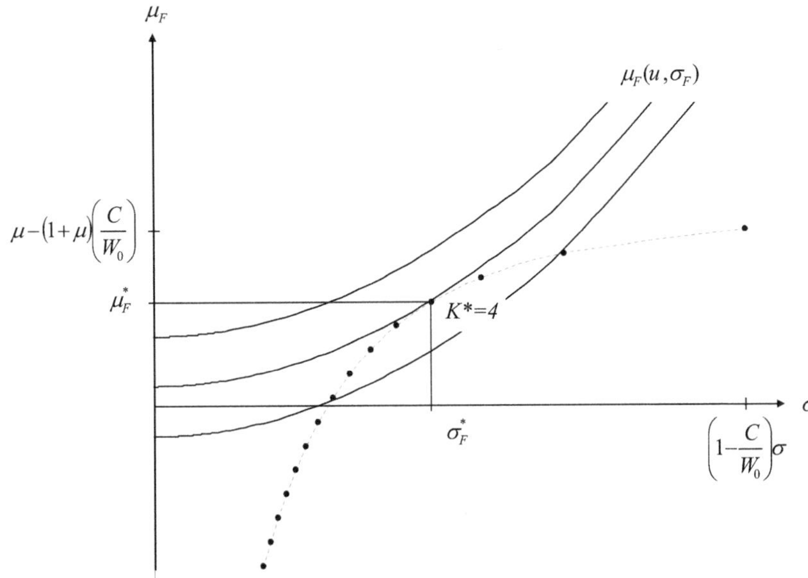

3.3.4 Interpretation of key findings

The model shows that a PE firm can choose between different combinations of expected rate of return and risk of its fund by investing in different numbers of investment clusters. By increasing the number of investment clusters a PE firm is able to lower the risk of its PE fund. However, by doing so the expected rate of return decreases. The higher the set-up costs are, the bigger the drop will be in the expected rate of return which is caused by the investment in an additional cluster. Thus, the set-up costs can be interpreted as the price of diversification, i.e., the price of risk reduction.

The negative relationship between the number of investment clusters and the expected risk of a PE fund explains the effects of 'naive' diversification reported by Weidig & Mathonet (2004) and Schmidt (2004). A random sample of companies selected from a large number of different companies will contain companies from several investment clusters. The more companies are included in the sample the larger the average number of investment clusters. Schmidt (2004) reports a diminishing marginal rate of risk reduction. This is in line with equation (3.15), which represents the expected risk of a PE fund as a function of the number of investment clusters. Moreover, one has to remember that in reality the correlation of the rate of return of companies belonging to the same investment cluster is not perfect. This fact fosters the effects of 'naive' diversification.

The PE firm chooses the number of investment clusters, which correspond to the utility maximizing portfolio of companies. Depending on the PE firm's preferences regarding the expected rate of return and risk, an optimal number of investment clusters exists, which determines the optimal level of diversification in PE funds. The simultaneous consideration of the expected rate of return and risk explains why PE firms neither put their money in one investment cluster only, nor spread it among all available investment clusters. This result is in line with the empirical findings of Gupta & Sapienza (1992) and Norton & Tenebaum (1993) who report that VC funds invest only in a few technologies, geographic areas, or financing stages.

Comparative statics reveal two further explanations for the empirical findings. First, the model confirms that larger PE funds invest in more investment clusters, ceteris paribus. Second and more important, the model provides a possible explanation for the observation of Gupta & Sapienza (1992) and Norton & Tenebaum (1993) that early stage VC funds contain less investment clusters than later stage VC funds. The first derivative of the optimal number of investment clusters with respect to the set-up costs is negative. Thus, the higher the set-up costs, the lower the optimal number of investment clusters. I argue that the set-up costs of investment clusters including early stage companies are higher than the set-up costs of investment clusters containing later stage companies. For instance, the more advanced a technology is in its life cycle, the more information is available about its possible uses, about its social acceptance, first successes, etc. Additionally, the costs for obtaining this information will be lower as the information becomes more widely spread. As a result, a PE firm has to invest less in assets which are specific for this technology. The same is true for countries. The more advanced a company is in its life cycle the more visible it becomes outside its country. Consequently, a PE firm specialized in later stage companies needs to invest less in country specific assets. In sum, the set-up costs for PE firms predominantly involved in early stage financing are higher than for PE firms predominantly involved in later stage or BO financing.

Comparative statics also suggest that the more attractive the average investment opportunity is, the less diversified PE funds are, ceteris paribus. A rise in the expected rate of return of portfolio companies leads to a decrease in the optimal number of investment clusters in a fund. Equivalent, the less riskier the investment opportunities are, i.e., the smaller the risk of portfolio companies is, the minor will be the optimal number of investment clusters in a PE fund.

Furthermore, the analysis may add an additional explanation for the popularity of syndication in VC financing. Manigart et al. (2004) reported that almost 30% of all European VC deals are syndicated according to statistics of the EVCA. Brander, Amit & Antweiler (2002) report a similar percentage for Canada. Many different reasons are mentioned for syndication in literature (Bygrave 1987, Bygrave 1988, Manigart, Lockett, Meuleman, Wright, Landstrom, Bruining, Desbriéres & Hommel 2004, Brander et al. 2002, Admati & Pfleiderer 1994, Sorenson & Stuart 2001, Lerner 1994). One argument is that syndication enables VC firms to increase portfolio diversification by allowing them to invest in deals which otherwise would be too large. According to my model, frequent syndication may enable the VC firm to lower the set-up costs for specific investment clusters. For instance, Sorenson & Stuart (2001) find that the probability that a VC firm invests in a company located far away increases, if there is a syndication partner with whom it has previously co-invested, and if the syndication partner is located near the company. Thus, the syndication partner reduces the set-up costs for its geographical area, which would otherwise be too costly for the VC firm.

3.3.5 Discussion of assumptions and further extensions

The assumptions of the previous sections are made for two reasons. First, the model should emphasize the trade-off between diversification and specialization in a clustered investment scope. Second, the model should be solvable without the use of simulation techniques. This implies that some of the assumptions can be extended to more realistic scenarios. In the following paragraphs the most important extensions and their consequences are briefly discussed.

First, I assume that the set-up costs are equal for all investment clusters. Due to the history of a PE firm and its team members, it is more realistic that some investment clusters are less costly to enter than others. The consequence for my model would be that the decline in the expected rate of return of the fund would no longer be linear. The PE firm would first choose to invest in the investment cluster with the lowest set-up costs, followed by the investment cluster with the second lowest set-up costs, and so on. Consequently, each PE firm would select different investment clusters according to its idiosyncratic abilities. However, the main result of my analysis would remain: with an increasing number of investment clusters the expected rate of return as well as the risk of the fund decreases.

Second, I presumed that all companies a priori have the same expected rate of return and risk. Letting μ_i und σ_i differ leads to a similar outcome than varying set-up costs. There would be an optimal order of investment clusters as well as an optimal set of companies in each of the clusters. The same result would be achieved if one allows a more realistic correlation structure between companies' rates of return, assuming that on average the correlation between the rates of return of two companies belonging to an investment cluster is higher than for two companies of different investment clusters. The only difference would be that the PE firms could also gain moderate risk reduction by investing in companies belonging to the same investment cluster. Permitting such a flexible structure of companies' returns requires the use of simulation and optimization techniques to determine the optimal number of investment clusters. Nonetheless, the relationship between the expected rate of return and the expected risk of a fund depending on the number of investment clusters stays positive.

A more restricting assumption is that PE firms act on the basis of unlimited liability. Sahlman (1990) first mentioned that the carried interest PE firms receive on the capital gain of a fund has the pay-off structure of an option. The carried interest does not participate in a negative outcome of the fund. Thus, the PE firm has only limited liability. Still, Golier, Koehl & Rochet (1995) have shown that in the case of limited liability a risk-averse decision maker with a Bernoulli utility function will choose only mean-variance efficient portfolios. Furthermore, PE firms are forced to invest at least one percent of the commitments as limited partners to participate in negative outcomes of a fund. Again, this suggests that the main result of the model remains.

The discussion shows that the model is quite robust against extensions of the assumptions. Making the model more realistic requires simulation and optimization techniques. However, the main results remain.

3.4 Summary: implications for empirical analysis

One major goal of this chapter was to provide a theoretical framework in order to derive hypotheses for the empirical work of this thesis. The model provides elementary hypotheses for both research questions, which will be empirically tested in chapters 5 and 6. It is possible to predict both the choice of portfolio strategies by PE firms as well as its impact on funds' return and risk. The most important predictions are: First, the more promising the expectation about future investment opportunities are, i.e., the better the return-risk characteristics of potential portfolio companies appear, the less diversified a PE fund should be. Second, risk aversion of a PE firm should have a positive effect on the level of diversification of PE funds. Third, the higher the set-up costs of investment clusters, in which the PE fund is acting, the lower the observed level of diversification. Furthermore, with an increasing level of diversification, the rate of return as well as total risk of a PE fund should diminish. Finally, as there is neither an investment in riskless asset, nor the possibility of short selling, nor a liquid secondary market for PE, the relationship between the expected rate of return and total risk of a PE fund should be positive.

To be able to test these predictions in multivariate analysis, two additional steps are taken in the following chapters. The hypotheses have to be further specified and the measurement of key variables has to be defined.

Chapter 4

Construction of data set and variables

4.1 Introduction

The term 'private' is indicative of one of the main challenges for empirical research of the PE industry. There is no liquid secondary market for PE investments comparable to public stock exchanges. Transactions are traded in private environments, and therefore, detailed information on PE investments is unavailable to the public. As long as the parties involved agree to keep transaction information private, no data is available to outsiders. Access to comprehensive data on PE transactions requires the collaboration of insiders.

The data set used in this thesis is derived from the records of a European fund-of-funds investor which were made available within a research cooperation between the fund-of-funds investor and the ODEON Center of Entrepreneurship at the Ludwig-Maximilian-University of Munich. The entire sample consists of 227 PE funds. The level of detail of the data set qualifies to calculate comprehensive measures for the level of diversification in a PE fund. The availability of the entire gross cash flow records between portfolio companies and its funds allows for an evaluation of the performance of PE funds through three measures: (1) rate of return, (2) intra-fund variation of return, and (3) shortfall probability. The additional variables utilized in this thesis are grouped into the categories: economic environment and PE market condition, as well as PE firm and fund characteristics.

This chapter aims at providing an overview of the data and variables used in this thesis. To indicate the advantage of the data set used in this thesis, *section 4.2* presents advantages and drawbacks of the most prominent PE data sets used by other authors. The overview aims at providing a point of reference for the data set used in this thesis. *Section 4.3* describes the data set used in this thesis discussing the source, composition, and potential selection biases. In order to test the theoretical conclusions of the previous chapter on the choice of portfolio strategies of PE firms and its impact on the performance of PE funds, a variety of variables have to be specified. *Section 4.4* defines the variables utilized in the empirical analyses of chapters 5 and 6.[26] A resume of the advantage and drawback of the data set used in this thesis in *section 4.5* ends the chapter.

4.2 Data sets used by other authors

4.2.1 Thomson Venture Economics

The most commonly used data set is an anonymous extraction of the TVE database. Different versions of this data set are used by Jones & Rhodes-Kropf (2003), Kaplan & Schoar (2005), Kaserer & Diller (2004*c*), and Gottschalg et al. (2004). Gottschalg et al. provide a detailed description of the TVE data, estimating that the records of TVE cover 88% of all VC funds and 50% of all BO funds in terms of capital committed. In terms of number of funds, it should cover cash-flow series for 40% of all European and US PE funds.

The biggest advantage of the TVE data set is its sample size as it covers the major parts of the PE universe. Additionally, the data set includes net cash flows and NAV on a quarterly basis.[27] Among its disadvantages are the lack of cash flows between portfolio companies and funds, making the calculation of portfolio companies' performance impossible. Additionally, the coverage and assignation of portfolio companies to funds varies heavily across different funds. Gottschalg et al. (2004, p. 35) state: "[...] despite all these efforts a complete coverage of all investments by all funds remains difficult to achieve." A comparison of the data set used in this thesis with the commercially available records of TVE reveals two sources of potential errors. On the one hand, the coverage of portfolio companies of a PE fund is often incomplete. On the other hand, portfolio companies are frequently assigned to the wrong fund in a sequence of funds managed by the same PE firm.[28] Finally, parts of the data of TVE are attained through self reporting by PE firms. Thus, there is a small but positive probability of error due to intentional reporting of better results than effectively achieved.

In summary, the data sets provided by TVE allow researchers to analyze the net performance of a large sample of PE funds. However, they do not qualify for studies aiming to evaluate the composition of PE funds nor do they allow to measure the performance of single portfolio companies. This judgement is confirmed by Gottschalg et al. (2004, p. 36): "We thus cannot compute performance at the investment level or decompose residual values into which type of on-going investment it is made of."

[26] The definition of variables in this chapter also avoids unnecessary duplications in chapters 5 and 6.

[27] The term net cash flows describes the cash flows between a PE fund and its investors (limited partners) net of management fees and carried interests. NAV is equal to the assets of a PE fund minus its liabilities at a certain point of time. The NAV of a PE fund consists mainly of the value of the unrealized portfolio companies.

[28] See also Ljungqvist & Richardson (2003*a*), footnote 15.

4.2.2 Dataset of Ljungqvist & Richardson

Ljungqvist & Richardson had access to the investment data of "one of the largest institutional investors in PE in the U.S." (Ljungqvist & Richardson 2003*a*, p. 6). Their data set contains the exact net cash flow history of all PE funds the institutional investor had funded between 1981 and 2001. Additionally, they are able to match nearly the entire sample to funds recorded in TVE. Yet, the data set only accounts for a small fraction of PE funds reported by TVE (73 mature funds started between 1981 and 1993 compared to 692 mature funds reported by Kaplan & Schoar (2005) for the same period of time). In terms of capital committed, the data set contains 17.5 % of total commitments to VC and 29.3 % of total commitments to BO compared to TVE.

The advantages of the data set are: (1) provision of the net cash flow records with size and timing, (2) coverage of more than a quarter of all capital committed to BO funds, and (3) little potential of erroneous data.[29] Nonetheless, the data set has the following shortcomings: (1) the data set is biased towards large BO funds, and VC funds are underrepresented (Ljungqvist & Richardson 2003*a*); (2) the sample size of 73 mature funds is relatively small; (3) only cash flows net of carried interests and management fees are reported; (4) the data set does not contain a complete listing of all portfolio companies of the funds.

In conclusion, the data set available to Ljungqvist & Richardson gives a very detailed insight into the cash flow and return patterns of large BO funds. However, a transfer of the results to small VC funds should be considered carefully. Moreover, results which refer to the composition of funds' portfolios might be biased.

4.2.3 CEPRES Center for Private Equity Research

The data set of the CEPRES Center of Private Equity Research is used by Schmidt (2004), Cumming & Walz (2004), and Ick (2005). CEPRES is a joint research initiative between VCM Venture Capital Management, a German PE fund-of-funds, and the chair of banking and finance of the Johann Wolfgang Goethe-University of Frankfurt/Main. It was founded in 2001 and aims to provide in-depth PE market data for quantitative analysis. For this purpose, CEPRES collects its own data set on PE funds. The most recent study of Ick (2005) states that the data set covers 243 PE funds containing 5,991 transactions in 4,819 portfolio companies. The data set contains anonymous information on the characteristics of the PE funds and their portfolio companies.

The key advantage of the data set is the coverage of the exact cash flow history of each investment, gross of management fees and carried interests. Additionally, it contains a large number of descriptive variables on both funds and its portfolio companies. A potential weakness of the data set is its representativeness. The three cited articles using the CEPRES data all focus

[29] Investors usually run a rigorous controlling of all data reported by a PE fund they invest in. Additionally, the annual reports of PE funds have to be certificated by public accountants. Thus, the probability of errors in the data is very low.

on the level of individual portfolio companies, and therefore, do not contain detailed information on the type of funds and possible biases. Ick (2005) only comments on a survivorship bias. Another shortcoming of the data seems to be a significant share of missing observations in some variables. For instance, Ick (2005) does not have information on the investment stage of 49% of his sample of 2,753 mature investments. Cumming & Walz (2004, p. 13) confirm this weakness: "For many firms in the data we were unable to obtain a reliable definition, and therefore use an 'unknown' category [...]".

To sum up, the data set of CEPRES contains very detailed information on a relatively large number of PE funds and its investments. Unfavorably, not much is known about potential biases of the included funds and the level of coverage of single variables.

4.3 Description of data set used in this thesis

4.3.1 Data source and sample

The data set utilized in this thesis is derived within the scope of a research cooperation with an European PE fund-of-funds investor. The data set was collected between April 2004 and October 2005. The information on PE firms, funds and its portfolio companies were extracted from the due diligence documents provided by the PE firms to the investor.

To secure the anonymity of the fund-of-funds investor as well as the PE firms, funds and portfolio companies included in the data set, several precautions were made. At first, each researcher had to sign a comprehensive confidentiality agreement which prohibits the researcher from revealing any information she learned through the cooperation. Secondly, the data set is only accessible in the office of the fund-of-funds investor. Only aggregated tables and outputs of econometric analyses, which do not enable reverse identification of a single PE firm, fund or portfolio company were allowed to be taken out of the office of the fund-of-funds investor. Finally, the fund-of-funds investor scrutinized any publication based on the data set for confidentiality issues before it was allowed to be published.

The data set contains detailed information on PE firms, their funds, and funds' investments. Concerning the PE firm, the year of firm foundation, the geographic location of offices, and the funds managed since foundation is available. For each fund of a PE firm the following data is collected: the vintage year, the total amount committed, and the investment focus as specified by the PE firm. Additionally, for each fund a complete listing of all investments is available. For each portfolio company a set of descriptive variables is gathered. In particular, the date of initial investment by the PE fund, the industry of main activity, the geographic location of the headquarters, and the financing stage at the time of initial investment is stored. In the case an observation is unknown, the variables are completed through external resources. If in existence, the website of the portfolio company is scanned for additional information. Additionally, the website of the PE firm is screened for supplementary data. If both sources do not reveal the necessary information, the commercially available records of TVE are investigated. The information found in TVE is only adopted if other variables for the portfolio company coincide with the information in the due diligence documents. To measure the financial performance of the PE funds the exact cash flow records between the fund and its investors net of carried interests and the management fees are collected (in the following called the net cash flows). For the same purpose, the exact timing and size of cash flows between the fund and each portfolio company at the time of data collection are saved (in the following called gross cash flows).

The entire sample includes 227 PE funds of 51 PE firms. The data set contains information on 6,758 PE transactions. The sample can be divided in 54 seed/early VC funds, 54 other VC funds, 61 BO funds, and 58 generalist funds.[30] 74.9% of the funds are managed by PE firms with headquarters in the USA. The headquarters of the remaining 25.1% of funds are located in Germany, France, Italy, Spain, Sweden, Switzerland, and the United Kingdom. 13.7% of the sample funds are first-time funds, 15.0% second-time funds, and 14.5% third-time funds. The rest (56.8%) are funds, which have sequence numbers of four or higher. 20.3% of the sample funds were liquidated at the time of data collection while the remaining 79.3% were still active. Table 4.1 summarizes the distribution of sample funds and descriptive statistics on fund size according to fund type, headquarters of PE firm, fund sequence number, and liquidation status. In order to secure the anonymity of all funds, the table does contain no minimum, no maximum, and no median values for fund size. Instead, Table 4.1 presents the mean fund size of the three smallest and the three largest funds.

Sample funds vary substantially by size. The three largest funds are on average 658 times larger than the three smallest funds with mean values of USD 7,242 million and USD 11 million, respectively. Seed/early VC funds have the smallest fund size with a mean of USD 191 million, whereas BO funds reach the largest size with an average of USD 1,206 million. The mean fund size for other VC funds is USD 400 million and for generalist funds USD 696 million. Fund size increases significantly with sequence number. The mean fund size grows from USD 107 million for first-time funds to USD 974 million for funds, which have sequence numbers of four or higher. Equivalently, liquidated funds in the sample have a much smaller size than active funds (USD 256 million compared to USD 741 million). Finally, US PE funds are on average one third larger than European funds (USD 697 million compared to USD 481 million).

Figure 4.1 displays the distribution of sample funds across vintage years. The oldest fund in the sample closed its first transaction in 1977; the youngest in 2003. The number of PE funds in each vintage year corresponds approximately to the development of the global PE industry.[31] Between the years 1977 and 1988 the yearly number of PE funds in the sample is small and approximately constant with an average of 2.6. In the years following 1988 the yearly number of PE funds in the sample grew until a maximum of 27 in 1998 and 26 in 2000. Thereafter, it declines sharply because of truncation.

30 Mezzanine funds and pre-fund vehicles were excluded.

31 For further comparison between the sample and the universe of PE funds reported by TVE see the sample selection regression in Table 4.2.

Table 4.1: Composition of entire sample

This table summarizes the entire sample according to fund type, headquarters of PE firm, fund sequence number, and liquidation status. It divides fund types in seed/early stage VC, other VC, BO and generalist funds. The sample contains only funds which are managed by PE firms with headquarters in USA or Europe. Fund sequence number describes the position of a fund within all funds managed by one particular PE firm. Active funds have a NAV larger than zero. Liquidated funds have no NAV any more. Columns 1 and 2 display the breakdown of the sample into different classifications. Columns 3 to 6 give information on the fund size defined as the total capital committed by investors to a fund. To secure the anonymity of all funds the mean, the mean of the three smallest funds and the mean of the three largest funds is tabulated.

	Funds		Fund Size (million USD 2000)			
	Obs.	%	Mean	Std. Dev.	Mean min. three funds	Mean max. three funds
All funds	227	100.0	642.6	1,150.7	11.3	7,241.9
Fund type						
Seed/early stage VC	54	23.8	190.9	188.2	12.1	766.8
Other VC	54	23.8	399.9	525.8	31.2	2,182.8
Buyout	61	26.9	1,206.3	1,722.6	33.1	7,241.9
Generalist	58	25.5	696.3	1,115.4	49.8	4,549.5
Headquarters of PE firm						
USA	170	74.9	696.9	1,260.5	12.1	7,241.9
Europe	57	25.1	480.6	716.2	30.0	2,797.4
Fund sequence number						
First-time	31	13.7	107.4	112.8	13.8	413.1
Second-time	34	15.0	217.7	237.8	32.1	879.3
Third-time	33	14.5	308.2	353.5	23.1	1,231.3
later	129	56.8	973.5	1,425.8	50.8	7,241.9
Liquidation status						
Active	181	79.7	740.9	1,255.7	21.9	7,241.5
Liquidated	46	20.3	255.9	389.3	11.3	1,449.9

Figure 4.1: Distribution of entire sample across vintage years

The figure shows the distribution of the observations across vintage years. The entire sample contains 227 PE funds with vintage years between 1977 and 2003. PE funds are divided into liquidated and active funds. Active funds have a NAV larger than zero. Liquidated funds have no NAV any more. Vintage year is defined as the year of the first investment of a fund.

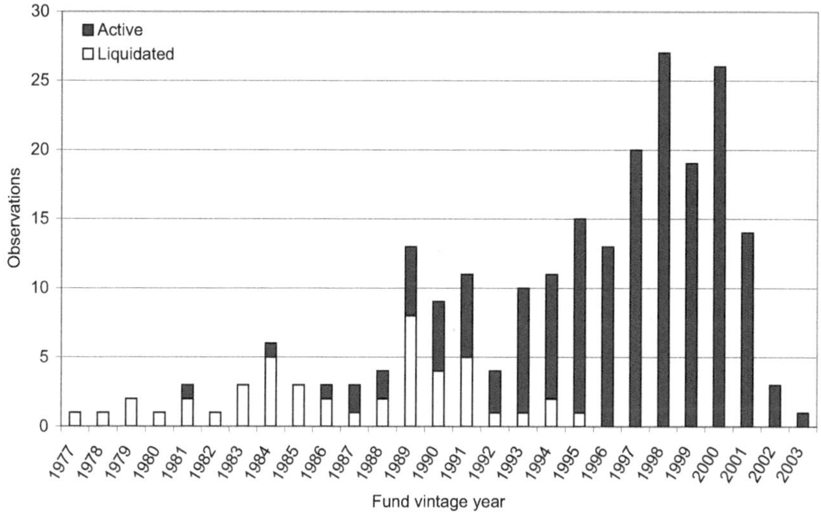

4.3.2 Selection biases

4.3.2.1 Origin of potential selection biases

One major issue in empirical research is the question to which extent the sample represents the population. In the strict sense, this is only the case if one has a random sample of the population. The data set used in this thesis is not a random sample and consists of all VC and BO funds which belong to a PE firm that (1) undertook fundraising activities for a new fund between 2000 and August 2005 and (2) were asked by the cooperation partner to provide due diligence documents. The time span of more than five years is larger than the usual fund raising cycle of PE funds of three to four years. Hence, the sampling period is not expected to cause any bias. However, it implies survivorship bias. No funds are included in the sample that have a vintage year before 2000 and were managed by a PE firm which did not try to raise a fund between 2000 and July 2005. This suggests that the funds of these PE firms started before 2000 generated a poor performance. Discussions with investment managers of the fund-of-funds investor indicate that PE firms creating poor returns in two subsequent funds have a very low probability of raising a new fund. Consequently, the funds included in the sample can be considered as a positive selection of the population in terms of return.

Additional selection biases could be caused by the investment preferences of the cooperation partner. Because of a regional focus, no funds of PE firms which have their headquarters outside USA or Europe are included in the sample. This does not restrict the analysis critically, as USA and Europe are by far the biggest PE markets.[32] Additionally, the fund-of-funds investor only does due diligence for funds of PE firms it rates as 'high-quality-teams'. Some part of the rating stems from past performance of PE firms implying again a positive selection with reference to return.

The potential selection biases are further analyzed in a two step approach. First, I compare the returns of sample funds with the aggregated return information available in TVE. Secondly, I evaluate additional sample selection with respect to fund type, fund size, headquarters of PE firm, and vintage year in a probit regression.

4.3.2.2 Superior returns of sample funds

The aim of this subsection is to compare the returns of sample funds with the return information provided by TVE. Unfortunately, TVE only creates aggregated return reports for groups of PE funds net of carried interest and management fees. Additionally, it is only possible to generate return statistics for either US funds or European funds. Consequently, I compare the upper quartile, median, and lower quartile of TVE funds' net IRRs with the median and lower quartile of sample funds' net IRRs separately for Europe and USA.[33] Funds are combined to groups of three vintage years between 1977 and 2000. Funds with vintage years of 2001 and later are not included because they are too young for reliable return statements. The TVE benchmark contains 1,462 US and 708 European PE funds.[34] In comparison, I am able to calculate the net IRR of 133 US and 48 European funds with a vintage year between 1977 and 2000 in the sample.[35]

As expected, Figure 4.2 presents superior returns of sample funds relative to the universe of PE funds. In eight out of twelve cases the sample median lies above the upper quartile of the TVE benchmark and the lower quartile of sample funds beats the median of TVE funds. These results confirm that the sample is a positive selection of the population in terms of return. Most of the PE funds included in the sample belong to the 'top-half' performers within their peer group. Consequently, the empirical results in chapters 5 and 6 are primarily valid for the 'top-half' of private equity funds. For 'bottom-half' funds the relationships might differ.

---

[32] The limitation to US and European based PE funds does not mean that no investments in companies outside USA and Europe are included in the data set. US and European PE firms also fund companies outside their home markets. The distribution of portfolio companies across countries is reported in panel C of Table B.1 in the appendix.

[33] IRR is the discount rate that yields a net present value of zero for a cash flow history. The Net IRR of a PE funds is calculated on the cash flow history between the fund and its investors (limited partners) net of management fees and carried interests. A mathematical definition of IRR is given in subsection 4.4.2.

[34] The return reports in TVE were generated on December 12, 2005.

[35] For 197 PE funds in the sample used in this thesis are net cash flows available. Of these 16 have vintages years of 2001 or later.

Figure 4.2: Return comparison between the funds in Thomson Venture Economics and the sample

The figure compares the IRR net of management fee and carried interest between TVE and the sample used in this thesis separately for US and European funds. Funds are joined to groups of three vintage years. Because of their young age no fund with a vintage year of 2001 or more is included in the comparison. The graphic shows upper quartile, median, and lower quartile of TVE funds' net IRR. For the sample used in this thesis it displays the median and lower quartile of net IRR. Net IRR was computable for 133 US and 48 European sample funds between 1977 and 2000. The TVE benchmark contains 1,462 US and 708 European PE funds.

Panel A: US PE funds

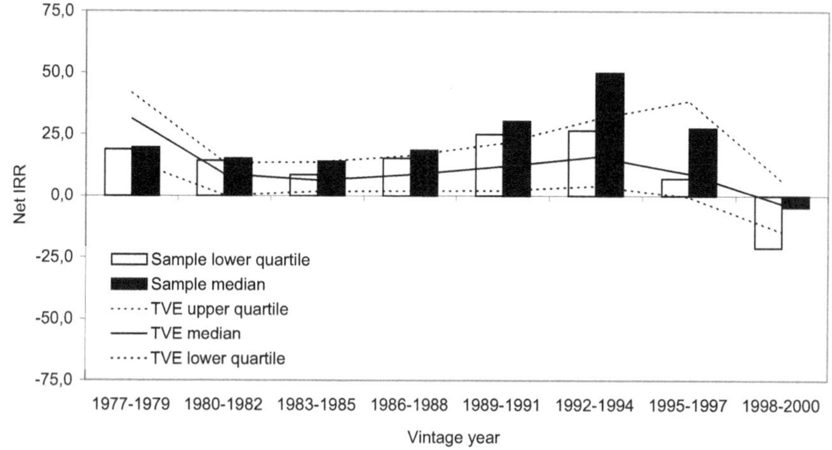

Panel B: European PE funds

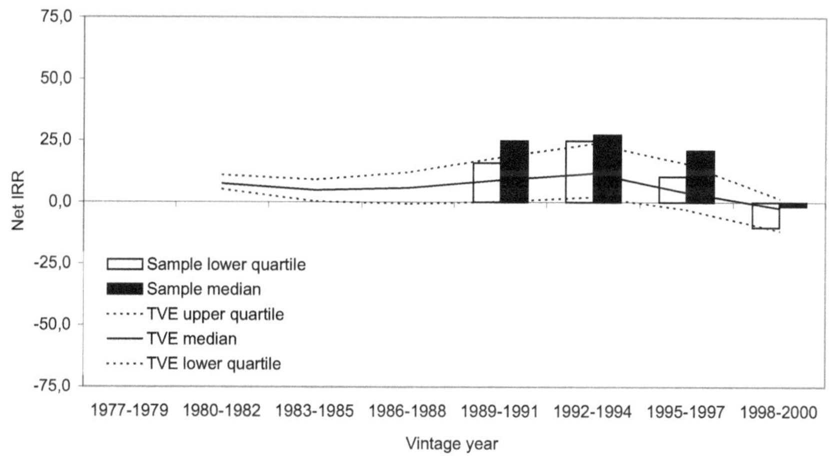

4.3.2.3 Further sample selection

In order to address further sample selection issues I analyze the probability of a PE fund in TVE to enter the sample in a probit regression. In order to do so, sample funds are identified in the universe of PE funds reported by TVE. All but two sample funds are matched to the records of TVE. Subsequently, the probit regression evaluates whether fund size, vintage year, the headquarters of the PE firm managing the fund, or the type of a fund have a significant influence on the probability of a PE fund to enter the sample.[36] Fund size is measured as the logarithm of the total amount committed in USD million in 2000 purchasing power. Vintage year is included as a quasi-continuous variable in the regression. A dummy variable denotes funds that are managed by PE firms with headquarters in Europe. For the probit regression, I distinguish between seed/early stage VC funds, other VC funds and BO funds. The reference case is seed/early stage VC funds. The dependent variable is a dummy variable that takes on the value of one if a fund belongs to the sample. Table 4.2 summarizes the results of the sample selection regression.

Table 4.2: Probit regression for sample selection

The regression contains 7,071 PE funds. The dependent variable is a dummy variable that takes on the value of one if the fund belongs to the sample. Independent variables include fund size (logarithm of total amount committed in USD million of 2000 purchasing power), vintage year (year of first investment), a dummy variable indicating funds managed by a PE firm with headquarters in Europe, dummy variables denoting other VC as well as BO funds, and a constant (not reported). The table reports marginal effects at the sample means of independent variables. For dummy variables the effect of a discrete change from zero to one is given.

	Dependent variable: Does fund belong to sample (0/1)	
Fund size (log million USD 2000)	0.0147	(0.0110)***
Vintage year	-0.0011	(0.0002)***
European headquarters (0/1)	0.0010	(0.0031)
Other VC fund (0/1)	-0.0031	(0.0034)
Buyout fund (0/1)	0.0009	(0.0036)
Log pseudo-likelihood	-862.5	
χ^2-statistic	296.3	
p-value	0.000	
pseudo-R^2	0.141	
no. of observations	7,071	

Standard errors are in parentheses.
* significant at 10%; ** significant at 5%; *** significant at 1%

The main results are that fund size and vintage year have a statistically significant effect on the probability of a fund to belong to the sample at the 1% level.[37] The probability of a BO fund with 1995 vintage year and US headquarters to be in the sample rises by 6.6% when its fund size changes from USD 56.4 million (lower quartile) to USD 389.1 million (upper quartile). The probability of a BO fund with an average size of USD 389.8 million and US headquarters

[36] For a detailed explanation of probit regression see Green (2003).

[37] In a unreported probit regression the quasi-continuous variable vintage year is substituted by eight dummy variables for the vintage year groups used in the previous subsection. Including dummy variables except for the period between 1998 and 2000, the dummy variables for the periods 1977-1979, 1980-1982, 1983-1985, 1986-1988, 1989-1991, 1992-1994, and 1995-1997 have positive and statistically significant coefficients.

to be in the sample decreases by 3.8% if the fund starts investing in 2000 (upper quartile) instead of 1991 (lower quartile). Thus, bigger funds are over-represented in the sample, while funds with later vintage years are slightly under-represented. These biases are not problematic as both variables are included as independent variables in the multivariate analyses presented in chapters 5 and 6. The dummy variables for European headquarters, other VC funds, and BO funds have no significant effect on the probability of a fund to belong to the sample. Consequently, there is no bias with reference to PE firms' headquarters and fund types in the sample.

4.4 Description of variables

4.4.1 Measurement of portfolio strategy

In this thesis the portfolio strategy of a PE fund is defined as the level of diversification according to five dimensions: (1) number of portfolio companies, (2) diversification across time, (3) diversification across financing stages, (4) diversification across industries, and (5) diversification across countries. To define the variables I use the following denominations: each PE fund contains N portfolio companies with $i = 1, 2, \dots, N$. In each portfolio company the fund invested the amount of money x_i.

(1) Number of portfolio companies (*no. of pcs*)

The variable *number of portfolio companies* evaluates 'naive' diversification across a randomly selected portfolio of risky assets (Evans & Archer 1968). It counts the number of portfolio companies N in a PE fund.

(2) Diversification across time (*div. a. time*)

Diversification across time reflects how fast a PE fund spends its capital. First, the start of a PE fund's investment activities is determined as the investment date of its first portfolio company. Secondly, for each portfolio company the time span between its date of investment and the date of investment of the first portfolio company, i.e., the start of the PE fund's investment activities is calculated:

$$\Delta t_i = t_i - t_{\text{first portfolio company}} \tag{4.1}$$

Thirdly, the time span Δt_i is weighted with the fraction of the fund invested in portfolio company i. Finally, the value-weighted average for a fund is calculated:

$$\textit{div. across time} = \sum_{i=1}^{N} \left(\Delta t_i \cdot \frac{x_i}{\sum_{i=1}^{N} x_i} \right) \tag{4.2}$$

(3) Diversification across financing stages (*div. a. fin. stages*)

I calculate a Herfindahl-Hirschmann-Index (HHI) to measure *diversification across financing stages* in a PE fund. HHI was first introduced by Herfindahl (1950) and Hirschman (1945) and has become a standard measure for all kinds of economic concentration phenomena. Originally developed for the assessment of concentration within a class (e.g. degree of market concentration within an industry) HHI is also often used for assessing diversification across different classes.[38] The following properties inherent to HHI have made it extremely popular (Hall & Tidemann 1967):

1. HHI integrates information in a single one-dimensional measure and is thus unambiguous.
2. The measure is independent of the size of the underlying whole. HHI takes on values between 0 and 1.
3. HHI reflects changes in diversification both due to the number of classes and to the distribution of shares across classes.

To measure the diversification of a PE fund across financing stages I assigned each portfolio company to one financing stage. The following five categories were used: (1) seed and early stage VC, (2) second, expansion and later stage VC, (3) BO, (4) listed securities, and (5) other financing stages.[39] In most cases the categorization of the portfolio companies provided by the PE firms was identical to my classification scheme and thus the categorization to the categories (1) to (5) was without difficulty. In cases where no direct correspondence existed further search on the status of the company at the date of initial investment was conducted in external resources. Through this method more than 99% of the portfolio companies could be classified.[40] Panel A in Table B.1 in the appendix contains the distribution of portfolio companies across the five groups.

Next, I calculated the fraction of capital invested in each financing stage. HHI is computed by squaring the fraction of each financing stage and then summing up the resulting numbers. Finally, for the purpose of easy interpretation I subtracted HHI from one. Hence, *diversification across financing stages* takes on the value of 0 for a fund, which is not diversified at all (i.e., a fund which invested only in one financing stage), and the value of 1 for a perfectly diversified fund (i.e., a fund which invested in an infinite number of financing stages):

$$\textit{div. across financing stages} = 1 - \left[\sum_{k=1}^{M}\left(\frac{\sum_{i=1}^{N}(x_i \cdot f_{ki})}{\sum_{i=1}^{N} x_i}\right)^2\right] \tag{4.3}$$

[38] For a recent example compare Schoar (2002).

[39] Definitions of VC and BO are described in section 1.3. In some cases PE firms buy shares of companies which are listed on public stock exchanges. Often these companies have been funded by the same PE firm years ago in a private transaction. The category other financing stages was used for companies, which did not fit in one of the other categories.

[40] The portfolio companies, which could not be classified to one of the financing stages because of missing information, were not considered for the calculation of HHI.

with $k = 1, 2, \ldots, M$ financing stages,

$$f_{ki} = \begin{cases} 1 & \text{if portfolio company i is assigned to financing stage k} \\ 0 & \text{else.} \end{cases}$$

(4) Diversification across industries (*div. a. industries*)

To measure *diversification across industries* each portfolio company was assigned uniquely to the industry class of its major operations. First, I used the industry classification of TVE at its two-digit-level. The categorization was based upon the description of the portfolio companies given by the PE firm in the due diligence documents. To verify the classification, it was compared with the record of TVE for each portfolio company. 94% of all portfolio companies could be classified.[41] Secondly, to minimize the subjectivity associated with the classification, the two-digit-classification was aggregated to nine industry segments used by Gompers, Kovner, Lerner & Scharfstein (2005): (1) Internet and Computers, (2) Communications and Electronics, (3) Business and Industrial, (4) Consumer, (5) Energy and Utilities, (6) Biotechnology and Healthcare, (7) Financial Services, (8) Business Services, and (9) Other. Gompers et al. claim that their classification scheme groups companies that have similarities in technology and markets. Therefore, it also qualifies for the evaluation of *diversification across industries*. Panel B in Table B.1 in the appendix describes the distribution of portfolio companies across the nine industry classes.

Based on the classification a HHI was computed, which is equivalently defined to the HHI applied in the measurement of diversification across financing stages. It takes on a value of 0 for funds, which specialize in only one industry, and a value close to 1 for funds, which are diversified across a large number of industries. It is computed as follows:

$$\textit{div. across industries} = 1 - \left[\sum_{k=1}^{M} \left(\frac{\sum_{i=1}^{N} (x_i \cdot t_{ki})}{\sum_{i=1}^{N} x_i} \right)^2 \right] \tag{4.4}$$

with $k = 1, 2, \ldots, M$ industries,

$$t_{ki} = \begin{cases} 1 & \text{if portfolio company i is assigned to industry k} \\ 0 & \text{else.} \end{cases}$$

(5) Diversification across countries (*div. a. countries*)

Finally, *diversification across countries* of sample funds was measured. Each portfolio company was assigned to the country of its headquarters and a HHI across the fraction of capital invested in each country was computed. The geographic location of the headquarters was available for all portfolio companies. Panel C in Table B.1 in the appendix summarizes the distribution of portfolio companies across countries. HHI takes the form:

[41] The portfolio companies, which could not be classified to one of the industries because of missing information, were not considered for the calculation of HHI.

$$div.\ across\ countries = 1 - \left[\sum_{k=1}^{M}\left(\frac{\sum_{i=1}^{N}(x_i \cdot c_{ki})}{\sum_{i=1}^{N} x_i}\right)^2\right] \tag{4.5}$$

with $k = 1, 2, \ldots, M$ countries,

$$c_{ki} = \begin{cases} 1 & \text{if portfolio company i is assigned to country k} \\ 0 & \text{else.} \end{cases}$$

4.4.2 Measurement of performance

4.4.2.1 Rate of return

As PE investments are only occasionally traded on secondary markets, return measurement usually relies on the cash flow history of a fund. In order to measure the rate of return of a PE fund a variety of measures are proposed and used in academics.[42] Among the most important are money multiple, IRR, excess-IRR, and public market equivalent (PME). The money multiple is often used by practitioners to measure the return of single portfolio companies. Instead, I aim at evaluating the return of PE funds with a lifetime of ten or more years. In this context money multiple is not considered as an appropriate return measure since it does not account for the time value of money.

As the objective of this thesis is to study the impact of diversification on the return of a PE fund and not to compare the achieved returns with other asset classes, the return is measured gross of management fees and carried interest. In summary, throughout this thesis I measure the rate of return of sample funds in terms of gross IRR, gross modified IRR (MIRR) and gross PME. All consider the exact timing and size of all cash flows between a PE fund and its portfolio companies gross of management fees and carried interests.

(1) Internal rate of return (*IRR*)

The *IRR* is the discount rate that yields a net present value of zero for the cash flow history of an investment:

$$0 = \sum_{t=0}^{T}\left(\frac{\sum_{i=1}^{N} CF_{it}}{(1+IRR)^t}\right) \tag{4.6}$$

with CF_{it} = cash flow of portfolio company i in period t.

Three shortcomings restrict the use of IRR (Martin 1995). First, mathematically for one cash flow stream there are as many IRRs as the cash flow stream has sign changes. Secondly, under some circumstances IRR is incalculable. Thirdly and most importantly, IRR implicitly

[42] For a more detailed discussion of the advantages and disadvantages of various return measures for PE funds see Kaserer & Diller (2004*a*).

assumes that interim cash flows are (re)invested at the same IRR. In most cases this reinvestment assumption is unrealistic. Neither PE firms nor investors are immediately able to reinvest in projects with the same IRR.

(2) Modified internal rate of return (*MIRR*)

The *MIRR* cures this problem making an explicit assumption about the discount rate for interim cash flows (Dorsey 2000). Negative interim cash flows occuring during the investment's lifetime are discounted at a specific discount rate to period 0. Accordingly, positive interim cash flows are reinvested at a specific discount rate until the last cash flow has occurred. In this thesis, I use a constant discount rate of 9%, which is equal to the annual rate of return of the MSCI World Index during 1979 and 2005. A further advantage of the MIRR is that it can be solved without iteration:

$$MIRR = \sqrt[T]{\frac{\sum_{t=0}^{T}\left[\left(\sum_{i=1}^{N} CF_{it}\right)\cdot(1+r)^{T-t}\cdot p_t\right]}{\sum_{t=0}^{T}\left[\left(\sum_{i=1}^{N} CF_{it}\right)\cdot(1+r)^{-t}\cdot n_t\right]}} \tag{4.7}$$

with $r =$ discount rate for interim cash flows,

$$p_t = \begin{cases} 1 & \text{if in period t } \sum_{i=1}^{N} CF_{it} \geq 0 \\ 0 & \text{else,} \end{cases}$$

$$n_t = \begin{cases} 1 & \text{if in period t } \sum_{i=1}^{N} CF_{it} < 0 \\ 0 & \text{else.} \end{cases}$$

(3) Public market equivalent (*PME*)

The *PME* compares the investment in a PE fund to the investment in a public market index (Kaplan & Schoar 2003). It is defined as the ratio of the present value of all cash inflows to the fund (i.e., realizations of portfolio companies) over the present value of all cash outflows from the fund (i.e., investments in portfolio companies) using the public market index as discount rate (Kaserer & Diller 2004*c*). As the sample contains European and US PE funds, I use the MSCI World Index as public market index. More precisely the PME is represented by:

$$PME = \frac{\sum_{t=0}^{T}\left[\left(\sum_{i=1}^{N} CF_{it}\right) / \left(\prod_{k=0}^{t}(1+r_k)\right)\cdot p_t\right]}{\sum_{t=0}^{T}\left[\left(\sum_{i=1}^{N} CF_{it}\right) / \left(\prod_{l=0}^{t}(1+r_l)\right)\cdot n_t\right]} \tag{4.8}$$

with $r_k, r_l =$ discrete return of the public market index in period k or l,

$$p_t = \begin{cases} 1 & \text{if in period t } \sum_{i=1}^{N} CF_{it} \geq 0 \\ 0 & \text{else,} \end{cases}$$

$$n_t = \begin{cases} 1 & \text{if in period t } \sum_{i=1}^{N} CF_{it} < 0 \\ 0 & \text{else.} \end{cases}$$

Finally, I include NAV in the calculation of IRR, MIRR, and PME. Gottschalg et al. (2004) document that the average ratio of present value of future cash flows to NAV in December of each year after the eighth birthday of a PE fund is 1.03. This implies that NAV in the last part of a funds' lifetime is a good proxy for future cash flows.

4.4.2.2 Intra-fund variation of return (*sd(Q-IRR), sd(Q-MIRR), sd(Q-PME)*)

The comparison of PE funds' risk is a challenging task (Reyes 1990). The illiquidity of PE investments prohibits the usual computation of standard measures of risk such as standard deviation of returns over time, beta factors, or value at risk. Consequently, no standard for risk measurement of PE funds exists so far. The attempts by various authors can be divided into two groups. The first group measures standard deviations and beta factors of returns in large groups of PE investments (Jones & Rhodes-Kropf 2003, Kaserer & Diller 2004*b*, Schmidt 2004, Cochrane 2005, Ick 2005), not suitable for the comparison of the risk of single PE funds. A second approach maps PE investments to public market companies and assumes equality in systematic risk (Ljungqvist & Richardson 2003*a*, Gottschalg et al. 2004). This technique proves unsatisfactory as the assumption of risk equality is questionable. The large difference in the results gives rise to the hypothesis that the betas depend more on the assumptions of mapping than on the characteristics of the portfolio companies in a PE fund.[43]

As a consequence, I do not try to measure the variance and covariance risk of PE funds and follow the approach of many investors. In order to appraise the performance of a PE firm, they do not stop at analyzing the rate of return at fund level. Instead, they step one level down evaluating the return distribution within PE funds. Accordingly, I propose *intra-fund variation of return* as a novel measure to characterize the performance of PE funds alongside the rate of return. It aims at comparing the dispersion across the outcomes of portfolio companies within PE funds.

However, analyzing the standard deviation of single portfolio companies' returns can be misleading because return measures like IRR, MIRR, and PME are relative measures, which do not depend on the amount of capital invested in a portfolio company. It is necessary to weigh portfolio companies' returns by the fraction of the fund's capital invested in the portfolio company. Unfavorably, IRR, MIRR, and PME prohibit the multiplication of portfolio companies' IRRs, MIRRs, or PMEs with their portfolio weights because IRR, MIRR, and PME consider the exact timing of cash flows. To solve this difficulty I propose the following technique: For each portfolio company the entire cash flow stream (including NAV) is omitted. Upon the aggregated cash flow history of the remaining $N-1$ portfolio companies a new, *quasi-rate of return* (*Q-IRR*, *Q-MIRR*, or *Q-PME*) for the fund is calculated. The difference between this quasi-rate of return and the original rate of return quantifies the importance of the omitted portfolio company for the fund's original rate of return and can be interpreted as the value-weighted rate of return of the omitted portfolio company. The fund's rate of return rises in the case the omitted portfolio company has a rate of return below the fund's original rate of return.

[43] For a detailed discussion of the articles compare section 2.2.

In the case that the omitted portfolio company returns more than the original fund's rate of return, the return difference is negative. The procedure is repeated for all portfolio companies resulting in N quasi-rates of return; each representing the value-weighted rate of return of one portfolio company. The technique is mathematically expressed by the following equations:[44]

(1) Quasi-internal rate of return (*Q-IRR*):

$$0 = \sum_{t=0}^{T} \left(\frac{\left(\sum_{i=1}^{N} CF_{it}\right) - CF_{it}}{(1 + Q - IRR_i)^t} \right) \quad \text{for all } i = 1, 2, \ldots, N \tag{4.9}$$

(2) Quasi-modified internal rate of return (*Q-MIRR*):

$$Q\text{-}MIRR_i = \sqrt[T]{\frac{\sum_{t=0}^{T} \left[\left(\left(\sum_{i=1}^{N} CF_{it}\right) - CF_{it} \right) \cdot (1+r)^{T-t} \cdot p_{it} \right]}{\sum_{t=0}^{T} \left[\left(\left(\sum_{i=1}^{N} CF_{it}\right) - CF_{it} \right) \cdot (1+r)^{-t} \cdot n_{it} \right]}} \quad \text{for all } i = 1, 2, \ldots, N \tag{4.10}$$

with discount rate for interim cash flows,

$$p_{it} = \begin{cases} 1 & \text{if for portfolio company i in period t } \left(\sum_{i=1}^{N} CF_{it}\right) - CF_{it} \geq 0 \\ 0 & \text{else,} \end{cases}$$

$$n_{it} = \begin{cases} 1 & \text{if for portfolio company i in period t } \left(\sum_{i=1}^{N} CF_{it}\right) - CF_{it} < 0 \\ 0 & \text{else.} \end{cases}$$

[44] The new, quasi-rate of return is calculated based on $N-1$ portfolio companies. Hence, the quasi-rate of return is computed on a total amount invested, which is inferior than the original total amount invested of the fund. As a result, one could think of an alternative idea that would replace the omitted portfolio company by an 'average' investment. This average investment should have the same amount of capital invested than the omitted portfolio company and should yield the original rate of return of the fund. However, this approach is mathematically not applicable because IRR, MIRR, and PME take into account the exact timing of a cash flow. To calculate the IRR, MIRR, and PME one has first to sum up the cash flows of all portfolio companies in each time period. A positive cash flow of one portfolio company compensates a negative cash flow in the same time period of another portfolio company. Subsequently, IRR, MIRR, or PME is computed on the aggregated cash flow stream. Consequently, neither IRR, nor MIRR, nor PME of a fund can be expressed as a weighted sum of the portfolio company IRRs, MIRRs, or PMEs. This fact inhibits the substitution of the omitted portfolio company by an 'average' investment. Furthermore, PE firms often do not invest the total amount committed of a fund. As a result, the assumption that the quasi-return is computed on a minor amount invested than the original amount invested is not critical.

(3) Quasi-public market equivalent (*Q-PME*):

$$Q\text{-}PME_i = \frac{\sum_{t=0}^{T}\left[\left(\left(\sum_{i=1}^{N} CF_{it}\right) - CF_{it}\right) / \left(\prod_{k=0}^{t}(1+r_k)\right) \cdot p_t\right]}{\sum_{t=0}^{T}\left[\left(\left(\sum_{i=1}^{N} CF_{it}\right) - CF_{it}\right) / \left(\prod_{l=0}^{t}(1+r_l)\right) \cdot n_t\right]}$$

$$\text{for all } i = 1, 2, \ldots, N \qquad (4.11)$$

with $r = r_k, r_l$ = discrete return of the public market index in period k or l,

$$p_{it} = \begin{cases} 1 & \text{if for portfolio company i in period t } \left(\sum_{i=1}^{N} CF_{it}\right) - CF_{it} \geq 0 \\ 0 & \text{else,} \end{cases}$$

$$n_{it} = \begin{cases} 1 & \text{if for portfolio company i in period t } \left(\sum_{i=1}^{N} CF_{it}\right) - CF_{it} < 0 \\ 0 & \text{else.} \end{cases}$$

Finally, *intra-fund variation of return* is computed applying standard deviation.[45] The resulting measures $sd(Q-IRR)$, $sd(Q-MIRR)$, and $sd(Q-PME)$ represent the dispersion across the value-weighted rates of return of portfolio companies at the end of a PE fund's lifetime.

Figure 4.3 illustrates intra-fund variation of return by an example from the data set. It shows *MIRR* and *sd(Q-MIRR)* for two funds with 22 portfolio companies each. Both funds yield a MIRR of 20.4%. Nonetheless, fund A displays a higher dispersion across the outcomes of its portfolio companies with a sd(Q-MIRR) of 0.0105 relative to 0.0061 for fund B. The MIRR of fund A changes on average by 1.1 percentage points if one portfolio company is taken out of fund A, whereas the MIRR of fund B only changes on average by 0.6 percentage points if one portfolio company is taken out of fund B.

Figure 4.3: Illustration of intra-fund variation of return

The figure compares two funds with 22 portfolio companies each based on MIRR and sd(Q-MIRR). Both funds have an equal MIRR of 20.4%. Fund A displays a higher dispersion across the outcomes of its portfolio companies than fund B because its sd(Q-MIRR) of 0.0105 is larger than the sd(Q-MIRR) of 0.0061 of fund B. The black dots represent single Q-MIRRs. Black crosses mark the MIRRs of the two funds.

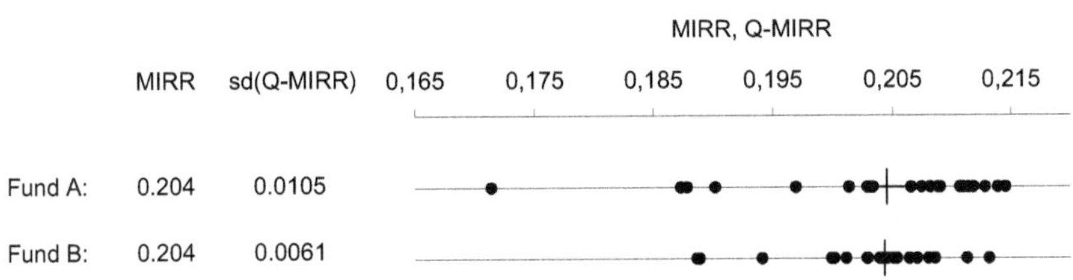

[45] In the strict sense, one needs to compute the standard deviation of the differences between the quasi-rates of return and the original rates of return across all portfolio companies. This is mathematically identical and hence leads to the same result.

Intra-fund variation of return can be interpreted as follows: On the one hand, it indicates different investment strategies of PE firms. A high intra-fund variation of return is equal to the strategy of putting all bets on only a few 'winners' (in an extreme case only one) accepting poor performance of the remaining portfolio companies in a PE fund. In contrast, a low intra-fund variation of return characterizes the strategy of growing all portfolio companies on an equal basis. On the other hand, one might also think of intra-fund variation of return as total risk of the investment strategy of a PE firm. To be able to grow a few portfolio companies so large as to offset the loss of the remaining portfolio companies, it is necessary to invest in portfolio companies with a high up-side potential, but also large down-side risk. In comparison, to achieve a low intra-fund variation of return, it might be necessary to invest in portfolio companies with low down-side risk, and consequently, a limited up-side potential.

4.4.2.3 Shortfall probability (*prob(loss), prob(tot. loss)*)

Many practitioners and some researchers (Dorsey 2000, Born 2004, Weidig & Mathonet 2004) characterize the risk profile of PE investments in terms of shortfall probability. *Shortfall probability* is defined as the probability of an investment to earn a return below a specific threshold (Roy 1965, Leibowitz & Henrickson 1989). It is equivalent to the lower partial moment of order zero. The underlying idea is that the riskier an investment strategy is, the higher the probability is that the return falls below the threshold, ceteris paribus. For PE funds usually two thresholds are used: zero percent and -100%. They are called probability of loss and total loss, respectively.

Shortfall probability is a very basic and crude performance measure. It only measures the fraction of the return distribution below the threshold. Neither does it consider deviations above the threshold, nor does it take into account the magnitude of the shortfalls. Empirically, the shortfall probability of a PE fund can be roughly estimated through the percentage of portfolio companies in a PE fund which return less than the threshold. Accordingly, probability of loss (*prop(loss)*) is estimated as the percentage of portfolio companies in a PE fund returning less than zero percent. Probability of total loss (*prob(tot. loss)*) is approximated as the percentage of portfolio in a PE fund companies with a rate of return of -100%.

4.4.3 Measurement of additional variables

4.4.3.1 Economic environment and PE market condition

The economic environment and PE market condition in which a PE firm was raised and executed is described through three variables.

(1) Return of MSCI World Index during fundraising (*return msci in vy*)

The expectations of a PE firm about future investment opportunities is influenced by the condition of the global economy during fundraising. Discussions with partners from the cooperation partner suggest that fundraising and fund formation require an average of twelve months. Consequently, I calculate the continuous return of the MSCI World Index the twelve months prior to the first investment of a PE fund in order to measure the condition of the global economy during fundraising. An equivalent variable was used by Kaserer & Diller (2004*c*). The values of the MSCI World Index are obtained from Thomson Financial Datastream.

(2) Return of MSCI World Index during investment period (*return msci investment period*)

In addition to the condition of the global economy during fundraising, the development of the global economy during investment period influences the investment behavior of a PE firm. Hence, I compute the annual continuous return of the MSCI World Index during the investment period of a PE fund. I define the investment period as the time span between the first and the last investment of a PE fund. The values of the MSCI World Index are obtained from Thomson Financial Datastream.

(3) New funds raised in vintage year (*funds raised in vy*)

The prospect of the PE market is measured in terms of new funds raised worldwide by PE firms in a year. Some authors refer the amount of the new funds raised by PE firms in a specific segment of the PE market to the level of competition in the PE market (Gompers & Lerner 2000, Ljungqvist & Richardson 2003*b*). However, Kaserer & Diller (2004*c*) as well as Gottschalg et al. (2004) find a positive relationship between the total capital committed to PE funds and the rate of return of PE funds. They argue that the amount of new funds raised by PE firms represents the economic prospect of the PE industry. Investors are able to accurately predict future fund returns and commit to PE funds in years with attractive investment opportunities. I follow this interpretation, and accordingly, I use the logarithm of the amount of new funds raised worldwide in the vintage year of a PE fund according to the statistics of TVE to measure the condition of the PE industry. I do not distinguish between European and US funds because of two reasons: First, a comparison with statistics published by the European Venture Capital Association suggests that TVE does not cover a reasonable fraction of the European PE market before 1998. Secondly, many US funds are also invested in Europe and vice versa. The amounts of USD were adjusted for inflation. The yearly consumer price index of the U.S. Department of Labor was used to express the purchasing power of new funds raised in 2000.

4.4.3.2 Private equity firm and fund characteristics

The characteristics of a PE firm and PE fund are evaluated through six variables.

(1) Firm internationalization (*firm internationalization*)

The variable *firm internationalization* counts the number of countries in which a PE firm has offices. It approximates different aspects of firm size: the quantity of offices and hence employees, the level of internationalization, and the complexity of the firm's organizational structure. Unfortunately, it is not possible to reconstruct the organizational history of most of the PE firms in the sample. It was only possible to observe the organizational structure of the PE firms as of 2005. Hence, the number of countries in which a PE firm had offices in 2005 was taken for all funds of the PE firm to measure firm internationalization.

(2) Firm experience (*firm experience*)

To measure the experience of a PE firm I count the fund sequence number. The variable reflects the experience a PE firm has accumulated since its inception. With each fund the PE firm acquires new knowledge. It is reasonable to argue that the learning process is not linear. I assume that the additional experience, which a PE firm gains in the management of an extra fund, decreases with the fund sequence number. Hence, *firm experience* is measured as the logarithm of the fund sequence number.

(3) Fund size (*fund size*)

The size of a fund is measured in terms of the total amount committed by investors to the PE fund. The total amount of commitments is the maximum a PE fund is able to invest. It is measured as the logarithm of USD million in 2000 purchasing power. European funds are accounted in EUR, GBP, CHF, or SEK. The amounts are converted to USD using the average monthly exchange rate in a fund's vintage year. The exchange rates are taken from Thomson Financial Datastream. To adjust for inflation the yearly consumer price index of the U.S. Department of Labor is utilized.

(4) Fund type (*seed/early VC, other VC, BO, generalist*)

PE funds are classified according to their focus on specific financing stages. I group sample funds based on the amount of capital invested in portfolio companies of specific development stages. A fund is categorized as *seed/early VC* if the fraction of its total invested capital in seed or early stage VC transactions is equal to or superior to 70%. Funds with a fraction of 70% or more invested in VC but less than 70% invested in seed or early stage VC were categorized as *other VC*. *BO* funds had to have 70% or more of its capital invested in BO transactions. The remaining funds, i.e., funds which invested 70% or more of their capital neither in VC nor in BO transactions were labelled as *generalist*. For each category a dummy variable was generated which takes on the value of one if the fund is assigned to the specific category and of zero else.

In chapter 6 I only distinguish between VC and BO funds. Accordingly, seed/early VC funds and other VC funds are grouped together as VC funds, BO funds and generalist funds as BO funds.

(5) Location of PE firm's headquarters (*European headquarters*)

Sample funds are divided into two groups: Funds which are managed by a PE firm with its headquarters in Europe and funds which are managed by a PE firm with its main operations in USA. The dummy variable *European headquarters* takes on the value of 1 for the first group of funds and 0 for the second group of funds. The variable captures cultural and governance differences in the management of PE funds as well as differences in the economic systems across the Atlantic.

4.4.3.3 Control variables

To test the robustness of results I use three control variables.

(1) First-time fund (*first-time fund*)

The first fund is particularly important for a PE firm. At that time, the PE firm is mainly unknown to investors and has no track record. Additionally, future fundraising possibilities will be dependent to a large extent on the success of the first fund. Discussions with partners of the cooperation partner indicate that PE firms which achieve a poor performance in its first fund have serious difficulties raising a second fund. To capture this particular situation, I include a dummy variable as a control variable, which takes on the value of one if the fund is the first fund of a PE firm and zero else.

(2) Time trend (*time trend*)

The PE industry developed and grew over the sample period. The business model of PE received greater acceptance and the barriers for entry in the PE industry lowered (Ljungqvist & Richardson 2003*a*). To consider this development, I include a linear time trend as control variable, which equals the vintage year of a PE fund scaled such that 1977 equals one.

(3) Year fixed effects (*year F.E.*)

I further include year fixed effects as control variables. Because of the limited sample size, I allocate funds to groups of three years. The groups are: 1977-1979, 1980-1982, 1983-1985, 1986-1988, 1989-1991, 1992-1994, 1995-1997, 1998-2000, and 2001-2003.

4.5 Summary: advantage and drawback of data set

This thesis uses a unique data set of 227 PE funds. It was manually collected between April 2004 and October 2005. To the best of my knowledge, it is one of the most comprehensive data sets on PE funds available to research. The data distinguishes itself from data sets used in previous studies through its high level of detail. For the first time it is possible to exactly measure the level of diversification in a PE fund along various dimensions. Moreover, the availability of the entire gross cash flow records between portfolio companies and its funds enables to calculate a new performance measure: intra-fund variation of return. It quantifies the dispersion of 'value-weighted' returns across the portfolio companies in a PE fund. Additionally, the rate of return and shortfall probability of sample funds are computed.

However, the data set is not a random sample. Intensive analysis shows that the data exhibit sample selection biases. Larger funds are over-represented in the sample, while funds with higher vintage years are slightly under-represented. These biases are not problematic since fund size and vintage year are included as independent variables in the multivariate analyses presented in chapters 5 and 6. More seriously, the data set includes a survivorship bias. As a result, sample funds earned superior returns compared to the universe of PE funds. This fact has to be considered when interpreting the results in chapters 5 and 6. The empirical results are primarily valid for the 'top-half' of PE funds. For 'bottom-half' funds the relationships might differ.

Chapter 5

Choice of portfolio strategies by private equity firms

5.1 Introduction

Very different portfolio strategies can be observed across PE funds. Some PE funds are highly specialized, whereas others are highly diversified. For instance, the least diversified PE fund in the sample invests only in one financing stage, three industries, and one country. In contrast, the most diversified PE fund includes portfolio companies in three financing stages, eight industries, and 22 countries. Furthermore, while the three smallest PE funds only contain an average of 5.3 portfolio companies, the mean of the three most numerous PE funds adds up to 110 portfolio companies. Finally, the fastest investing PE fund spends its capital in only 4.0 months, whereas the slowest investing PE fund takes 46.5 months to commit its capital.

However, not much is known thus far about factors determining the level of diversification in PE funds. The few studies dealing with aspects of the choice of portfolio strategies by PE firms agree that VC firms predominantly involved in seed and early stage financing prefer less industry diversity and a narrower geographic scope in their portfolio than VC firms predominantly involved in later stage financing (Gupta & Sapienza 1992, Norton & Tenebaum 1993). Secondly, larger VC firms prefer greater industry diversity and broader geographic scope relative to smaller VC firms, and older VC firms prefer more industry diversity relative to younger VC firms (Gupta & Sapienza 1992). Also, larger funds (measured by total commitments) as well as larger VC firms (measured by number of managers) invest in a larger number of portfolio companies than smaller VC funds and smaller VC firms, respectively (Cumming 2004). Lastly, principal agent theory supposes that in periods with high acquisition prices VC firms fund a smaller number of companies (Kanniainen & Keuschnigg 2003, Bernile & Lyandres 2003). Nevertheless, only the study of Cumming (2004) is based on actual PE transactions. As a result, there is a lack of systematic understanding of the choice of portfolio strategies by PE firms

According to chapters 1 and 3, PE firms choose their portfolio strategies based on their expectations as well as their return and risk preferences. The objective of this chapter is to examine external factors influencing expectations and preferences of PE firms during fund formation. Since expectations and preferences of a PE firm are unobservable, I evaluate the impact of external factors on observed portfolio strategies of PE funds. In particular, the influence of the following variables is analyzed: the rate of return of MSCI World Index during fundraising, annual rate of return of MSCI World Index during investment period, new funds raised in vintage year, firm internationalization, firm experience, fund size, location of PE firm's headquarters and fund type.

Portfolio strategies of sample funds are measured along five dimensions classified into three groups: (1) 'naive' diversification across number of portfolio companies, (2) 'systematic' diversification across financing stages, industries as well as countries, and (3) 'dynamic' diversification across time. 'Naive' diversification enables a PE firm to lower the risk of its portfolio to the average systematic risk of its portfolio companies by increasing the number of companies (Evans & Archer 1968). Additionally, 'systematic' diversification takes specific characteristics of portfolio companies into account. 'Systematic' diversification benefits from the fact that portfolio companies belonging to different investment clusters usually share less systematic risk than portfolio companies within one investment cluster. Diversification across time adds a dynamic perspective accounting for changes in the economic conditions and relationships over the lifetime of a PE fund. Presumably, it allows PE firms to diversify the liquidity risk of their investments by spreading their funds over a long period of time (Cumming, Flemming & Schwienbacher 2004).

The chapter is organized as follows: *section 5.2* describes subsample 1 used in this chapter. In *section 5.3* 'naive' diversification across portfolio companies is analyzed empirically. *Section 5.4* studies 'systematic' diversification across financing stages, industries and countries. In *section 5.5* I take a closer look at factors determining 'dynamic' diversification across time. In each of the three previous sections, first a set of hypotheses is formulated, before descriptive and multivariate analyses are run. *Section 5.6* consolidates the major results of the various sections and highlights further research opportunities in this area.

5.2 Data and key variables

The objective of this chapter is to evaluate portfolio strategies of PE funds. As a result, subsample 1 utilized in this chapter is restricted to funds which appear to be entirely invested. A fund is assumed to be entirely invested if it fulfills one of the following criteria:

First, I include all PE funds which had invested equal or more than 75% of their commitments at the time of data collection, assuming that the remaining 25% or less of the capital are retained only for follow-on investments in existing portfolio companies. The capital is retained to finance further growth or to prepare a successful exit. Since it is difficult to forecast these activities, PE funds are often unable to invest their total commitments (Ljungqvist & Richardson 2003*b*). According to this criteria 166 PE funds were included in subsample 1. Second, some sample funds raised between 1977 and 1995 never invested more than 75% of their commitments. In order to not exclude these funds from the analysis, PE funds with a time span of at least 72 months between their first investment and the time of data collection are also assumed to be entirely invested. Due to this rule, eight additional funds were added to subsample 1.

Table 5.1 displays the composition of subsample 1. Subsample 1 includes 174 PE funds divided into 42 seed/early stage VC funds, 41 other stage VC funds, 42 BO funds, and 49 generalist funds. 77.0 % of the funds are managed by PE firms with their headquarters in the USA. The remaining 23.0% of funds are located in Europe. 17.8% of the sample funds are first-time, 14.9% second-time, and 16.1% third-time funds. The rest (51.1%) are funds which have sequence numbers of four or higher. 26.4% of the sample funds were liquidated at the time of data collection, while the remaining 73.6% were still active.[46] The average fund has a size of USD 500.5 million in 2000 purchasing power. Fund size varies substantially across funds in subsample 1. The mean size of the three smallest funds is USD 11.3 million, while the average size of the three largest funds adds up to USD 7,093.8 million. The distribution of fund size across the various groups exhibits the same patterns as the entire sample and is therefore not discussed further here. The oldest fund in sample 1 closed its first transaction in 1977 and the youngest in 2000 (Figure C.1).

Summary statistics for the variables used in this chapter are shown in Table 5.2.[47] The average PE fund in subsample 1 has a size of USD 500.5 million (Table 5.1), invests in 31 portfolio companies, spends its capital in 20.5 months, and has a level of diversification across financing stages of 0.36, across industries of 0.62, and across countries of 0.16. PE firms show a mean experience equivalent to 3.3 funds and run on average offices in 2.4 countries. The average annual rate of return of the MSCI World Index during fundraising is 11.1% and during the investment period 8.9%. The mean logarithm of new funds raised in vintage year is equivalent to USD 46.8 billion.

To end the data description, I comment on collinearity between the independent variables. There is no perfect multi-collinearity between the independent variables, which would inhibit regression analysis. Appendix C shows Pearson product-moment correlations (Table C.1) and variance inflation factors (Table C.2) for the set of independent variables.[48] Excluding control variables all variance inflation factors (VIF) are below 2.5. However, the VIF of the logarithm of new funds raised in vintage year increases dramatically to a value of 11.02, when the time trend is included. Both variables have a correlation of 0.93. This can be explained by the fact that the yearly amount of new funds raised grew nearly steadily during the sample period according to the statistics of TVE (Figure C.2). Only in 1990 and 1991 does TVE quote a decrease in the amounts of new funds raised compared to the previous year. When year fixed effects are included, the VIF for the logarithm of new funds raised in vintage year rises to

[46] Active funds have a NAV larger than zero. Liquidated funds do not have a NAV any more.

[47] A detailed definition of variables is included in chapter 4.

[48] The higher a VIF for a variable is, the higher the estimated variance of the corresponding coefficient, and hence, the greater the chance that seriuos multi-collinearity issues are present (Neter, Wasserman & Kutner 1990). However, no theory provides a threshold value for VIF to judge for serious multi-collinearity. Neter et al. state 10 to be a useful threshold.

Table 5.1: Composition of subsample 1

The table summarizes subsample 1 according to fund type, headquarters of PE firm, fund sequence number, and liquidation status. It divides fund types into seed/early stage VC, other VC, BO and generalists. The sample contains only funds which are managed by PE firms with headquarters in USA or Europe. Fund sequence number describes the position of a fund within all funds managed by one particular PE firm. Active funds have a NAV larger than zero. Liquidated funds do not have a NAV any more. Columns 1 and 2 display the breakdown of the sample into the different classifications. Columns 3 to 6 give information on the fund size. Fund size is the total capital committed by investors to a fund. To secure the anonymity of all funds the mean, the mean of the three smallest funds and the mean of the three largest funds is tabulated.

	Funds		Fund Size (million USD 2000)			
	Obs.	%	Mean	Std. Dev.	Mean min. three funds	Mean max. three funds
All funds	174	100.0	500.5	1,061.5	11.3	7,093.8
Fund type						
Seed/early stage VC	42	24.1	168.9	187.4	12.1	716.1
Other VC	41	23.6	290.0	419.1	31.2	1,453.6
Buyout	42	24.1	995.4	1,760.5	33.1	6,385.4
Generalist	49	28.2	536.6	942.0	49.8	3,601.8
Headquarters of PE firm						
USA	134	77.0	555.5	1,183.6	12.1	7,093.8
Europe	40	23.0	316.2	418.2	30.0	1,520.3
Fund sequence number						
First-time	31	17.8	107.4	112.8	13.8	413.1
Second-time	26	14.9	162.8	159.2	32.1	504.1
Third-time	28	16.1	226.3	235.1	23.1	780.8
later	89	51.2	822.3	1,395.5	50.8	7,093.8
Liquidation status						
Active	128	73.6	588.4	1,204.8	21.9	7,093.8
Liquidated	46	26.4	255.9	389.3	11.3	1,449.5

Table 5.2: Summary statistics for subsample 1

Subsample 1 consists of 174 PE funds. The table exhibits the mean, median, standard deviation, minimum, and maximum for dependent and independent variables used in chapter 5.

	Mean	Median	Std. Dev.	Min.	Max.
Dependent variables					
Number of portfolio companies [a]	31.30	26.50	20.60	5.33	110.00
Diversification across time (months)	20.52	18.67	9.40	4.04	46.53
Diversification across financing stages	0.36	0.42	0.20	0.00	0.72
Diversification across industries	0.62	0.65	0.18	0.00	0.84
Diversification across countries	0.16	0.05	0.22	0.00	0.85
Independent variables					
Return msci in vy	0.111	0.111	0.100	-0.126	0.432
Return msci invest period (p.a.)	0.089	0.105	0.076	-0.151	0.331
Funds raised in vy (log billion USD 2000)	3.846	3.903	1.056	-0.547	5.560
Firm internationalization [a]	2.368	1.0	2.490	1.0	9.667
Firm experience [a]	1.200	1.390	0.750	0.0	2.770
Fund size (log million USD 2000)	5.302	5.156	1.265	2.251	9.155
European headquarters (0/1)	0.230	0.0	0.422	0.0	1.0
Seed/early VC fund (0/1)	0.241	0.0	0.429	0.0	1.0
Other VC fund (0/1)	0.236	0.0	0.426	0.0	1.0
Buyout fund (0/1)	0.241	0.0	0.492	0.0	1.0
Generalist fund (0/1)	0.282	0.0	0.451	0.0	1.0
Time trend (1977 = 1)	16.868	18.0	5.344	1.0	24.0
First-time fund (0/1)	0.178	0.0	0.383	0.0	1.0

[a] To guarantee the confidentiality of PE firms and funds, the mean of the three smallest and the mean of the three largest values is displayed instead of the minimum and maximum.

14.05. This high collinearity might cause estimation difficulties when the time trend or year fixed effects are included in the regression analysis.

5.3 'Naive' diversification across portfolio companies

5.3.1 Determinants of 'naive' diversification

'Naive' diversification is measured as the number of portfolio companies in a PE fund. Although the number of portfolio companies of a PE fund is determined to some extent by its size, PE firms still can decide about the size of their portfolio. Means by which a PE firm can vary the number of portfolio companies in a fund of fixed size include: percentage of ownership in portfolio companies, use of syndication, and amount of debt employed in the transactions. In the following, I present six hypotheses about determinants of the number of portfolio companies in a PE fund which can be observed and, thus, tested in an empirical analysis.

The first hypothesis concerns the influence of the global economy on the number of portfolio companies in a PE fund. The better the global economy is performing during the investment period of a fund, the higher the prices for companies. Holding the size of a fund constant, I therefore assume:

H1: The higher the annual rate of return of the MSCI World Index during the investment period of a PE fund, the fewer portfolio companies it contains.

The larger the amount of new funds raised in vintage year, the better the perception of the PE industry. Investors expect a high quantity of attractive investment opportunities and commit a large amount of money to PE funds. It has been shown that PE funds that begin activity in a year of high commitments achieve larger returns than funds formed in years of low commitments (Kaserer & Diller 2004*c*, Gottschalg et al. 2004). As a result, in times of high commitments to the PE industry, PE firms expect high returns of their investments, and therefore, are disposed to invest a larger fraction of their money in single portfolio companies. Hence, it is supposed:

H2: The larger the amount of new funds raised in the vintage year of a PE fund, the lower the number of portfolio companies in the fund.

The opening of an office in a new country is a long term decision and involves investments. These investments have to be justified by a minimum amount of transactions managed by the new office. Consequently, I expect a positive relationship between firm internationalization and number of portfolio companies:

H3: The higher the number of countries in which a PE firm has an office, the more portfolio companies contain a fund of the PE firm.

The average amount of capital needed to fund a company depends on its development stage. The further a company is in its life cycle, the more money is typically needed to buy a significant stake in the company. In addition, VC funds usually buy only minority stakes, whereas BO funds usually purchase a controlling interest in their portfolio companies. Accordingly, PE funds focusing on different stages contain different numbers of portfolio companies:

H4: The number of portfolio companies decreases in the order: (1) seed/early stage VC funds, (2) other VC funds, (3) generalist funds, and (4) BO funds.

With each fund a PE firm manages it collects additional experience. It is able to enhance its reputation and to enlarge its network. The enhanced reputation and enlarged network should allow PE firms to generate proprietary deal flow and to strengthen their bargaining power. As a result, the prices an experienced PE firm has to pay for a share in a portfolio company should be lower than for less experienced PE firms:

H5: The more experience a PE firm has at the time of fund formation, the more portfolio companies contain a fund of the PE firm.

The more capital a PE fund has raised, the higher the number of portfolio companies it can invest in. Thus, fund size has the following effect on the number of portfolio companies in a PE fund:

H6: The bigger a PE fund, the more portfolio companies it contains.

The basic organization and governance structure of PE firms and funds is similar in Europe and the USA. As a result, I do not expect a statistically significant difference between the number of portfolio companies in European and US PE funds. The prices a PE firm has to pay for companies depends on the performance of the global economy at the time of investment (H1), but not at the time of fund formation. Hence, I do not presume a statistically significant relationship between the rate of return of the MSCI World Index in vintage year of a PE fund and its number of portfolio companies.

5.3.2 Descriptive analysis

This section presents descriptive statistics for the number of portfolio companies in subsample 1. I use correlation analysis and mean comparison tests to evaluate bivariate relationships between the number of portfolio companies and the independent variables. The average PE fund in subsample 1 contains 31.3 portfolio companies, while the median fund invests in 26.5 portfolio companies. There is a large range between the smallest and largest funds according to the number of portfolio companies. The three least numerous portfolios include an average

Table 5.3: Number of portfolio companies by fund classifications

The table contains cross tables for number of portfolio companies and fund classifications. Funds are grouped according to fund type, headquarters of PE firm, and fund sequence number. For each group the number of observations, mean, and standard deviation are shown. Moreover, the table displays results of mean comparison tests.

	No. of portfolio companies			Mean comparison test	
	Obs.	Mean	Std. Dev.	Test statistic	p-value
All funds	174	31.3	20.6		
Fund type[a]				13.42	0.0000
Seed/early stage VC	42	34.6	19.0		
Other VC	41	37.5	18.5		
Buyout	42	15.5	10.4		
Generalist	49	36.9	23.5		
Headquarters of PE firm[b]				3.11	0.0025
USA	134	33.4	21.8		
Europe	40	24.3	14.1		
Fund sequence number[b]				4.25	0.0001
First-time	31	21.7	11.7		
Follow-on	143	33.4	21.5		

[a] An one-way analysis of variance is applied to compare means. The test statistic is a F-statistic.

[b] Based on a variance ratio test a double-sided t-test with unequal variances was calculated to compare means. The test statistic is a t-statistic.

of 5.3 portfolio companies, whereas the three most numerous portfolios fund on average 110.0 companies (Table 5.2).

Table 5.3 displays cross tables and mean comparison tests for the various groups of funds in subsample 1. Generalist funds and other VC funds invest in the largest number of portfolio companies with a mean of 36.9 and 37.5, respectively. Seed/early stage VC funds include slightly fewer portfolio companies with an average of 34.6. BO funds contain substantially fewer portfolio companies with a mean of 15.5. In an one-way analysis of variance the differences between the means are statistically significant at the 1% level.

PE funds managed by PE firms with headquarters in the USA invest on average in 33.4 portfolio companies, whereas PE firms with their headquarters in Europe only invest in a mean of 24.3 portfolio companies. Hence, at the 1% level US PE funds contain a statistically significant larger number of portfolio companies than their European counterparts. First-time funds include significantly fewer portfolio companies at the 1% level than follow-on funds (21.7 compared to 33.4).

Pearson product-moment correlations show the following relationships (Table 5.4). The annual rate of return of the MSCI World Index during investment period has a negative correlation with number of portfolio companies which is statistically significant at the 5% level. Firm internationalization, firm experience and fund size have positive correlations with number of portfolio companies which are statistically significant at the 1% level. Correlation analysis

Table 5.4: Correlation analysis for number of portfolio companies

The table displays Pearson product-moment correlations between number of portfolio companies and independent variables. All correlations are based on 174 observations.

	Pearson product-moment correlation	
	No. of pcs	p-value
Return msci in vy	0.1064	0.1622
Return msci invest period (p.a.)	-0.1875**	0.0132
Funds raised in vy (log billion USD 2000)	0.0459	0.5476
Firm internationalization	0.1987***	0.0086
Firm experience	0.3204***	0.0000
Fund size (log million USD 2000)	0.2795***	0.0002
Time trend (1977 = 1)	-0.0197	0.7965

* significant at 10%; ** significant at 5%; *** significant at 1%

reveals no significant relationship between number of portfolio companies and rate of return of the MSCI World index during vintage year, nor between number of portfolio companies and new funds raised in vintage year, nor between number of portfolio companies and time trend.

5.3.3 Multivariate analysis

The bivariate analysis shed some light on the relationships between number of portfolio companies and the exogenous factors. However, they cannot test hypotheses 1 to 5 rigorously. Bivariate analysis is not able to extract the effect of single variables under the ceteris-paribus assumption. Consequently, I continue analyzing number of portfolio companies in a multivariate regression analysis.

Number of portfolio companies in a PE fund is a count variable. It can only take on non-negative integer values. Accordingly, I estimate a negative binomial regression model (NBRM) with y_i denoting the number of portfolio companies in fund i.[49] $\mathbf{x}_i$ is the line vector of the independent variables of fund i and contains unity as its first element. $\boldsymbol{\beta}$ is the vector of parameters including a constant. The NBRM assumes that the distribution of y_i given $\mathbf{x}_i$ is negative binomial with conditional mean and variance of (Wooldridge 2002):

$$E\left(y_i|\mathbf{x}_i\right) = m\left(\mathbf{x}_i, \boldsymbol{\beta}\right)$$

$$V\left(y_i|\mathbf{x}_i\right) = m\left(\mathbf{x}_i, \boldsymbol{\beta}\right) + \alpha \cdot \left[m\left(\mathbf{x}_i, \boldsymbol{\beta}\right)\right]^2 \tag{5.1}$$

The NBRM maximizes the following log-likelihood function:

49 A likelihood ratio test for overdispersion rejects the use of a Poisson regression model with a pseudo-χ^2-test-statistic of 433.0 and a p-value of 0.000.

$$\sum_{i=1}^{N} \ell_i(\boldsymbol{\beta}, \alpha) = \sum_{i=1}^{N} \left[\alpha^{-1} \cdot log \left(\frac{\alpha^{-1}}{\alpha^{-1} + m(\mathbf{x}_i, \boldsymbol{\beta})} \right) + \right. \left. + y_i \cdot log \left(\frac{m(\mathbf{x}_i, \boldsymbol{\beta})}{\alpha^{-1} + m(\mathbf{x}_i, \boldsymbol{\beta})} \right) + log \left(\frac{\Gamma(y_i + \alpha^{-1})}{\Gamma(\alpha^{-1})} \right) \right] \quad (5.2)$$

where α represents the degree of overdispersion and $\Gamma(\cdot)$ is the gamma function defined for $r > 0$ by $\Gamma(r) = \int_0^\infty z^{r-1} exp(-z)\, dz$. The NBRM can be estimated using standard maximum likelihood methods.[50] The mean is estimated as exponential function of the parametric model $\mathbf{x}\boldsymbol{\beta}$. Analyzing the number of portfolio companies the parametric model has the form:

$$m(\mathbf{x}, \boldsymbol{\beta}) = exp\left(\beta_0 + \sum_{k=1}^{K} \beta_k \cdot x_k\right) \quad (5.3)$$

with β_0 = constant,
β_k = parameter of variable x_k, and
x_k = independent variables (compare Table 5.5).

I estimate Huber-White standard errors which are robust against violation of the assumption of homoscedasticity (White 1980). Moreover, the observations in subsample 1 are clustered because an average of 3.5 funds belong to one PE firm. The observations belonging to one PE firm might not be independent from each other. As a result, standard errors are also adjusted for 50 clusters, i.e., PE firms (Rogers 1993). Table 5.5 displays the estimation results containing marginal effects at the sample means of independent variables, robust standard errors, and summary statistics. Table C.3 in the appendix contains the estimated coefficients. Regression (1) estimates the basic model. Specification (2) includes the control variables time trend and first-time fund. Regression (3) controls for year fixed effects. The χ^2-tests on joint significance of all parameters are significant at the 1% level for all specifications.

In the basic model, rate of return of the annual MSCI World Index during investment period, firm internationalization, firm experience, fund size, as well as the dummy variables, seed/early VC funds, other VC funds, and BO funds have statistically significant influence on number of portfolio companies at least at the 10% level. Rate of return of the MSCI World Index during vintage year, new funds raised during vintage year and the dummy variable indicating funds managed by a PE firm with headquarters in Europe have no significant effect on number of portfolio companies in the basic model.

Hypothesis 1 is supported by the data. The rate of return of the MSCI World Index during the investment period has a negative effect on the number of portfolio companies which is significant at the 1% level. In times of a well performing economy, prices for companies rise. Ceteris paribus, PE firms are only able to invest in a lower number of portfolio companies. An increase of one standard deviation in the annual rate of return of the MSCI World Index during

[50] For further explanations of the NBRM see Cameron & Trivedi (1986), Wooldridge (2002), and Long & Freese (2001).

investment period reduces number of portfolio companies by 7.8%, holding all other variables constant (Table 5.5, column (1)).[51] The parameter stays significant at the 5% level but loses some of its magnitude when time trend is included. Controlling for year fixed effects leads to an insignificant parameter for annual rate of return of the MSCI World Index during investment period.

As expected, the parameter of firm internationalization is positive and statistically significant at least at the 1% level. An additional country is associated with an increase in number of portfolio companies by 4.5%, holding all other variables constant (Table 5.5, column (1)). The bigger a PE firm is in terms of international subsidiaries, the larger is the number of portfolio companies in its funds. Each country has to manage a minimum of transactions in order to justify its existence. This result is in line with Cumming (2004), who reports a positive relationship between number of portfolio companies and firm size measured in terms of fund managers for VC funds.

Under the ceteris paribus assumption, seed/early VC funds contain the largest number of portfolio companies followed by other VC funds, generalist funds, and BO funds. Hence, hypothesis 3 as well as the result of Cumming (2004) are confirmed by the data. Assuming an average fund size of USD 500.5 million, a seed/early VC fund would have invested in 47.1, an other VC fund in 43.6, a generalist in 34.5, and a BO fund in 15.7 portfolio companies (Table 5.5, column (1)).[52]

Also, I find weak evidence in favor of hypothesis 5. Although the marginal effect of firm experience is only statistically significant at the 10% level in specification (3) (Table 5.5), the coefficient is statistically significant at the 10% level in specification (1) and (3) (Table C.3). There appears to be a positive relationship between number of portfolio companies and firm experience. A doubling of fund sequence number increases number of portfolio companies by 12.3%, holding all other variables constant (Table 5.5, column (1)). Experienced PE firms seem to pay less for their investments than their unexperienced counterparts. The track record and reputation of experienced PE firms enhance proprietary deal flow and bargaining power resulting in lower prices compared to unexperienced PE firms.

Not surprisingly, fund size has a positive effect on number of portfolio companies in a PE fund, which is statistically significant at the 5% level. The more capital a PE fund has raised, the larger is the number of portfolio companies in which it can invest. For instance, rising fund size of an average seed/early VC fund from USD 150 million to USD 250 million increases number of portfolio companies from 38.2 to 41.7 (Table 5.5, column (1)). This confirms once more the results of Cumming (2004), who also reports a positive relation between fund size and number of portfolio companies in a VC fund.

[51] The numerical interpretation of continuous effects in this subsection are given as percentage changes, because percentage change in the NBRM does not depend on the level of any variable.

[52] An average fund is assumed to have the following characteristics: US headquarters, offices in two countries, fund sequence number of three, a rate of return of the MSCI World Index during vintage year of 11.1%, an annual rate of return of the MSCI World Index during investment period of 8.9%, and an amount of new funds raised in vintage year of USD 46.8 billion.

Table 5.5: Negative binomial regression for number of portfolio companies
Subsample 1 consists of 174 PE funds. The dependent variable is number of portfolio companies. Independent variables include rate of return of the MSCI World Index in vintage year, annual rate of return of the MSCI World Index during investment period, new funds raised in vintage year, firm internationalization, firm experience, fund size, and time trend. Additionally, the regressions contain dummy variables indicating funds managed by PE firms with headquarters in Europe, seed/early VC funds, other VC funds, BO funds, and first-time funds as well as a constant (not reported). The table reports marginal effects at the sample means of independent variables. For dummy variables the effect of a discrete change from zero to one is displayed.

	Dependent variable: Number of portfolio companies		
	(1)	(2)	(3)
Return msci in vy	1.875	-6.56	-8.553
	(8.315)	(5.818)	(8.008)
Return msci invest period (p.a.)	-30.092***	-24.352**	-16.053
	(11.445)	(12.439)	(15.299)
Funds raised in vy (log bil. USD 2000)	-3.373	3.627*	3.015
	(2.217)	(2.184)	(3.123)
Firm internationalization	1.228*	1.292**	1.269**
	(0.683)	(0.652)	(0.613)
Firm experience	4.700	4.653	4.650*
	(2.976)	(3.927)	(2.677)
Fund size (log mil. USD 2000)	4.885**	4.512*	4.986**
	(2.437)	(2.345)	(2.199)
European headquarter (0/1)	-2.582	-1.675	-1.849
	(3.334)	(3.163)	(3.017)
Seed/early VC fund (0/1)	9.547*	9.185*	9.884*
	(5.668)	(5.403)	(5.636)
Other VC fund (0/1)	7.031**	7.647**	7.590**
	(3.159)	(3.178)	(3.263)
Buyout fund (0/1)	-18.435***	-18.238***	-18.447***
	(3.2508)	(3.441)	(3.500)
Time trend (1977 = 1)		-1.397**	
		(0.559)	
First-time fund (0/1)		-2.079	
		(3.546)	
Year F.E.	No	No	Yes
Log pseudo-likelihood	-670.2	-666.5	-663.9
χ^2-statistic	131.9	221.3	1241.8
p-value of χ^2-test	0.000	0.000	0.000
Number of observations	174	174	174

Standard errors are in parentheses and are adjusted for serial correlation, heteroscedasticity and dependence between observations from one PE firm.
* significant at 10%; *** significant at 5%; *** significant at 1%

The effects of fund type, fund size, firm internationalization, and firm experience are stable in direction and magnitude across the various specifications. Furthermore, there seems to have been a trend to smaller portfolios in the sample period. The time trend included in regression (2) has a negative coefficient and is statistically significant at the 5% level. One possible explanation is that the average amount of money in VC investments (i.e., the amount of capital necessary for the development and marketing of new products) and BO transactions (i.e., the size and complexity of buyout transactions) has grown from 1979 to 2000. Finally, neither new funds raised during vintage year nor the location of PE firm headquarters has a significant influence on the number of portfolio companies. The bivariate difference in number of portfolio companies between European and US PE funds is explained through other independent variables. In particular, US PE funds have remarkably larger fund sizes than their European equivalents leading to larger numbers of portfolio companies of US PE funds in the bivariate analysis.

5.4 'Systematic' diversification across financing stages, industries, and countries

5.4.1 Determinants of 'systematic' diversification

'Naive' diversification only counts the number of companies in a portfolio. In contrast, 'systematic' diversification considers the specific characteristics of portfolio companies. Chapter 3 derives the optimal level of 'systematic' diversification in PE funds in a theoretical model. Diversification is measured in terms of investment clusters, in which a PE fund invests its capital. Comparative statics exhibit the relationship between model parameters and the optimal level of diversification in PE funds. First, an increase in the set-up costs leads to a decrease in the optimal number of investment clusters. Second, an extension of fund size results in a rise in the optimal number of investment clusters. Third, the more risk-averse the PE firm is, the higher the optimal number of investment clusters. Fourth, growth in the expected rate of return of portfolio companies induces a reduction in the optimal number of investment clusters. Last, the larger the risk of portfolio companies is, the higher the optimal number of investment clusters. These relations build the basis for the hypotheses presented in this section.

The expected development of the global economy influences the perception of future investment opportunities by PE firms. In times of a well performing economy PE firms expect their portfolio companies to earn high returns. Thus, according to comparative statics in chapter 3 it is proposed:

H1: The higher the rate of return of the MSCI World Index in the vintage year of a PE fund is, the less diversified is its portfolio across financing stages, industries, and countries.

A PE firm may change its expectations on the rate of return of its portfolio companies when there is a significant change in the development of the global economy. As a response, a PE firm may try to adjust its portfolio strategy. The possibility to make adjustments is limited to the investment period of a fund:

H2: The higher the annual rate of return of the MSCI World Index during the investment period of a PE fund is, the less diversified is its portfolio across financing stages, industries, and countries.

A positive perception of PE market condition at the time of fund formation causes PE firms to expect high returns for future investments, and simultaneously, attracts commitments by investors anticipating the high future returns (Kaserer & Diller 2004*c*, Gottschalg et al. 2004). Hence, I assume a negative relationship between new funds raised in vintage year and the level of 'systematic' diversification in PE funds:

H3: The higher the amount of new funds raised in the vintage year of a PE fund is, the less diversified is its portfolio across financing stages, industries, and countries.

To run an office in a country, a PE firm has to pay set-up costs associated with country specific investments. Since some part of the costs are sunk, the set-up costs for continuing investments in the country are lower compared to a PE firm entering the country for the first time. According to comparative statics in chapter 3, lower set-up costs are related to a higher level of 'systematic' diversification:

H4: The higher the number of countries, in which a PE firm runs offices, the more diversified is a PE fund of this PE firm across financing stages, industries, and countries.

With the management of each additional fund a PE firm acquires new knowledge. The entire experience of a PE firm at the time of fund formation has an ambiguous effect on the level of 'systematic' diversification of PE funds. On the one hand, the more experience a PE firm has in specific investment clusters, the lower are its set-up costs for these clusters:

H5a: The more experience a PE firm has at the time of fund formation, the more diversified is its portfolio across financing stages, industries, and countries.

On the other hand, the more funds a PE firm has successfully managed, the longer is its track record. A long track record compensates a negative impact of a badly performing fund on future fundraising. Hence, the more experienced, the less risk-averse is a PE firm leading to the contrary hypothesis:

H5b: The more experience a PE firm has at the time of fund formation, the less diversified is its portfolio across financing stages, industries, and countries.

Which effect dominates cannot be judged ex ante. Furthermore, the number of investment clusters grows with increasing fund size. Thus, fund size is supposed to foster 'systematic' diversification in a PE fund:

H6: The bigger a PE fund is, the more diversified is its portfolio across financing stages, industries, and countries.

Whereas the USA is one country with a huge economy, Europe consists of numerous countries with small economies relative to the US economy. The small size of European economies translates into a lower quantity of attractive investment opportunities in each investment cluster of a European country in comparison to the USA. The relative lack of attractive investment opportunities forces European PE firms to enter more investment clusters than their US counterparts.

H7: European PE funds are more diversified across financing stages, industries, and countries compared to US PE funds.

In chapter 3, I argue that set-up costs are decreasing with the development of portfolio companies. The older and further developed companies are, the more information is available about their products, operations, and financial potential. Additionally, the costs for obtaining this information decrease with the development of companies because the information becomes more widely spread. As a result, set-up costs for PE firms predominantly involved in seed and early stage financing are higher than for PE firms specialized in later stage financing. Hence, PE funds of different fund types have different levels of diversification across industries and countries:

H8: The level of diversification across industries and countries increases in the order: (1) seed/early stage VC funds, (2) other VC funds, (3) generalist funds, and (4) BO funds.

Diversification across financing stages is not included in hypothesis 8. The variables fund type and diversification across financing stages are calculated based on the same information. By definition, I expect an increasing diversification across financing stages of the following order: (1) BO funds, (2) seed/early VC funds, (3) other VC funds, and (4) generalist funds.

5.4.2 Diversification across financing stages

5.4.2.1 Descriptive analysis

Diversification across financing stages measures the distribution of a PE fund's capital across the financing stages (1) seed/early stage VC, (2) second, expansion and later stage VC, (3) BO, (4) listed securities, and (5) other financing stage in terms of HHI. Table 5.6 displays cross tables and mean comparison tests for diversification across financing stages. The average PE fund in subsample 1 has a level of diversification across financing stages of 0.36. As expected, BO funds are least diversified across financing stages with a mean of 0.12. Generalist funds have the highest level of diversification with a mean of 0.56. Seed/early VC funds and other VC funds are in between with means of 0.28 and 0.47, respectively. This order follows from the definition of the variable fund type. An one-way analysis of variance reveals that the differences in means are statistically significant at the 1% level.

Table 5.6: Diversification across financing stages by fund classifications

The table contains cross tables for diversification across financing stages and fund classifications. Funds are grouped according to fund type, headquarters of PE firm, and fund sequence number. For each group the number of observations, mean, and standard deviation are shown. Moreover, the table displays results of mean comparison tests.

	Div. a. financing stages			Mean comparison test	
	Obs.	Mean	Std. Dev.	Test statistic	p-value
All funds	174	0.363	0.205		
Fund type[a]				129.170	0.0000
Seed/early stage VC	42	0.275	0.125		
Other VC	41	0.465	0.124		
Buyout	42	0.123	0.131		
Generalist	49	0.558	0.075		
Headquarters of PE firm[b]				0.780	0.4392
USA	134	0.371	0.187		
Europe	40	0.337	0.257		
Fund sequence number[b]				1.311	0.1968
First-time	31	0.318	0.210		
Follow-on	143	0.373	0.203		

[a] An one-way analysis of variance was applied to compare means. The test statistic is a F-statistic.

[b] Based on a variance ratio test a double-sided t-test with equal or unequal variances was calculated to compare means. The test statistic is a t-statistic.

US funds are on average slightly more diversified across financing stages than European funds (0.37 compared to 0.34). However, a mean comparison test is not significant. The hypothesis that US and European funds are equally diversified across financing stages can not be rejected.

First-time funds have a lower level of diversification across financing stages relative to follow-on funds. First-time funds show an average diversification across financing stages of 0.32, while follow-on funds are diversified across financing stages with a mean of 0.37. Though, in a double sided t-test with equal variances the difference between the means is not significant.

The relationship between firm internationalization and diversification across financing stages is positive and statistically significant at the 1% level with a Pearson product-moment correlation of 0.227. Diversification across financing stages also correlates positively with firm experience. The Pearson product-moment correlation between both variables adds up to 0.145 and is statistically significant at the 10% level. The remaining independent variables do not show statistically significant correlations with diversification across financing stages (Table 5.7).

Table 5.7: Correlation analysis for diversification across financing stages
The table displays Pearson product-moment correlations between diversification across financing stages and independent variables. All correlations are based on 174 observations.

	Pearson product-moment correlation	
	Div. a. fin. stages	p-value
Return msci in vy	-0.0332	0.6636
Return msci invest period (p.a.)	-0.0385	0.6143
Funds raised in vy (log billion USD 2000)	-0.0073	0.9239
Firm internationalization	0.2270***	0.0002
Firm experience	0.1451*	0.0561
Fund size (log million USD 2000)	-0.0373	0.6248
Time trend (1977 = 1)	0.0173	0.8211

* significant at 10%; ** significant at 5%; *** significant at 1%

5.4.2.2 Multivariate analysis

The aim of this section is to evaluate the influence of the exogenous factors on diversification across financing stages in a multivariate regression analysis. Diversification across financing stages is measured as HHI taking on continuous values between zero and one. Eighteen PE funds in subsample 1 have a level of diversification across financing stages of zero because they invest all their capital in one financing stage. All 18 are BO funds.

Consequently, I use a Tobit regression model with left censoring at zero. The Tobit model can be estimated with standard maximum likelihood methods. The log likelihood function of the Tobit model has the following form:[53]

$$\sum_{i=1}^{N} \ell_i(\boldsymbol{\beta}, \sigma) = \sum_{i=1}^{N} d_i \cdot log\left[\frac{1}{\sigma}\phi\left(\frac{y_i - \mathbf{x}_i\boldsymbol{\beta}}{\sigma}\right)\right] + \sum_{i=1}^{N} c_i \cdot log\left[1 - \Phi\left(\frac{\mathbf{x}_i\boldsymbol{\beta}}{\sigma}\right)\right] \quad (5.4)$$

with y_i = div. a. fin. stages of fund i,
$\boldsymbol{\beta}$ = vector of parameters including a constant,
$\mathbf{x}_i$ = line vector of independent variables of fund i containing unity as its first element (compare Table 5.8),
d_i = 1 if $y_i > 0$ and 0 else,
c_i = 1 if $y_i = 0$ and 0 else,
σ = standard deviation of residuals in latent variable model,
ϕ = standard normal density function, and
Φ = standard cumulative normal density function.

[53] For further explanations of Tobit regression compare Wooldridge (2002).

The estimation results are displayed in Table 5.8. The table contains marginal effects at the sample means of independent variables:

$$\frac{\partial E\left(y|\overline{\mathbf{x}}\right)}{\partial x_j} = \Phi\left(\frac{\overline{\mathbf{x}}\beta}{\sigma}\right)\beta_j$$

with $\mathbf{x}_j$ = independent variable of interest (compare Table 5.8) and
β_i = parameter of independent variable j,

It also includes standard errors, as well as summary statistics of the regressions. Table C.4 in the appendix contains the estimated coefficients. Standard errors in both tables are robust against the violation of the assumption of homoscedasticity and are adjusted for 50 clusters, i.e. PE firms (White 1980, Rogers 1993). As mentioned before, the variables fund type and diversification across financing stages are both calculated based on the fraction of invested capital in the various financing stages. As a result, the variable fund type explains a large part of the variance in diversification across financing stages. To capture this speciality, specifications (1) to (3) do not include the dummy variables seed/early VC, other VC, and BO. They are added in regressions (4). The χ^2-tests on joint significance of all parameters are significant at the 1% level for all specifications.

Neither the development of the global economy nor the condition of the PE industry has an impact on diversification across financing stages in PE funds. Rate of return of the MSCI World Index in vintage year, annual rate of return of the MSCI World Index during investment period, and new funds raised in vintage year have statistically insignificant coefficients across all specifications.

In contrast, the data strongly supports hypothesis 4. Diversification across financing stages rises with the number of countries in which a PE firm runs offices. The coefficient for firm internationalization is statistically significant at the 1% level across all regressions. With each additional country diversification across financing stages rises by 0.19 standard deviations, holding all other variables at their mean (Table 5.8, column (1)).[54] Controlling for fund types the impact of an additional country decreases to 0.07 standard deviations, holding all other variables at their mean, but stays statistically significant at the 1% level (Table 5.8, column (4)).

Firm experience fosters diversification across financing stages. A doubling in fund sequence number increases diversification across financing stages by 0.27 standard deviations, holding all other variables at their mean (Table 5.8, column (1)). The effect is statistically significant at the 5% level and stable across specifications (1) to (3). This result supports hypothesis 5a and neglects hypothesis 5b. The set-up cost effect appears to dominate the risk aversion effect. An increasing experience presumably lowers the set-up costs, and hence, raises the level of diversification across financing stages, ceteris paribus. Introducing fund types supports this argumentation leading to an insignificant effect of firm experience in regression (4). Generalist

[54] The marginal and discrete effects in this subsection are interpreted relative to the standard deviation of diversification across financing stages of 0.205 in subsample 1.

funds in subsample 1 have a significant higher fund sequence number than the other fund types. On average, generalist funds have a fund sequence number of 5.8, while seed/early VC funds have an average fund sequence number of 3.4, other VC funds of 3.6, and BO funds of 4.1. The parameter of firm experience in regressions (1) to (3) shows, that with an increasing number of funds a PE firm diversifies its capital more across financing stages. At a certain point the PE fund no longer invests more than 70% of its capital in one financing stage and thus is categorized as generalist fund.

Table 5.8: Tobit regression for diversification across financing stages

Subsample 1 consists of 174 PE funds. The dependent variable is diversification across financing stages. Independent variables include rate of return of the MSCI World Index in vintage year, annual rate of return of the MSCI World Index during investment period, new funds raised in vintage year, firm internationalization, firm experience, fund size, and time trend. Additionally, the regressions contain dummy variables indicating funds managed by PE firms with headquarters in Europe, seed/early VC funds, other VC funds, BO funds, and first-time funds, as well as a constant (not reported). The table reports marginal effects at the sample means of independent variables. For dummy variables the effect of a discrete change from zero to one is displayed.

	Dependent variable: Diversification across financing stages			
	(1)	(2)	(3)	(4)
Return msci in vy	-0.176	-0.161	-0.112	0.019
	(0.156)	(0.143)	(0.168)	(0.111)
Return msci invest period (p.a.)	-0.202	-0.207	-0.065	-0.110
	(0.171)	(0.179)	(0.200)	(0.153)
Funds raised in vy (log bil. USD 2000)	0.020	0.007	0.046	0.013
	(0.028)	(0.030)	(0.056)	(0.026)
Firm internationalization	0.040***	0.039***	0.042***	0.014***
	(0.010)	(0.010)	(0.010)	(0.005)
Firm experience	0.055**	0.059*	0.065**	0.008
	(0.027)	(0.033)	(0.029)	(0.022)
Fund size (log mil. USD 2000)	-0.053**	-0.052**	-0.057**	-0.004
	(0.026)	(0.026)	(0.025)	(0.013)
European headquarter (0/1)	-0.163**	-0.164**	-0.169**	-0.058
	(0.077)	(0.076)	(0.075)	(0.040)
Seed/early VC fund (0/1)				-0.257***
				(0.028)
Other VC fund (0/1)				-0.093***
				(0.025)
Buyout fund (0/1)				-0.404***
				(0.028)
Time trend (1977 = 1)		0.003		
		(0.006)		
First-time fund (0/1)		0.012		
		(0.048)		
Year F.E.	No	No	Yes	Yes
Log likelihood	7.15	7.21	11.15	96.84
χ^2-statistic	27.22	31.51	85.64	580.89
p-value of χ^2-test	0.000	0.000	0.000	0.000
Number of left-censored observations	18	18	18	18
Number of observations	174	174	174	174

Standard errors are in parentheses and are adjusted for serial correlation, heteroscedasticity and dependence between observations of one PE firm.
* significant at 10%; *** significant at 5%; *** significant at 1%

In contrast to hypothesis 6, fund size has a negative effect on diversification across financing stages in regressions (1) to (3) which is statistically significant at the 5% level. However, this result has to be interpreted carefully as controlling for fund types in specification (4) yields to an insignificant coefficient of fund size. The negative sign for fund size in regression (1) to (3) can be explained by the characteristics of BO funds in subsample 1. BO funds have the lowest level of diversification across financing stages (compare specification (4) in Table 5.8), and are by far the biggest funds (compare Table 5.1). Restricting subsample 1 to VC and generalist funds, an unreported regression shows a positive coefficient for fund size, which is significant at the 1% level. A doubling in fund size increases diversification across financing stages by 0.20 standard deviations, holding all other variables at mean. To conclude, fund size has a positive impact on diversification across financing stages for VC and generalist funds. However, this relationship is not valid for BO funds.

In specification (1) to (3) PE firms with their headquarters in Europe diversify less across financing stages than PE firms with their headquarters in the USA. The level of diversification across financing stages of European PE funds is 0.80 standard deviations less than that of equivalent US funds, holding all other variables at mean (Table 5.8, column (1)). This result is in contrast to hypothesis 7. However, the result can be explained by the different distribution of funds across fund types between European and US funds in subsample 1. Of European funds 37.5% are BO funds which have by far the lowest level of diversification across financing stages (compare Table 5.6), whereas for US funds only 20.2% are BO funds. Consequently, in regression (4) there is no statistical significant difference in diversification across financing stages between European and US funds at the 10% level (Table 5.8, column (4)).

Finally, regression (4) indicates the same order of fund types according to diversification across financing stages as the bivariate analysis. BO funds have the least level of diversification across financing stages, followed by early stage VC funds, other VC funds, and generalist funds. The difference between BO funds and generalist funds adds up to 1.97 standard deviations, holding all other variables at their mean. The deviation between seed/early VC funds and generalist funds averages 1.25 standard deviations, holding all other variables at their mean. Most similar are other VC funds and generalist funds with a difference of 0.45 standard deviations, holding all other variables at their mean (Table 5.8, column (4)).

5.4.3 Diversification across industries

5.4.3.1 Descriptive analysis

Diversification across industries measures the distribution of PE funds' capital across nine industry segments suggested by Gompers et al. (2005): (1) Internet and Computers, (2) Communications and Electronics, (3) Business and Industrial, (4) Consumer, (5) Energy and Utilities, (6) Biotechnology and Healthcare, (7) Financial Services, (8) Business Services, and (9) Other. The average fund in subsample 1 has a level of diversification across industries of 0.62.

This value cannot be compared to values of diversification across financing stages or countries because the number of classes on which HHI is calculated differ.

Table 5.9 contains cross tables and mean comparison test for diversification across industries and the various groups of funds. According to an one-way analysis of variance the difference in diversification across industries between the four fund types is statistically significant at the 1% level. Seed/early VC funds have the lowest level of diversification across industries with a mean of 0.53, succeeded by other VC funds with a mean of 0.63, BO funds with a mean of 0.64, and generalist funds with a mean of 0.67.

European PE funds diversify their capital across industries more than US PE funds. The difference adds up to 0.084 and is statistically significant at the 1% level. Though first-time funds have a lower level of diversification across industries than follow-on funds (0.57 compared to 0.63), the hypothesis that first-time funds and follow-on funds have the same level of diversification across financing stages cannot be rejected at the 10% level.

Moreover, firm internationalization, firm experience, and fund size correlate positively and statistically significant at the 1% level with diversification across industries (Table 5.10). Pearson product-moment correlations are 0.32 for firm internationalization, 0.24 for firm experience, and 0.24 for firm size. The remaining independent variables do not have statistically significant correlations with diversification across industries.

Table 5.9: Diversification across industries by fund classifications

The table contains cross tables for diversification across industries and fund classifications. Funds are grouped according to fund type, headquarters of PE firm, and fund sequence number. For each group number of observations, mean, and standard deviation are shown. Moreover, the table displays results of mean comparison tests.

	Div. a. industries			Mean comparison test	
	Obs.	Mean	Std. Dev.	Test statistic	p-value
All funds	174	0.618	0.178		
Fund type[a]				5.450	0.0013
Seed/early stage VC	42	0.529	0.176		
Other VC	41	0.631	0.135		
Buyout	42	0.638	0.160		
Generalist	49	0.669	0.201		
Headquarters of PE firm[b]				-3.092	0.0027
USA	134	0.599	0.184		
Europe	40	0.683	0.139		
Fund sequence number[b]				1.616	0.1080
First-time	31	0.572	0.185		
Follow-on	143	0.628	0.175		

[a] An one-way analysis of variance was applied to compare means. The test statistic is a F-statistic.

[b] Based on a variance ratio test a double-sided t-test with unequal variances was calculated to compare means. The test statistic is a t-statistic

Table 5.10: Correlation analysis for diversification across industries
The table displays Pearson product-moment correlations between diversification across industries and independent variables. All correlations are based on 174 observations.

	Pearson product-moment correlation	
	Div. a. industries	p-value
Return msci in vy	0.0441	0.5633
Return msci invest period (p.a.)	-0.0367	0.6306
Funds raised in vy (log billion USD 2000)	-0.0830	0.2764
Firm internationalization	0.3221***	0.0000
Firm experience	0.2356***	0.0018
Fund size (log million USD 2000)	0.2434***	0.0012
Time trend (1977 = 1)	-0.1114	0.1434

* significant at 10%; ** significant at 5%; *** significant at 1%

5.4.3.2 Multivariate analysis

Diversification across industries is measured as HHI equivalent to diversification across financing stages. It can only take on values between zero and one. Three funds in subsample 1 show a level of diversification across industries of zero, investing their entire capital in only one industry. Accordingly, the same Tobit regression model is estimated as for diversification across financing stages.[55] Table 5.11 contains the regression results and displays marginal effects at the sample means of independent variables, standard errors and summary statistics of the estimations. Table C.5 in the appendix includes the estimated coefficients. Standard errors in both tables are robust against the violation of the assumption of homoscedasticity and are adjusted for 50 clusters, i.e., PE firms (White 1980, Rogers 1993). Column (1) presents the basic model. Column (2) controls for a time trend and first-time funds. In column (3) year fixed effects are added. The χ^2-tests on joint significance of all parameters are significant at the 1% level for all specifications.

The data does not confirm hypothesis 1, 2 and 3. Neither rate of return of the MSCI World Index in vintage year, nor annual rate of return of the MSCI World Index during investment period, nor new funds raised during vintage year have statistically significant coefficients. Hence, neither the development of the global economy nor the condition of PE markets at the time of fund formation do have an impact on diversification across industries in PE funds.

The effect of firm internationalization has the predicted direction on diversification across industries. However, it is only statistically significant at the 10% level in specification (2) controlling for a linear time trend. An additional country, in which a PE firm has an office, increases diversification across industries by 0.06 standard deviations, holding all other variables at their mean (Table 5.11, column (2)). The opening of a new office seems to lower the set-up costs, and hence, leads to more diversification.

The same is true for firm experience. A larger experience at the time of fund formation presumably decreases the set-up costs, and therefore, increases diversification across industries.

[55] For a detailed description of the estimated Tobit model see section 5.4.2.2.

As for diversification across financing stages the set-up cost effect appears to dominate the risk aversion effect. Though, the effect is only statistically significant at the 10% level in specification (2). A doubling in fund sequence number rise diversification across industries by 0.39 standard deviations, holding all other variables at their mean (Table 5.11, column (2)).

Table 5.11: Tobit regression for diversification across industries

Subsample 1 consists of 174 PE funds. The dependent variable is diversification across industries. Independent variables include rate of return of the MSCI World Index in vintage year, annual rate of return of the MSCI World Index during investment period, new funds raised in vintage year, firm internationalization, firm experience, and fund size. Additionally, the regressions contain dummy variables indicating funds managed by PE firms with headquarters in Europe, seed/early VC funds, other VC funds, BO funds, and first-time funds, as well as a constant (not reported). The table reports marginal effects at the sample means of independent variables. For dummy variables the effect of a discrete change from zero to one is displayed.

	Dependent variable: Diversification across industries		
	(1)	(2)	(3)
Return msci in vy	0.064	-0.039	-0.010
	(0.109)	(0.100)	(0.110)
Return msci invest period (p.a.)	-0.115	-0.046	-0.149
	(0.150)	(0.149)	(0.181)
Funds raised in vy (log bil. USD 2000)	-0.035	0.038	0.036
	(0.026)	(0.035)	(0.046)
Firm internationalization	0.010	0.011*	0.009
	(0.007)	(0.007)	(0.007)
Firm experience	0.042	0.069*	0.046
	(0.034)	(0.041)	(0.034)
Fund size (log mil. USD 2000)	0.024	0.018	0.025
	(0.017)	(0.017)	(0.017)
European headquarter (0/1)	0.085*	0.095**	0.105**
	(0.046)	(0.046)	(0.046)
Seed/early VC fund (0/1)	-0.050	-0.046	-0.047
	(0.064)	(0.063)	(0.060)
Other VC fund (0/1)	0.036	0.048	0.047
	(0.052)	(0.052)	(0.053)
Buyout fund (0/1)	-0.019	-0.010	-0.023
	(0.049)	(0.050)	(0.050)
Time trend (1977 = 1)		-0.014***	
		(0.005)	
First-time fund (0/1)		0.044	
		(0.037)	
Year F.E.	No	No	Yes
Log likelihood	66.65	69.23	70.83
χ^2-statistic	40.43	45.41	103.98
p-value of χ^2-test	0.000	0.000	0.000
Number of left-censored observations	3	3	3
Number of observations	174	174	174

Standard errors are in parentheses and are adjusted for serial correlation, heteroscedasticity and dependence between observations of one PE firm.
* significant at 10%; *** significant at 5%; *** significant at 1%

The regressions corroborate hypothesis 7, supposing that European funds are more diversified across industries than their US counterparts. The level of diversification across industries of European PE funds is 0.48 standard deviations larger than that of equivalent US PE funds, holding all other variables at their mean (Table 5.11, column (1)). The effect is significant at least at the 5% level and stable across all specifications. The relative lack of attractive investment opportunities in one investment cluster between a European country and the USA economy forces European PE firms to diversify their capital across more industries than their US counterparts. A further incentive fostering diversification across industries in European PE funds is the absence of a pan-European fund structure. The different tax laws of European countries make the structuring and administration of transactions outside the home country of a PE fund complicated and expensive (Commission 2005). Hence, European PE firms may prefer diversification across industries to diversification across countries.

Although neither seed/early VC funds, nor other VC funds, nor BO funds show a level of diversification across industries statistically different from generalist funds, a Wald test on the joint significance of the fund type dummies is statistically significant at the 10% level in specification (2) with a p-value of 0.078 and in specification (3) with a p-value of 0.89. As expected, seed/early VC funds have the lowest level of diversification across industries. In contrast, other VC funds show the highest level of diversification across industries. BO funds and generalist funds lie between the extremes with similar levels of diversification across industries. The difference between the extremes adds up to 0.53 standard deviations, holding all other variables at their mean (Table 5.11, column (2)). This order describes one of the specialities of seed and early stage VC investing. Since seed and early stage projects are still in product or technical development, it is very difficult to assess the technical success of the project. In order to be able to select successful projects, seed/early VC funds significantly have to invest in specialized knowledge. As soon as the companies start producing and shipping, the technical uncertainties mainly disappear, and hence, the set-up costs for interacting in different industries fall drastically. This explains the high level of diversification across industries in other VC funds compared to seed/early VC funds.

Finally, during the sample period PE funds have become less diversified across industries. The linear time trend in specification (2) has a negative coefficient which is statistically significant at the 1% level. An additional year decreases diversification across industries by 0.08 standard deviations, holding all other variables at their mean (Table 5.11, column (2)).

5.4.4 Diversification across countries

5.4.4.1 Descriptive analysis

While diversification across financing stages or industries is possible within one country, diversification across countries forces PE firms to cross borders. The variable diversification across financing stages measures the distribution of PE funds' capital across the countries in which their portfolio companies have their main operations. Mean diversification across countries in subsample 1 sums up to 0.16. Arranging fund types by diversification across countries in an ascending order leads to the following sequence: (1) other VC funds with a mean of 0.14, (2) seed/early VC funds with a mean of 0.15, (3) BO funds with a mean of 0.16, and (4) generalist funds with a mean of 0.19. However, according to an one-way analysis of variance, the differences in means are not statistically significant (Table 5.12).

Table 5.12: Diversification across countries by fund classifications

The table contains cross tables for diversification across countries and fund classifications. Funds are grouped according to fund type, headquarters of PE firm, and fund sequence number. For each group number of observations, mean, and standard deviation are shown. Moreover, the table displays results of mean comparison tests.

	Div. a. countries			Mean comparison test	
	Obs.	Mean	Std. Dev.	Test statistic	p-value
All funds	174	0.157	0.217		
Fund type[a]				0.440	0.7215
Seed/early stage VC	42	0.147	0.201		
Other VC	41	0.135	0.227		
Buyout	42	0.155	0.242		
Generalist	49	0.185	0.201		
Headquarters of PE firm[b]				-4.774	0.0000
USA	134	0.109	0.176		
Europe	40	0.318	0.260		
Fund sequence number[b]				2.647	0.0103
First-time	31	0.083	0.156		
Follow-on	143	0.173	0.225		

[a] An one-way analysis of variance was applied to compare means. The test statistics is a F-statistic.

[b] Based on a variance ratio test a double-sided t-test with unequal variances was calculated to compare means. The test statistic is a t-statistic.

There is a huge difference in diversification across countries between PE funds managed by European and US PE firms. Whereas the average level of diversification across countries in European PE funds totals up to 0.32, diversification across countries in US PE funds only averages 0.11. A mean comparison test is statistically significant at the 1% level. The large difference supports the hypothesis that the relatively small economies in Europe force PE firms to invest a significant fraction of their capital outside their home country.

Moreover, firm experience seems to play a significant role in diversification across countries. First-time funds have a statistically significant lower level of diversification across countries than follow-on funds at the 5% level (0.08 compared to 0.17).

Correlation analysis shows significant Pearson product-moment correlations between diversification across countries and the following variables: new funds raised in vintage year, firm internationalization, firm experience, fund size, as well as time trend. All correlations are statistically significant at the 1% level except for the relationship between diversification across countries and firm experience, which is statistically significant at the 5% level (Table 5.13). The positive correlations of firm internationalization, firm experience, and fund size with diversification across countries are in line with expectations. However, the positive sign of the correlation between new funds raised and diversification across countries is at odds with the argumentation of hypothesis 3 supposing a negative relationship between both variables.

Table 5.13: Correlation analysis for diversification across countries
The table displays Pearson product-moment correlations between diversification across countries and independent variables. All correlations are based on 174 observations.

	Pearson product-moment correlation	
	Div. a. countries	p-value
Return msci in vy	-0.0304	0.6903
Return msci invest period (p.a.)	-0.0856	0.2617
Funds raised in vy (log billion USD 2000)	0.2561***	0.0006
Firm internationalization	0.5339***	0.0000
Firm experience	0.1501**	0.0480
Fund size (log million USD 2000)	0.2728***	0.0003
Time trend (1977 = 1)	0.2907***	0.0001

* significant at 10%; ** significant at 5%; *** significant at 1%

5.4.4.2 Multivariate analysis

To evaluate the impact of the independent variables on diversification across countries in a multivariate analysis, I estimate the same Tobit regression, which is used to study diversification across financing stages and across industries.[56] A remarkable large fraction of 71 PE funds in subsample 1 are left-censored at a level of diversification across countries of zero investing their capital in only one country. Of these, 63 are US PE funds and 8 European PE funds. Table 5.14 displays the results of the Tobit regressions. It contains marginal effects at the sample means of independent variables, standard errors and summary statistics for three specifications. Table C.6 in the appendix contains the estimated coefficients. Standard errors in both tables are robust against the violation of the assumption of homoscedasticity and adjusted for 50 clusters, i.e., PE firms (White 1980, Rogers 1993). Regression (1) is the basic model. In specification (2) I introduce time trend and a dummy variable for first-time funds as control variables. Regression (3) controls for year fixed effects. The χ^2-tests on joint significance of all parameters are significant at the 1% level for all specifications.

In line with hypothesis 1, a well performing global economy during fund formation is associated with a lower level of diversification across countries. An one standard deviation rise in rate of return of the MSCI World Index in vintage year leads to a decline in diversification across countries by 0.14 standard deviations, holding all other variables at their mean (Table 5.14, column (1)).[57] The effect is statistically significant at the 1% level and stable across all specifications. At odds, annual rate of return of the MSCI World Index during the investment period has no statistically significant impact on diversification across countries. The two results suggest that the level of diversification across countries is set during fund formation. PE firms appear not to make major corrections during the investment period.

[56] A detailed description of the estimated Tobit regression can be found in section 5.4.2.2.

[57] The marginal and discrete effects in this subsection are interpreted relative to the standard deviation of diversification across countries of 0.217 in subsample 1.

In regression (1) the amount of new funds raised in the vintage year has a positive effect on diversification across countries, which is statistically significant at the 5% level. A doubling in the amount of new funds raised in the vintage year increases diversification across countries by 0.17 standard deviations, holding all other variables at their mean, contradicting hypothesis 3 (Table 5.14, column (1)). However, the effect loses its significance when controlling for time trend or fixed year effects. The insignificance of the amount of new funds raised in specification (2) and (3) can be explained by the high correlation between new funds raised in vintage year and time trend (compare Table C.1). Over the sample period, PE funds increased diversification across countries. At the same time the amount of new funds raised grew nearly constantly enabling two possible explanations. On the one hand, a general development in the PE market led to the rise in new funds raised, which then might have caused the increase in diversification across countries. On the other hand, the general development might has accounted for both the rise in new funds raised and the increase in diversification across countries. Due to the high collinearity between the logarithm of new funds raised in vintage year and time trend it is not possible to distinguish between the two explanations. A Wald test on the joint significance of the logarithm of new funds raised in vintage year and time trend is significant at a 10% level in specification (2).

According to hypothesis 4, firm internationalization correlates positively with diversification across countries. An additional country increases diversification across countries by 0.13 standard deviations, holding all other variables at their mean (Table 5.14, column (1)). The effect is statistically significant at the 1% level and confirms the observation of Gupta & Sapienza (1992) that bigger PE firms prefer broader geographic scope of their investments relative to smaller PE firms.

Contrary to correlation analysis firm experience has no significant influence on diversification across countries. The positive correlation between the two variables can be entirely explained by the other variables in the regression analysis.

Fund size has the expected effect on diversification across countries. A doubling in fund size increases diversification across countries by 0.18 standard deviations, holding all other variables at their mean (Table 5.14, column (1)). The effect is statistically significant at the 5% level and robust against the introduction of control variables.

Because of the relatively small size of European economies, European PE firms face a limited quantity of attractive investment opportunities in their home country. They are forced to diversify their capital across countries more than their US counterparts. Accordingly, the level of diversification across countries of European PE funds is 0.61 standard deviations higher than that of equivalent US PE funds, holding all other variables at mean (Table 5.14, column (1)). The effect is statistically significant at the 5% level in regressions (1) and (2). In specification (3) it is only statistically significant at the 10% level.

Under ceteris paribus assumptions, seed/early VC funds have the highest level of diversification across countries, followed by other VC funds and generalist funds. BO funds display

Table 5.14: Tobit regression for diversification across countries

Subsample 1 consists of 174 PE funds. The dependent variable is diversification across countries. Independent variables include rate of return of the MSCI World Index in vintage year, annual rate of return of the MSCI World Index during investment period, new funds raised in vintage year, firm internationalization, firm experience, fund size, and time trend. Additionally, the regressions contain dummy variables indicating funds managed by PE firms with headquarters in Europe, seed/early VC funds, other VC funds, BO funds, and first-time funds, as well as a constant (not reported). The table reports marginal effects at the sample means of independent variables. For dummy variables the effect of a discrete change from zero to one is displayed.

	Dependent variable: Diversification across countries		
	(1)	(2)	(3)
Return msci in vy	-0.299***	-0.273***	-0.265***
	(0.112)	(0.101)	(0.099)
Return msci invest period (p.a.)	-0.048	-0.065	0.098
	(0.153)	(0.159)	(0.203)
Funds raised in vy (log bil. USD 2000)	0.036**	0.014	0.041
	(0.018)	(0.041)	(0.041)
Firm internationalization	0.029***	0.029***	0.029***
	(0.011)	(0.010)	(0.009)
Firm experience	0.008	0.004	0.007
	(0.031)	(0.045)	(0.027)
Fund size (log mil. USD 2000)	0.040**	0.042**	0.037**
	(0.019)	(0.020)	(0.018)
European headquarter (0/1)	0.133**	0.130**	0.114*
	(0.064)	(0.066)	(0.062)
Seed/early VC fund (0/1)	0.102*	0.102*	0.097*
	(0.056)	(0.056)	(0.051)
Other VC fund (0/1)	0.047	0.045	0.055
	(0.052)	(0.049)	(0.050)
Buyout fund (0/1)	-0.034	-0.036	-0.023
	(0.032)	(0.031)	(0.032)
Time trend (1977 = 1)		0.004	
		(0.009)	
First-time fund (0/1)		-0.005	
		(0.051)	
Year F.E.	No	No	Yes
Log likelihood	-39.8	-39.6	-36.8
χ^2-statistic	68.7	92.4	437.2
p-value of χ^2-test	0.000	0.000	0.000
Number of left-censored observations	71	71	71
Number of observations	174	174	174

Standard errors are in parentheses and are adjusted for serial correlation, heteroscedasticity and dependence between observations of one PE firm.
* significant at 10%; *** significant at 5%; *** significant at 1%

the lowest level of diversification across countries. The difference between seed/early VC funds and BO funds adds up to 0.63 standard deviations (Table 5.14, column (1)). A Wald-test on joint significance of the fund type dummies rejects the hypothesis that there are no differences in diversification across countries between fund types at the 1% level. The observed order is contrary to hypothesis 8, which suggests that seed/early funds are least diversified and generalists most diversified. There are two alternative views explaining the results. On the one hand, the set-up costs for entering a new country might be increasing with the development stage of companies instead of decreasing. However, I cannot present a rationale for this argument. On the other hand, the risk associated with investments in portfolio companies might decline with their development from seed to BO transactions (Kaserer & Diller 2004*c*). My results suggest that PE firms predominantly involved in early stage financing diversify the high risk of their portfolio companies by spreading their investments across countries.

5.5 'Dynamic' diversification across time

5.5.1 Determinants of 'dynamic' diversification

'Dynamic' diversification across time measures the value-weighted period of time in which PE funds spend their capital. It adds a dynamic perspective to diversification acknowledging changes in the economic conditions over the lifetime of a PE fund. Cumming et al. (2004) claim that PE firms should be able to diversify the liquidity risk of its funds by investing over a long period of time.

In times of a well performing economy, exit markets are in good condition. The IPO market is 'open' and high prices can be achieved in trade sales. Accordingly, PE firms consider the liquidity risk of their portfolio companies to be low and want to use the exit window before it closes. Hence, I propose:

H1: The higher the rate of return of the MSCI World Index during the vintage year of a PE fund, the less diversified is its portfolio across time.

A PE firm may change its perception of future exit markets when there is a significant change in the development of the global economy. The PE firm may respond to changes in the global economy and try to adjust its portfolio strategy. The possibility of making adjustments is limited to the investment period of a fund:

H2: The higher the annual rate of return of the MSCI World Index during the investment period of a PE fund, the less diversified is its portfolio across time.

A large quantity of money flowing into the PE industry indicates a positive perception of future investment opportunities. The more attractive investment opportunities are available, the faster PE firms are able to invest their capital:

H3: The higher the amount of new funds raised during the vintage year of a PE fund, the less diversified is its portfolio across time.

With each fund a PE firm accumulates experience. It enlarges its network and its reputation among entrepreneurs. The larger the network and reputation of a PE firm, the more attractive investment opportunities it receives per unit of time. As a consequence, experienced PE firms are capable of spending their capital at a faster rate than unexperienced PE funds, leading to:

H4: The more experience a PE firm has at the time of fund formation, the less diversified is its portfolio across time.

I do not expect an impact of firm internationalization and fund size on diversification across time. Also, I presume no differences in diversification across time neither between US and European PE funds nor between fund types.

5.5.2 Descriptive analysis

Diversification across time is measured as the value-weighted average of the time spans between each portfolio companies' date of investment and the date of investment of the first investment of a fund. The average PE fund in subsample 1 diversifies its capital across 20.5 months. There is a huge difference between the fastest and slowest investing fund in the sample. The fastest investing fund spends its money in only 4.0 months whereas the slowest investing fund reaches a weighted average of 46.5 months (Table 5.2). Table 5.15 displays summary statistics and mean comparison tests for the different classifications of funds.

Seed/early VC funds invest their capital the fastest with a mean of 17.2 months. On the contrary, the highest diversification across time is shown by generalist funds with a mean of 23.6 months. Other VC funds and BO funds lie between the two extremes with means of 19.5 and 21.3 months, respectively. According to an one-way analysis of variance the differences in means are statistically significant at the 1% level. In contrast, there is no statistically significant difference in the level of diversification across time between PE funds managed by US and European PE firms. US funds invest their capital only slightly faster than European funds in 20.3 months compared to 21.1 months. Similarly, the difference in diversification across time between first-time funds and follow-on funds is not statistically significant. First-time funds spend their capital on average in 20.4 months, whereas follow-on funds invest their money in 20.9 months.

Diversification across time has negative and statistically significant Pearson product-moment correlations at the 1% level with the following variables: rate of return of the MSCI World index during vintage year, new funds raised in vintage year, fund size, and time trend (Table 5.16). The correlation between diversification across time and rate of return of the MSCI World Index during investment period is also negative, but only statistically significant at the

Table 5.15: Diversification across time by fund classifications

The table contains cross tables for diversification across time and fund classifications. Funds are grouped according to fund type, headquarters of PE firm, and fund sequence number. For each group number of observations, mean, and standard deviation are shown. Moreover, the table displays results of mean comparison tests.

	Div. across time			Mean comparison test	
	Obs.	Mean	Std. Dev.	Test statistic	p-value
All funds	174	20.5	9.4		
Fund type[a]				4.030	0.0084
Seed/early stage VC	42	17.2	9.2		
Other VC	41	19.5	8.8		
Buyout	42	21.3	9.3		
Generalist	49	23.6	9.3		
Headquarters of PE firm[b]				-0.461	0.6451
USA	134	20.3	9.8		
Europe	40	21.1	7.9		
Fund sequence number[b]				-0.260	0.7951
First-time	31	20.4	9.6		
Follow-on	143	20.9	8.4		

[a] An one-way analysis of variance was applied to compare means. The test statistics is a F-statistic.

[b] Based on a variance ratio test a double-sided t-test with equal variances was calculated to compare means. The test statistic is a t-statistic.

10% level. There is neither a significant correlation between diversification across time and firm internationalization nor between diversification across time and firm experience.

Table 5.16: Correlation analysis for diversification across time

The table displays Pearson product-moment correlations between diversification across time and independent variables. All correlations are based on 174 observations.

	Pearson product-moment correlation	
	Div. a. time	p-value
Return msci in vy	-0.2354***	0.0018
Return msci invest period (p.a.)	-0.1424*	0.0609
Funds raised in vy (log billion USD 2000)	-0.4021***	0.0000
Firm internationalization	0.0531	0.4862
Firm experience	-0.0192	0.8016
Fund size (log million USD 2000)	-0.2885***	0.0001
Time trend (1977 = 1)	-0.3629***	0.0000

* significant at 10%; ** significant at 5%; *** significant at 1%

5.5.3 Multivariate analysis

In order to test hypotheses 1 to 4 an OLS regression analysis is used. The linear model estimated has the following form:

$$diversification\ across\ time = \beta_0 + \sum_{k=1}^{K} \beta_k \cdot x_k + \varepsilon \tag{5.5}$$

with β_0 = constant,
β_k = parameter of independent variable x_k,
x_k = independent variables (compare Table 5.17), and
ε = residual.

I estimate again three specifications: Regression (1) is the basic model, specification (2) controls for time trend and first-time funds, and regression (3) adds year fixed effects. Table 5.17 summarizes the regression results. It displays the estimated parameters, standard errors, and summary statistics. Standard errors in both tables are robust against the violation of the assumption of homoscedasticity and are adjusted for 50 clusters, i.e., PE firms (White 1980, Rogers 1993). The F-tests on joint significance of all parameters are significant at the 1% level for all specifications. Moreover, regression (3) explains 53% of the variance in diversification across time.

Hypothesis 1 and 2 are confirmed by the data. In times of a well performing economy PE firms perceive a low liquidity risk of their investments and want to use the open exit window. Hence, the better the global economy is performing during the vintage year and the investment period of a PE fund, the faster PE firms spend their capital. A rise of one standard deviation in rate of return of the MSCI World Index during vintage year decreases diversification across time by 1.3 months, ceteris paribus (Table 5.17, column (1)). The effect is statistically significant at the 5% level. An increase of one standard deviation in annual rate of return of the MSCI World Index during investment period leads to a decline of 2.9 months in diversification across time, all else equal (Table 5.17, column (1)). The effect is statistically significant at the 1% level. These results hold when control variables are included.

According to hypothesis 3, a large amount of new funds raised in the vintage year of a PE fund leads to faster investing. A doubling in new funds raised in vintage year declines diversification across time by 2.8 months, all else equal (Table 5.17, column (1)). However, the effect is not robust against the introduction of time trend and year fixed effects. The insignificance of the amount of new funds raised in specification (2) and (3) can be explained by the high correlation between new funds raised in vintage year and time trend (compare Table C.1). During the sample period there has been a trend of faster investing and at the same time a growth in new funds raised. Because of the cross-sectional design of the analysis, it is not possible to decide whether the growth in the amount of new funds raised caused the acceleration in investment time or whether both have been caused simultaneously through the general development of the PE industry during the sample period. A F-test on the joint significance of the logarithm of new funds raised in vintage year and time trend is significant at the 1% level in specification (2).

Hypothesis 4 suggests that experienced PE firms spend their capital faster than unexperienced PE firms because of a larger network and better reputation among entrepreneurs.

Table 5.17: OLS regression for diversification across time

Subsample 1 consists of 174 PE funds. The dependent variable is diversification across time. Independent variables include rate of return of the MSCI World Index in vintage year, annual rate of return of the MSCI World Index during investment period, new funds raised in vintage year, firm internationalization, firm experience, fund size, and time trend. Additionally, the regressions contain dummy variables indicating funds managed by PE firms with headquarters in Europe, seed/early VC funds, other VC funds, BO funds, and first-time funds, as well as a constant. The table reports marginal effects.

	Dependent variable: Diversification across time		
	(1)	(2)	(3)
Return msci in vy	-12.951**	-14.510**	-14.123***
	(5.904)	(6.434)	(5.027)
Return msci invest period (p.a.)	-37.810***	-37.137***	-30.112***
	(8.827)	(9.466)	(12.000)
Funds raised in vy (log bil. USD 2000)	-2.833***	-1.500	-0.764
	(0.817)	(2.370)	(1.925)
Firm internationalization	0.247	0.259	0.215
	(0.263)	(0.264)	(0.239)
Firm experience	2.967***	2.714**	2.499***
	(1.105)	(1.807)	(0.744)
Fund size (log mil. USD 2000)	-3.505***	-3.596***	-2.781***
	(0.811)	(0.861)	(0.744)
European headquarter (0/1)	-1.791	-1.634	-2.122
	(1.703)	(1.719)	(1.803)
Seed/early VC fund (0/1)	-6.995***	-7.138***	-5.399***
	(2.008)	(2.016)	(1.706)
Other VC fund (0/1)	-4.295**	-4.243***	-3.529**
	(1.800)	(1.852)	(1.511)
Buyout fund (0/1)	0.607	0.603	0.046
	(1.290)	(1.296)	(1.520)
Time trend (1977 = 1)		-0.268	
		(0.485)	
First-time fund (0/1)		-0.986	
		(2.560)	
Constant	53.598***	54.030***	44.028***
	(4.709)	(4.954)	(7.455)
Year F.E.	No	No	Yes
F-statistic	22.637	19.903	22.195
p-value of F-test	0.000	0.000	0.000
R^2	0.414	0.417	0.526
Number of observations	174	174	174

Standard errors are in parentheses and are adjusted for serial correlation, heteroscedasticity and dependence between observations of one PE firm.
* significant at 10%; *** significant at 5%; *** significant at 1%

However, firm experience has the opposite effect in all three specifications. A doubling in fund sequence number extends diversification across time by 3.0 months, ceteris paribus (Table 5.17, column (1)). The effect is statistically significant at the 1% level and stable across all specifications in direction and magnitude. Gompers (1996) gives a potential reason for the positive effect: grandstanding of young VC firms. He reports young VC firms to rush their successful portfolio companies to IPOs in order to signal their ability to investors and, hence, to increase the fundraising success of their subsequent fund. Experienced VC firms with a long track record hold their portfolio companies longer before taking them public. The probability of an early and successful exit via an IPO or trade sale increases the faster a young PE firm invests its money. Consequently, the higher incentive for unexperienced PE firms to grandstand compared to experienced PE firms may lead to less diversification across time in PE funds with low sequence numbers than for PE funds with high sequence numbers.

Contrary to expectations, I find a negative relationship between fund size and diversification across time. The effect is significant at the 1% level and holds in all specifications. A doubling in fund size reduces diversification across time by 3.5 months, all else equal (Table 5.17, column (1)). One possible explanation for this result is that fund size is a proxy for the success of a PE firm. Kaplan & Schoar (2005) have shown that fund size correlates positively with the performance of preceding funds managed by the same PE firm. Successful PE firms with bigger funds receive more attractive investment opportunities, and hence, are able to spend their money at a higher rate than less successful PE firms with smaller funds explaining the negative relation between fund size and diversification across time.

Finally, under the ceteris paribus assumption VC funds spend their capital faster than BO and generalist funds. PE funds focusing on seed and early stage VC invest their capital in 7.0 months less time than generalist funds. Other VC funds need on average 4.3 months less to spend their capital compared to generalist funds (Table 5.17, column (1)). The differences are statistically significant at least at the 5% level. BO funds do not differ significantly from generalist funds in terms of diversification across time. The effects are robust in direction and magnitude against the introduction of control variables. Though the results are not intuitive, one might think of three possible explanations. First, the necessary holding period to grow an early stage company is longer than the period to harvest a BO company. Given the usual lifetime of ten plus two years of potential prolongation for all PE funds, VC funds would be consequently forced to spend their money faster. However, calculating the holding period for all entirely exited portfolio companies (i.e., with a residual value of zero) in the sample tells the opposite story. The mean holding period for seed and early stage VC investments are 50.6 months (1,288 observations), for later stage VC investments 54.9 months (1,315 observations) and for BO investments 56.3 months (1,095 observations). Secondly, the selection, evaluation, and negotiation process for BO deals is more time consuming than for VC transactions. Although established companies contain less technological and market uncertainties than young companies in their first development stage, the size and complexity of BO transactions makes selection and evaluation very time consuming. Thirdly, the difference in diversification across time between VC funds and BO funds might reflect a cultural difference between the VC and BO business.

5.6 Summary: importance of market conditions and firm characteristics

Though very different levels of diversification can be observed across PE funds, not much is known on the choice of portfolio strategies by PE firms. This chapter aims at understanding external factors influencing expectations and preferences of PE firms during fund formation. Since, expectations and preferences of PE firms are unobservable, the impact of external factors on the observed level of diversification of PE funds is evaluated. The results show that the conditions of public stock and PE markets at fund formation have only a limited impact on the portfolio strategies applied by PE firms, whereas characteristics of PE firms and PE funds explain a large part of the level of diversification in PE funds. Table 5.18 summarizes the results of the regression analyses. A plus represents a positive and a minus a negative relationship between the pair of variables. Signs are only displayed if the relation is statistically significant at least at the 10% level. For fund types the joint significance in a Wald test is considered. A sign in parentheses denotes that the effect is only significant in some of the estimated specifications.

Table 5.18: Summary of regression analyses of chapter 5

The tables summarizes the results of the regression analyses conducted in this chapter. A plus represents a positive and a minus a negative relationship between the pair of variables. Signs are only displayed if the relation is statistically significant at least at the 10% level. For fund types the joint significance in a Wald test is considered. A sign in parentheses denotes that the effect is only significant in some of the estimated specifications.

	No. of pcs	Div. a. fin. stages	Div. a. industries	Div. a. countries	Div. a. time
Economic environment and PE market condition					
Return msci in vy				-	-
Return msci invest period	(-)				-
Funds raised in vy				(+)	(-)
PE firm and fund characteristics					
Firm internationalization	+	+	(+)	+	
Firm experience	(+)	+	(+)		+
Fund size	+	+[a]		+	-
European headquarters			+	+	
Seed/early VC fund	+	-[b]	(-)	+	-
Other VC fund	+	-[b]	(+)	+	-
BO fund	-	-[b]	(-)	-	+

[a] Relationship is only valid for VC and generalist funds.
[b] Relationship holds per definition.

PE firms adjust their speed of investment according to the development of the global economy and its public stock markets. Diversification across time declines substantially with an increase in rate of return of the MSCI World Index in vintage year as well as annual rate of return of the MSCI World Index during investment period. In 'boom' times of the global economy, PE firms invest very quickly in order to benefit from good exit opportunities. In contrast, neither 'naive' nor 'systematic' diversification vary considerably with the development of the global economy. Only diversification across countries decreases with a growing rate of return of the MSCI World Index in vintage year and number of portfolio companies declines with an increasing rate of return of the MSCI World Index during investment period.

PE market condition has a weak influence on portfolio strategies applied by PE firms. Only diversification across financing stages and diversification across time correlate significantly with the annual amount of new funds raised worldwide by the PE industry. The level of diversification across countries rises, while diversification across time decreases with an increase in new funds raised in vintage year. Since the amount of new funds raised by the PE industry has grown nearly steadily over the sample period, these results are associated with a general development in portfolio strategies of PE firms over the period from 1977 to 2000. Introducing a linear time trend in the regression analysis, portfolio strategies show the following pattern over the sample period: PE funds invested in fewer portfolio companies, at a higher speed, and more specialized on industries. However, they have become more international and globalized.[58]

Firm internationalization has a clear impact on the level of diversification in PE funds. A larger number of international subsidiaries is associated with an increase in number of portfolio companies, as well as in 'systematic' diversification across financing stages, industries, and countries. There is no influence of firm internationalization on diversification across time.

Equivalently, firm experience leads to a higher level of 'naive' and 'systematic diversification in PE funds. The regressions find positive and significant relations between firm experience and number of portfolio companies, diversification across financing stages and industries. Additionally, the effect of firm experience on diversification across countries has a positive sign, although it is not statistically significant. The experience PE firms attain with the management of each additional fund presumably lowers their set-up costs for the investment clusters they had invested in, and hence, gives space for entering new investment clusters. The positive sign for number of portfolio companies can be explained through an increasing reputation with firm experience. The reputation enhances proprietary deal flow and raises bargaining power of experienced PE firms, resulting in lower prices for companies. Furthermore, there is a positive influence of firm experience on diversification across time. The incentives for young PE firms to present their investors successful exits early in the life time of their funds appear to enhance their rate of investment.

Fund size, in terms of total commitments, has also a clear impact on portfolio strategies of PE funds. The bigger a PE fund is, the more portfolio companies it contains and the more diversified it is across financing stages and countries.[59] Furthermore, bigger PE funds invest their capital faster than smaller PE funds.

---

58 In the regressions run in this section, I tried to distinguish between the time trend and the variation in new funds raised in vintage year. However, because of the high collinearity between both variables, it is not possible to disentangle both effects.

59 The positive relationship between fund size and diversification across financing stages is only valid for VC and generalist funds. It can not be observed for BO funds.

Moreover, the findings back the hypothesis that European PE funds compose their portfolios differently than US PE funds. Though European PE funds invest in an equal quantity of portfolio companies and with an equal speed as their US counterparts, they show differences according to 'systematic' diversification. European PE firms diversify their funds across industries and countries more than equivalent US PE funds. The relatively small economies of the European countries, compared to the US economy, force European PE firms to spread their funds more across industries and countries than their US counterparts.

Finally, portfolio strategies differ between fund types. Ranking fund types according to diversification across number of portfolio companies, industries, and countries creates the following pattern: Diversification in PE funds declines with the development stage of funded portfolio companies from seed/early stage VC funds to other VC funds, from other VC funds to generalist funds, and from generalist funds to BO funds.[60] PE firms focusing on early stage transactions seem to compensate the higher risk of their investments through a higher level of diversification compared to PE firms predominantly involved in later stage transactions. There is one interesting exception to this order: Seed/early VC funds have the lowest level of diversification across industries relative to the other fund types, describing one of the specialities of seed and early stage VC investing. Since seed and early stage projects are still in product or technical development, it is very difficult to assess the technical success of the project. In order to be able to select successful projects, seed/early VC firms have to invest significantly in specialized knowledge in very few industries. As soon as the companies start producing and shipping, the technical uncertainties mainly disappear. Hence, the high specialization is not necessary any more and more diversification across industries, i.e., a less risky portfolio strategy is preferred by PE firms focused on later development stages. Diversification across time ranks fund types in the opposite order. Seed/early VC funds invest their capital fastest, followed by other VC, generalist, and BO funds. The evaluation, selection, and negotiation process for BO investments appears to be more time consuming than for VC investments.

The analysis presented in this chapter contributes to the stream of literature aiming to understand the investment behavior of PE firms (Gupta & Sapienza 1992, Norton & Tenebaum 1993, Ljungqvist & Richardson 2003*b*, Cumming 2004, and others). The chapter gives a thorough picture of the choice of portfolio strategies by PE funds. It is shown that 'naive' and 'systematic' diversification of a PE fund are mainly related to the characteristics of PE firms and funds. In contrast, diversification across time is predominantly an opportunistic reaction to market conditions. The results offer PE firms as well as investors valuable insights. PE firms are able to question their own behavior in comparison to the results. Investors are enabled to predict more accurately the portfolio strategies of PE funds in order to allocate their capital according to their own investment strategy.

The results open paths for future research on portfolio strategies of PE firms. One interesting question, which could not be analyzed here, is the influence of the management team of a PE

[60] Diversification across financing stages is not interpreted because the ranking is caused by the definition of fund types.

firm on the portfolio strategy of a PE fund. How much impact do education and professional experience of the management team have on the level of diversification of PE funds? Moreover, how much influence do limited partners have on portfolio strategies of a PE fund? The more limited partners are involved in a PE fund, the more preferences compete, and hence, the more diversified a fund should be. Another important issue for future research is to compare the portfolio strategy communicated during fundraising and the portfolio strategy actually employed by a PE firm. Possible research questions in this field are: Do PE firms stick to their portfolio strategies communicated during fundraising or do they deviate from their plans? What determines observed discrepancies? Are changes in the portfolio strategy done in agreement with investors or not? Finally, do changes in the portfolio strategy have an impact on the performance of a PE fund? Exploring these questions will provide a deeper understanding of the investment behavior of PE firms.

Chapter 6

Performance of private equity funds: does diversification matter?

6.1 Introduction

There is a large and growing literature analyzing the return of PE investing (Cochrane 2005, Ljungqvist & Richardson 2003*a*, Ljungqvist & Richardson 2003*b*, Cumming & Walz 2004, Ick 2005, Jones & Rhodes-Kropf 2003, Kaplan & Schoar 2005, Kaserer & Diller 2004*c*, Gottschalg et al. 2004).[61] The majority of these articles study the relative performance of PE compared to public markets. There is less understanding about the impact of diversification on the performance of PE funds. In this chapter, I try to fill this gap by examining the influence of diversification on the rate of return, intra-fund variation of return, and shortfall probability of PE funds.

In the literature two statements can be found about the relationship between diversification and performance of PE funds. One view is that PE funds should focus on specific industries and countries in order to acquire specialized knowledge. The expertise is necessary to overcome the information asymmetries and principal agent problems inherent in the selection and oversight of private companies. By means of this specialization, PE firms are able to make superior selection decisions and to manage the risk of their funds (Gupta & Sapienza 1992, Norton & Tenebaum 1993). A contrary view is provided by modern portfolio theory (Markowitz 1952, Markowitz 1959, Sharpe 1964, Lintner 1965). It states that an investor can diversify the unsystematic risk of its portfolio by investing in assets with different characteristics.[62] Modern portfolio theory accounts for the fact that the risk of a portfolio depends not only on the variance of its assets, but also on the covariances between these assets. Since PE funds are portfolios of risky assets, their total risk should decrease with diversification. This view is corroborated by the studies of Weidig & Mathonet (2004) and Schmidt (2004) which report risk reduction through 'naive' diversification.

---

[61] For a detailed summary of the literature compare chapter 2.

[62] Strictly, this is only true if the rates of return of different assets do not perfectly correlate. However, in reality this will be always the case.

In chapter 3, I developed a model based on modern portfolio theory which combines both views. 'Systematic' diversification across industries, countries or financing stages lowers the risk of a PE fund but is costly. Each PE firm chooses the level of diversification which maximizes its expected utility depending on the expected rate of return and risk of the PE fund. As a result, some PE firms will prefer less diversified funds than others although this might involve a substantial quantity of risk.

The objective of this chapter is twofold: First, it aims at studying the impact of diversification on PE funds' performance empirically. Due to the illiquidity of PE markets, it is not possible to calculate total risk in terms of variation of PE funds' valuation over time. As a consequence, I evaluate the influence of diversification on three performance measures which rely on the cash flow history of PE funds: rate of return, intra-fund variation of return, and shortfall probability. Secondly, the chapter aims at analyzing the relationship between rate of return and intra-fund variation of return, as well as rate of return and shortfall probability, controlling for a variety of variables.

The remainder of the chapter is as follows: *section 6.2* briefly reviews previous research and derives a set of hypotheses for the empirical analysis. *Section 6.3* summarizes the subsample used in this chapter and shows summary statistics on key variables. The multivariate analysis is presented in *section 6.4*. *Section 6.5* concludes the chapter, discusses implications of the findings, and indicates caveats of the analysis.

6.2 Impact of diversification on private equity funds' performance

This section aims at deriving hypotheses on the relationship between diversification and performance of PE funds. In order to do so, the first part briefly revises results of previous studies on determinants of PE funds' performance. In the second part, I derive a set of hypotheses for the empirical analysis conducted in this chapter.

Since the year 2000, the number of articles on the rate of return of PE investments has grown steadily revealing the following characteristics:[63] Firstly, Kaplan & Schoar (2005) and Gottschalg et al. (2004) report a positive and concave relationship between fund size and rate of return of PE funds. The concave shape of the relationship suggests a decreasing return to scale of fund size. Secondly, their results also suggest a positive impact of firm experience on the rate of return of PE funds. The more experience a PE firm has at the time of fund formation, the higher the rate of return of PE funds, ceteris paribus. Thirdly, Kaserer & Diller (2004*c*) find a negative influence of the annual rate of return of the MSCI Europe Index in the vintage year of European PE funds on their rate of return. Fourthly, an increasing amount of new funds raised by the PE industry in the vintage year of a PE fund is associated with a rise of its rate of return (Kaserer & Diller 2004*c*, Gottschalg et al. 2004). Moreover, Gottschalg et al.

[63] For a detailed summary of the cited articles compare section 2.2.

(2004) report a negative influence of the fraction of the capital invested in Europe on the rate of return of a PE fund. Hence, European PE funds achieve a lower rate of return than their US counterparts, ceteris paribus. Finally, some authors report a superior return of VC funds over BO funds (Kaplan & Schoar 2005, Kaserer & Diller 2004*c*), whereas other studies find no difference (Gottschalg et al. 2004) or a negative difference between VC funds and BO funds (Ljungqvist & Richardson 2003*a*). In order to review and control for these effects I will include corresponding variables in my analysis.[64]

Much less is known on the impact of diversification on the performance of PE funds so far. Ljungqvist & Richardson (2003*a*) find no significant influences of diversification across number of portfolio companies and industries on IRR for their sample of mainly BO funds. Schmidt (2004) reports a decreasing variation of returns across simulated PE portfolios with a rising number of companies in the portfolio. Moreover, Weidig & Mathonet (2004) show that the probability of loss and total loss of VC investments decline from direct investments in portfolio companies to VC funds, and from VC funds to simulated VC fund-of-funds.

Chapter 3 models the relationship between diversification and performance of PE funds based on modern portfolio theory. The global investment scope of potential portfolio companies is divided into investment clusters of financing stages, industries, and countries. It is assumed that companies, which have different economic characteristics, i.e., that do not belong to the same investment cluster, are more likely to have lower covariances than companies, which show similar economic characteristics, i.e., which belong to the same investment cluster. Acting in an investment cluster is costly for the PE firm. It has to invest in cluster specific assets (e.g. cluster specific human capital and network ties) in order to overcome the informational asymmetries and agency problems inherent in the investment in private companies. Without paying these set-up costs the PE firm is not able to make successful transactions in an investment cluster.

This set-up allows to evaluate the relationship between 'systematic' diversification and expected rate of return of PE funds. A PE firm has to pay set-up costs for each investment cluster it is actively investing in. In other words, the amount of set-up costs increases with 'systematic' diversification. As a consequence, under ceteris paribus assumptions, the observable rate of return of PE funds should decrease with 'systematic' diversification. 'Systematic' diversification is possible across financing stages, industries, or countries, giving rise to the three hypotheses:

H1a: The higher the level of diversification across financing stages in a PE fund, the lower is its rate of return.

H1b: The higher the level of diversification across industries in a PE fund, the lower is its rate of return.

[64] Additionally, Kaplan & Schoar (2005) and Kaserer & Diller (2004*c*) find a performance persistence across funds of the one PE firm. PE firms who outperform the industry in one fund are likely to outperform the industry in the next fund. Unfortunately, the return of preceding fund is only available for 69 of the 100 sample funds. Hence, the return of preceding fund is not included in the regression analysis of this chapter. In an unreported regression with only 69 PE funds I also find a positive and statistically significant persistence across fund of one PE firm.

H1c: The higher the level of diversification across countries in a PE fund, the lower is its rate of return.

Furthermore, the covariance of companies' returns which belong to the same investment cluster is higher than the covariance of companies' returns which belong to different investment clusters. Thus, with an increase in 'systematic' diversification, the total risk of a PE fund diminishes. However, due to the illiquidity of PE markets it is not possible to observe time series of objective valuations for PE investments. This fact prohibits the calculation of total risk in terms of variation in PE funds' valuation over time. As a consequence, I compute intra-fund variation of return in order to approximate the total risk of PE funds. Assuming that intra-fund variation of return reflects the total risk of the investment strategy of PE firms, I propose that the higher the level of 'systematic' diversification in a PE fund is, the lower is its intra-fund variation of return, ceteris paribus. Again, 'systematic' diversification can be divided into financing stages, industries, and countries. Additionally, a PE firm can leverage the ups and downs in the economic development by investing its funds over a long period of time. Considering 'systematic' and 'dynamic' diversification one gets four hypotheses:

H2a: The higher the level of diversification across financing stages in a PE fund, the lower is its intra-fund variation of return.

H2b: The higher the level of diversification across industries in a PE fund, the lower is its intra-fund variation of return.

H2c: The higher the level of diversification across countries in a PE fund, the lower is its intra-fund variation of return.

H2d: The higher the level of diversification across time in a PE fund, the lower is its intra-fund variation of return.

Though the assumption was made in chapter 3, the correlation between the rates of return of portfolio companies belonging to the same investment cluster is in reality not perfect. Consequently, PE funds can also gain risk reduction through 'naive' diversification by investing in a large number of companies. Additionally, the more portfolio companies a PE fund contains, the less exposed it is to the outcome of a single company. Both arguments give rise to the hypothesis:

H2e: The more portfolio companies a PE fund contains, the lower is its intra-fund variation of return.

Weidig & Mathonet (2004) characterize the risk profile of PE investments in terms of shortfall probability. They report a decline in mean probability of loss and total loss from direct VC investments to VC funds and from VC funds to simulated VC fund-of-funds. As a consequence, I assume that shortfall probability is also a proxy for the total risk in PE funds leading to hypothesis 3a to 3e:

H3a: The higher the level of diversification across financing stages in a PE fund, the lower is its shortfall probability.

H3b: The higher the level of diversification across industries in a PE fund, the lower is its shortfall probability.

H3c: The higher the level of diversification across countries in a PE fund, the lower is its shortfall probability.

H3d: The higher the level of diversification across time in a PE fund, the lower is its shortfall probability.

H3e: The more portfolio companies a PE fund contains, the lower is its shortfall probability.

Additionally, this chapter aims at studying the influence of intra-fund variation of return and shortfall probability on the rate of return of PE funds. Previous research is differing on whether the return of PE funds is driven by systematic and/or unsystematic risk. Whereas Ljungqvist & Richardson (2003*a*) find no significant effect of weighted portfolio betas on the rate of return of PE funds, Gottschalg et al. (2004) report a positive relationship between funds' betas and returns. Following a different approach, Jones & Rhodes-Kropf (2003) document a positive relationship between the idiosyncratic risk of PE funds and its rates of return.

The model in chapter 3 combines the results of Jones & Rhodes-Kropf (2003) and Gottschalg et al. (2004) supposing a positive relationship between expected rate of return and total risk of PE equity funds. A higher amount of total risk is rewarded with a higher rate of return, and vice versa. Since it is not possible to compute total risk in terms of variation in PE funds' valuation over time, I am not able to test this relationship directly. However, I am able to test the relationship between intra-fund variation of return and rate of return as well as between shortfall probability and rate of return. According to hypotheses 2 and 3, I assume that intra-fund variation of return as well as shortfall probability represent the total risk of a PE fund implicating:

H4: The higher the intra-fund variation of return in a PE fund, the higher is its rate of return, ceteris paribus.

H5: The higher the shortfall probability in a PE fund, the higher is its rate of return, ceteris paribus.

6.3 Descriptive analysis

6.3.1 Data and key variables

In this chapter I use another subsample of the entire data set. The entire sample has to be restricted because of two reasons: First, in the strict sense the final performance can only be measured of entirely liquidated PE funds. This would reduce the number of observations to 40.[65] However, Kaplan & Schoar (2005) report a correlation of 0.89 between the final IRR and interim IRR after five years for a large sample of PE funds. Their result suggests that the interim performance of a mature PE fund is a valid proxy of final performance. The extent to which the interim performance can differ from the final performance depends on the amount of NAV at the time of interim calculation. Kaserer & Diller (2004*c*) include PE funds in their analysis if their NAV is less than 20% of the absolute value of all previously accrued cash flows. I follow this approach, however, with a small distinction: I use the total value of a PE fund as reference for the NAV. Total value is defined as the sum of realized proceeds and NAV. I define PE funds as mature and include them in the analysis which have a NAV of less than 20% relative to their total value. Hundred-twenty-three funds in the entire sample fulfill this criteria. Secondly, to calculate the IRR, MIRR, and PME) and intra-fund variation of IRR, MIRR, and PME the complete cash flow history between a fund and each portfolio company has to be available. This information is not available for 23 of the mature funds. To conclude, subsample 2 which will be used throughout this chapter consists of 100 PE funds. Table 6.1 summarizes the composition of subsample 2. It contains the distribution of subsample 2 across various classifications of PE funds. Additionally, it includes summary statistics on the size of sample funds.

Subsample 2 can be divided into 38 VC and 62 BO funds.[66] 72 funds belong to PE firms with headquarters in the USA and 28 funds are managed by PE firms located in Europe. Subsample 2 includes 21 first-time, 17 second-time, and 14 third-time funds. The remaining 48 are PE funds with sequence numbers of four or higher. Forty funds were already liquidated at the time of data collecting while the remaining 60 funds were still active.[67] The active funds have an average fraction of NAV compared to total value of 6.4%.

The average fund has a size of USD 440.2 million in 2000 purchasing power. Fund size varies substantially across funds in subsample 2. The mean size of the three smallest funds is USD 21.3 million, while the average size of the three largest funds totals up to USD 4,761 million. The distribution of fund size across the various groups shows the same patterns as the entire sample and is therefore not further discussed here.[68] The oldest fund in sample 2 closed its first transaction in 1979 and the youngest fund in 1998 (Figure D.1).

Table 6.2 displays summary statistics for the variables used in this chapter. The average PE fund in subsample 2 has an IRR of 50.2% and a MIRR of 19.9% gross of management

[65] Compare Table 6.1.

[66] In this chapter, I only distinguish between VC and BO funds (including generalist funds). This is done because of three reasons: First, the regression analysis in this chapter aims at evaluating the impact of diversification across financing stages on the performance of PE funds amongst others. The four fund types used in chapter 5 (seed/early VC, other VC, BO, and generalist) are calculated on the same information as the variable diversification across financing stages, and hence, explain most of the variation in diversification across financing stages. In order to prevent collinearity difficulties it is necessary to group the four fund types into VC and BO. Secondly, this division is in line with most of the previous studies on the performance of PE funds and facilitates the comparison of results. Finally, subsample 2 has a limited size. The classification into only two groups saves two degrees of freedom in the regression analysis.

[67] Active funds have NAV larger than zero. NAV of liquidated funds is equal to zero.

[68] Compare section 4.3.

Table 6.1: Composition of subsample 2

The table summarizes subsample 2 according to fund type, headquarters of PE firm, fund sequence number, and liquidation status. It divides fund types in VC and BO. The sample contains funds, which are managed by PE firm with headquarters in USA and Europe. Fund sequence number describes the position of a fund within all funds managed by one PE firm. Active funds have NAV larger than zero, while NAV of liquidated funds is equal to zero. Columns 1 and 2 display the breakdown of the sample into the different classifications. Columns 3 to 6 give information on fund size. Fund size is the total capital committed by investors to a fund. To secure the anonymity of all funds only mean, standard deviation, mean of the three smallest funds and mean of the three largest funds is given.

	Funds		Fund Size (mil. USD 2000)			
	Obs.	%	Mean	Std. Dev.	Mean min. three funds	Mean max. three funds
All funds	100	100.0	440.2	1,048.4	21.3	4,761.4
Fund type						
Venture capital	38	38.0	172.2	394.1	26.4	1,082.1
Buyout	62	62.0	604.4	1,271.8	37.7	4,717.7
Headquarters of PEF						
USA	72	72.0	498.2	1,215.7	26.4	4,761.4
Europe	28	28.0	291.0	334.8	36.7	1,002.6
Fund sequence number						
First-time	21	21.0	83.6	47.9	25.7	171.6
Second-time	17	17.0	196.6	187.5	38.3	504.2
Third-time	14	14.0	177.2	175.1	34.2	456.2
later	48	48.0	759.2	1,430.9	50.3	4,761.4
Liquidation status						
Active	60	60.0	542.4	1,306.6	28.3	4,761.4
Liquidated	40	40.0	286.8	408.9	25.7	1,449.5

fees and carried interests. The large difference between the average IRR and the average MIRR challenges the assumption of the IRR that interim cash flows are reinvested at same IRR. The reinvestment assumption of IRR artificially enhances the spread between top and low performing PE funds. The minimum IRR and minimum MIRR are nearly equal with values of 3.5% and 6.7% respectively. In contrast, the maximum IRR and maximum MIRR differ by 130.3 percentage points. Hence, a big part of the high cross-sectional variance in the returns of PE funds reported by many previous studies may be explained by the inappropriate reinvestment assumption of the IRR. Still, there is a substantial variation across sample funds in terms of MIRR with a standard deviation of 7.2 percentage points and a spread between minimum and maximum MIRR of 38.7 percentage points. With a mean PME of 3.1 gross of management fees and carried interests the average fund in subsample 2 returned three times more than the MSCI World Index. The minimum PME is 0.79 and the maximum PME totals up to 11.9.

Mean intra-fund variation of IRR in sample 2 is 0.056. IRR varies on average 5.6 percentage points if one portfolio company is taken out of the average sample fund. Mean intra-fund variation of MIRR is lower with a value of 0.012. On average MIRR changes by 1.2 percentage points taking one portfolio company out of a sample fund. PME changes on average by 0.26 if one portfolio company is taken out of a sample fund. There is a huge difference in intra-fund variation of return across sample funds. In the minimal case IRR only varies by 0.1 percentage points, whereas in the maximum case IRR changes by 34.9 percentage points if one portfolio company is taken out of the fund. The difference between the minimum and maximum intra-fund variation of MIRR is 4.3 percentage points and between the minimum and maximum intra-fund variation of PME 1.7.

On average 34.9% of the portfolio companies in a sample fund returned less than their investment. Of these, 15.7% did not return anything at all. Shortfall probabilities vary remarkably across sample funds. The maxima are reached with 76.9% of losses and 42.9% of total losses in a single fund. In contrast, there are funds in the sample without any loss or total loss.

The average fund in subsample 2 contains 28.9 portfolio companies and invests its money in 22.3 months. It has a mean level of diversification across financing stages of 0.36 and across industries of 0.64. While the mean level of diversification across countries is 0.14, the median is only 0.05. Thus, most sample funds invested their capital in one country, most likely their home country, whereas a few funds spread their capital across a large number of countries. The maximum level of diversification across countries totals up to 0.85. Furthermore, the mean of the logarithm of fund size is equivalent to USD 175.0 million and average experience is equivalent to a fund sequence number of 3.1.

Table 6.3 shows the development of rate of return, intra-fund variation of return and shortfall probability over time. Because of the limited sample size, funds are arranged in groups of three vintage years. I use the same groups as in chapter 5. There is a time trend towards larger returns in the sample from a mean IRR of 26.2% in the period of 1980-1982 to a mean IRR of

64.0% in 1995-1997. Neglecting the years of 1979 and 1998, only the period between 1986-1988 shows a decrease in mean IRR compared to the previous period. Looking at MIRR, the trend is even more apparent with a steady rise from a mean MIRR of 13.9% in 1980-1982 to a mean MIRR of 21.4% in 1992-1994. Only the period between 1995-1997 shows a MIRR which is slightly lower than in the previous period. However, the MIRR in 1995-1997 is still superior to all periods before 1992. This trend suggests that the development of the global PE market over the sample period enabled the PE firms to increase their returns. A similar pattern is reported by Kaplan & Schoar (2005).[69] PME shows a slightly different development. The mean PME first increases from 1.37 in 1980-1982 to a maximum of 3.90 in 1986-1988. Subsequently, it declines somewhat but stays at a high level above 3. The difference in the development of IRR and MIRR to PME can be explained by the influence of the MSCI World Index on the PME.

Intra-fund variation of IRR, MIRR, and PME show more changes over the sample period so that no systematic pattern can be detected by looking at Table 6.3. The shortfall probabilities depict a U-shaped pattern over the sample period. Probability of loss and probability of total loss fall from a level of 49.0% and 22.2% in 1979 to a minimum of 27.1% and 10.8% in 1989-1991. Thereafter, they grow again to a level of 52.9% and 30.1% in 1998.

Finally, a closer look is taken at the distribution of the performance variables. Previous results suggest returns of VC investments to be right-skewed and to be best represented by means of a lognormal distribution (Cochrane 2005). Figure D.2 in the appendix shows histograms of the performance variables. As expected, IRR, MIRR, PME, intra-fund variation of IRR, intra-fund variation of MIRR, and intra-fund variation of PME show right skewed distributions. Also, the distribution of probability of total loss appears to be right skewed. In contrast, probability of loss seems to be distributed symmetrically around its mean.

6.3.2 Bivariate relationships

To approach the research questions, the expected relationships are first evaluated with the help of mean comparison tests and correlations. Table 6.4 applies mean comparison tests for the performance measures between VC and BO funds as well as between European and US PE funds. BO funds earn slightly more than VC funds, achieving an average IRR of 51.1%, an average MIRR of 19.9%, and an average PME of 3.22, whereas VC funds return an average IRR of 48.9%, an average MIRR of 19.7%, and an average PME of 2.84. However, the differences are not statistically significant.

Intra-fund variation of return shows the opposite pattern. VC funds have a higher intra-fund variation of return than BO funds. For VC funds the average intra-fund variation of IRR, MIRR, and PME add up to 5.7 percentage points, 1.4 percentage points, and 0.26, respectively. For BO funds the mean intra-fund variation of IRR, MIRR, and PME are 5.5 percentage points,

[69] Calculating average IRRs for the same three years groups, Table V of Kaplan & Schoar (2005) also shows an increase in return from the period 1980-1982 to the period 1992-1994 with a small decline in the period 1986-1988 compared to the previous period.

Table 6.2: Summary statistics for subsample 2

The table exhibits mean, median, standard deviation, minimum, and maximum for dependent and independent variables used in the regressions of this chapter. Subsample 2 consists of 100 PE funds.

	Mean	Median	Std. Dev.	Min.	Max.
Dependent variables					
Gross IRR	0.502	0.423	0.317	0.035	1.763
Gross MIRR	0.199	0.189	0.072	0.067	0.460
Gross PME	3.076	2.293	2.151	0.786	11.940
Sd(Q-IRR)	0.056	0.038	0.058	0.001	0.349
Sd(Q-MIRR)	0.012	0.010	0.009	0.0003	0.043
Sd(Q-PME)	0.257	0.179	0.264	0.011	1.831
Prob(loss)	0.349	0.354	0.167	0.0	0.769
Prob(tot. loss)	0.157	0.138	0.108	0.0	0.429
Independent variables					
Number of portfolio companies [a]	28.9	23.0	16.8	5.3	71.0
Diversification across time (months)	22.3	20.7	9.1	7.8	46.5
Diversification across financing stages	0.36	0.432	0.218	0.0	0.675
Diversification across industries	0.638	0.678	0.177	0.0	0.845
Diversification across countries	0.141	0.046	0.203	0.0	0.813
Funds raised in vy (log bil. USD 2000)	3.439	3.500	0.816	1.067	5.034
Return msci in vy	0.096	0.092	0.100	-0.126	0.423
Fund size (log mil. USD 2000)	5.162	4.987	1.228	2.677	9.155
Firm experience [a]	1.132	1.099	0.771	0.0	2.707

[a] To guarantee the confidentiality of PE firms and funds the mean of the three smallest and the mean of the three largest values is displayed instead of minimum and maximum.

Table 6.3: Performance by vintage years

The table displays the development of IRR, MIRR, PME, intra-fund variation of IRR, intra-fund variation of MIRR, intra-fund variation of PME, probability of loss, and probability of total loss over the sample period from 1979 to 1998. Funds are arranged to groups of three vintage years.

		Mean							
		Rate of return			Intra-fund variation of return			Shortfall probability	
Vintage year	Obs.	Gross IRR	Gross MIRR	Gross PME	Sd(Q-IRR)	Sd(Q-MIRR)	Sd(Q-PME)	P(loss)	P(tot. loss)
All funds	100	0.502	0.199	3.076	0.056	0.012	0.257	0.349	0.157
1979	2	0.323	0.145	1.861	0.029	0.006	0.134	0.490	0.222
1980-1982	4	0.262	0.139	1.366	0.027	0.007	0.158	0.374	0.216
1983-1985	10	0.408	0.157	2.046	0.061	0.009	0.226	0.321	0.130
1986-1988	8	0.391	0.184	3.899	0.019	0.005	0.198	0.282	0.109
1989-1991	29	0.471	0.193	3.381	0.049	0.008	0.254	0.271	0.108
1992-1994	21	0.596	0.234	3.584	0.060	0.015	0.338	0.379	0.175
1995-1997	21	0.640	0.226	3.057	0.075	0.017	0.278	0.407	0.185
1998	5	0.344	0.151	1.855	0.077	0.020	0.142	0.529	0.301

1.0 percentage point, and 0.25, respectively. The difference in intra-fund variation of MIRR is statistically significant at the 10% level with a p-value of 0.086.

VC and BO funds also differ significantly across shortfall probabilities. With a probability of loss of 45.3%, close to half of the portfolio companies in VC funds return less than their investment. Additionally, a fifth of the portfolio companies in VC funds do not return any money. BO funds have lower shortfall probabilities. Yet, with a probability of loss of 28.6% more than a quarter of the portfolio companies of a BO fund return less than their investment and 12.6% of the portfolio companies of a BO fund return nothing. Double sided t-tests reveal that the differences are statistically significant at the 1% level. In summary, the BO funds in subsample 2 display a preferable combination of performance measures. They earn higher rates of return, have lower intra-fund variation of return and lose fewer of their portfolio companies.

PE funds managed by US PE firms return more than their European counterparts. The average US PE fund achieves an IRR of 51.5%, a MIRR of 20.6%, and a PME of 3.36. Mean IRR, mean MIRR, and mean PME of European PE funds are 47.0%, 17.9%, and 2.36 respectively. The differences in MIRR and PME are statistically significant at the 10% level with p-values of 0.053 and 0.006, respectively. The differences in intra-fund variation of return between US and European PE funds are mixed. Intra-fund variation of IRR for US PE funds is lower than for European PE funds (5.3 percentage points compared to 6.3 percentage points), while intra-fund variation of MIRR and intra-fund variation of PME are higher for US PE funds than for their European counterparts (1.4 percentage points compared to 1.0 percentage points and 0.29 compared to 0.18). However, only the difference in intra-fund variation of PME is statistically significant at the 5% level. Finally, US PE funds have higher shortfall probabilities. On average 36.4% of the portfolio companies of US PE funds return less than their investment and 16.9% of the portfolio companies earn nothing. For European funds the means are lower with 31.2% of losses and 12.5% of total losses. However, only the difference in probability of total loss is statistically significant at the 10% level with a p-value of 0.061. To summarize, US PE funds yield higher returns, have similar intra-fund variation of return, but lose a bigger share of their portfolio companies than European PE funds.

Correlation analysis reveals the following relationships between the level of diversification and performance of PE funds (Table 6.5). There is no significant correlation between IRR and MIRR and one of the dimensions of diversification. PME correlates positively and statistically significant at the 1% level with number of portfolio companies and diversification across time. In comparison, diversification appears to lower intra-fund variation of return in PE funds. The correlations between intra-fund variations of return and the diversification measures are all but one negative and mostly statistically significant. Only the correlation between diversification across time and intra-fund variation of PME is positive, but not statistically significant. The correlations between diversification and intra-fund variation of return in PE funds appear to be economically important with values between -0.40 and -0.05.

Diversification also correlates statistically significant with shortfall probability of PE funds. However, the direction of influence is mixed. Number of portfolio companies has a positive correlation with probability of loss, which is statistically significant at the 1% level. Likewise, diversification across financing stages correlates positively with probabilities of loss and total loss. Both coefficients of correlation are statistically significant at the 5% level. In contrast, the correlations between diversification across time and probabilities of loss and total loss, as well as the correlation between diversification across industry and the probability of total loss are negative and statistically significant at the 5% level.

Furthermore, correlation analysis shows a positive relation between the amount of new funds raised in the vintage year of a fund and all performance measures. The correlation coefficients lie between 0.07 and 0.42. Except for PME and intra-fund variation of PME the correlations are statistically significant at least at the 10% level. Correlations also show a positive relationship between firm experience and rate of return of a PE fund. The Pearson product-moment correlation between firm experience and IRR is 0.09, between firm experience and MIRR 0.18 and between firm experience and PME 0.26. The last two are statistically significant at the 10% and 1% level, respectively.

Another aim of this chapter is to study the influence of intra-fund variation of return and shortfall probability on the rate of return of PE funds. Table D.1 in the appendix shows Pearson product-moment correlations within the six performance measures. As supposed by hypothesis 4, the relationship between rate of return and intra-fund variation of return is positive and statistically significant. The correlation between IRR and intra-fund variation of IRR is 0.67, the correlation between MIRR and intra-fund variation of MIRR 0.47 and the correlation between PME and intra-fund variation of PME 0.74. Contrary to hypothesis 5, the relationship between return and shortfall probabilities is negative. However, only the correlations between PME and probability of loss as well as probability of total loss are statistically significant at the 10% level.

6.4 Multivariate analysis

6.4.1 Methodology

The descriptive analysis gives a comprehensive overview of the data. This section aims at testing hypothesis 1 to 5 in multivariate regressions. Throughout this chapter, I use OLS estimation methods. The linear model has the following form:

$$y = \beta_0 + \sum_{k=1}^{K} \beta_k \cdot x_k + \varepsilon \tag{6.1}$$

with y = dependent variable,
β_0 = constant,
β_k = parameter of independent variable x_k,
x_k = independent variables, and
ε = residual.

Table 6.4: Performance by fund classifications

The table contains mean comparison tests for the performance measures. Funds are grouped according to fund type and headquarters of PE firm. For each group the mean of IRR, MIRR, PME, intra-fund variation of IRR, intra-fund variation of MIRR, intra-fund variation of PME, probability of loss, and probability of total loss are tabulated. Additionally the table includes t-statistics and p-values of mean comparison tests.

		Mean							
		Rate of return			Intra-fund variation of return			Shortfall probability	
	Obs.	Gross IRR	Gross MIRR	Gross PME	Sd(Q-IRR)	Sd(Q-MIRR)	Sd(Q-PME)	P(loss)	P(tot. loss)
All funds	100	0.502	0.199	3.076	0.056	0.012	0.257	0.349	0.157
Fund Type									
Venture Capital	38	0.489	0.197	2.841	0.057	0.014	0.263	0.453	0.207
Buyout	62	0.511	0.199	3.221	0.055	0.010	0.254	0.286	0.126
t-statistic[a]		0.335	0.118	0.857	-0.154	-1.751	-0.143	5.568	3.915
p-value		0.738	0.907	0.394	0.878	0.086	0.887	0.000	0.000
Headquarters of PEF									
USA	72	0.515	0.206	3.356	0.053	0.012	0.287	0.364	0.169
Europe	28	0.470	0.179	2.355	0.063	0.011	0.182	0.312	0.125
t-statistic[a]		0.638	1.965	2.827	0.671	0.752	2.326	1.411	1.894
p-value		0.525	0.053	0.006	0.506	0.455	0.022	0.161	0.061

[a] Based on a variance ratio test a double-sided t-test with equal or unequal variances was calculated to compare means

Table 6.5: Correlation analysis between performance measures and independent variables

The table displays Pearson product-moment correlations between performance measures and independent variables. All correlations are based on 100 observations.

	Pearson product-moment correlation							
	Rate of Return			Intra-fund variation of return			Shortfall probability	
	IRR	MIRR	PME	Sd(Q-IRR)	Sd(Q-MIRR)	Sd(Q-PME)	p(loss)	p(tot loss)
No. of portfolio companies	0.011	0.126	0.287***	-0.387***	-0.400***	-0.168*	0.297***	0.063
	(0.912)	(0.210)	(0.004)	(0.000)	(0.0000)	(0.095)	(0.003)	(0.536)
Div. a. time (months)	-0.056	0.026	0.311***	-0.319***	-0.375***	0.010	-0.220**	-0.233**
	(0.582)	(0.795)	(0.002)	(0.001)	(0.000)	(0.924)	(0.028)	(0.020)
Div. a. fin. stages	-0.033	-0.025	0.078	-0.237**	-0.189*	-0.0855	0.358***	0.232**
	(0.745)	(0.808)	(0.440)	(0.017)	(0.060)	(0.399)	(0.000)	(0.020)
Div. a. industries	0.016	0.003	0.153	-0.168*	-0.300***	-0.051	-0.132	-0.203**
	(0.871)	(0.979)	(0.128)	(0.094)	(0.002)	(0.613)	(0.190)	(0.043)
Div. a. countries	-0.061	0.006	-0.054	-0.163	-0.156	-0.180*	0.067	-0.028
	(0.544)	(0.956)	(0.595)	(0.105)	(0.122)	(0.073)	(0.508)	(0.782)
Return msci in vy	-0.144	-0.124	-0.138	-0.082	-0.083	-0.138	0.083	0.060
	(0.154)	(0.220)	(0.172)	(0.420)	(0.413)	(0.170)	(0.413)	(0.554)
Funds raised in vy	0.194*	0.225**	0.069	0.187*	0.423***	0.067	0.253**	0.247**
(log bil. USD 2000)	(0.053)	(0.025)	(0.494)	(0.063)	(0.000)	(0.508)	(0.011)	(0.013)
Fund size	-0.128	-0.109	-0.115	-0.197**	-0.141	-0.158	-0.127	-0.075
(log mil. USD 2000)	(0.205)	(0.279)	(0.253)	(0.049)	(0.161)	(0.115)	(0.209)	(0.460)
Firm experience	0.089	0.175*	0.262***	-0.146	-0.001	0.031	-0.050	-0.071
	(0.379)	(0.083)	(0.008)	(0.148)	(0.993)	(0.763)	(0.623)	(0.482)

p-values are in parentheses.

* significant at 10%; ** significant at 5%; *** significant at 1%

To avoid biased standard errors because of heteroscedasticity, I estimate Huber-White-standard errors, which are robust against violation of the assumption of homoscedasticity (White 1980). Moreover, the observations in subsample 2 are clustered according to PE firms. The observations belonging to one PE firm might not be independent from each other. Hence, standard errors are adjusted for 34 clusters, i.e., PE firms (Rogers 1993). The sample size of 100 PE funds is limited. Hence, before I start with the regression analysis, a closer look is taken at the functional form of the dependent variables as well as on collinearity issues.

In line with previous articles, the descriptive analysis in section 6.3 presents the distributions of rate of return and intra-fund variation of return to be right skewed (Figure D.2). Cochrane (2001) and Jones & Rhodes-Kropf (2003) suggest that the return of PE investments and funds can be represented best by means of a lognormal distribution. Consequently, some authors used a logarithmic transformation of returns as dependent variables in their analyses instead of the returns themselves (Hege et al. 2003, Cumming & Walz 2004, Gottschalg et al. 2004).

I use the Box-Cox transformation in order to test whether logarithmic transformations of rates of return and intra-fund variations of return better fit the data than the variables themselves.[70] The results of the Box-Cox estimations are presented in table D.2 in the appendix. For all variables of rate of return and intra-fund variation of return the hypothesis that the data is best represented by a linear functional form is rejected at the 1% level. In contrast, for MIRR, PME, intra-fund variation of IRR, and intra-fund variation of PME the hypothesis that the data is best represented by a logarithmic transformation cannot be rejected at least at the 10%level. For IRR and intra-fund variation of MIRR the hypothesis is rejected, but still at a lower level of significance than the hypothesis that the data follows a linear functional form. In summary, the tests favor a logarithmic transformation in four of six cases. Hence, I use the logarithm of IRR, MIRR, PME, intra-fund variation of IRR, intra-fund variation of MIRR, and intra-fund variation of PME as dependent variables rather than the variables themselves. To be consistent with previous studies I take the logarithm of (1+IRR) and (1+MIRR) so that log(1+IRR) and log(1+MIRR) equals zero when IRR and MIRR are zero (Cumming & Walz 2004).

Though the logarithmic transformation makes the interpretation of the estimated coefficients a little bit more complicated, it improves estimation. In comparison, appendix D contains alternative regressions for non-logarithmized rates of return and non-logarithmized intra-fund variations of return. The results are qualitatively equal to the regressions for logarithmized variables. However, accuracy of some parameters is less. Since probability of loss seems to be distributed symmetrically, probability of loss and total loss are not logarithmized.

Another issue when working with small sample sizes is multi-collinearity. High collinearity between dependent variables lowers the accuracy of parameter estimation. As a first indicator for multi-collinearity, Table D.3 contains Pearson product-moment correlations between the independent variables. No correlation is above 0.45. More information about multi-collinearity provides variance inflation factors (VIFs) (Neter et al. 1990). Tables D.4 and D.5 in the

[70] For further details on Box-Cox transformation and its use see Box & Cox (1964).

appendix enclose VIFs for the regressions conducted in this chapter.[71] All VIFs are below 3.5 so that no serious multi-collinearity issues are expected without one exception. When year fixed effects are included in the regressions, the VIFs for new funds raised in vintage year increase to values between 8.3 and 9.2. This might cause estimation difficulties of new funds raised in vintage year in the corresponding regressions.

6.4.2 Impact of diversification on rate of return

The first question I address is whether diversification has an impact on the rate of return of a PE fund. I regress log(1+IRR), log(1+MIRR), and log(PME) on the five dimensions of diversification. Additionally, I include a set of variables which have been shown to impact the rate of return of PE funds in previous studies.

Tables 6.6, 6.7, and 6.8 summarize the regression results.[72] They display the estimated parameters, robust standard errors, and summary statistics. For each return variable I estimate three specifications, which vary among the dimensions of diversification. Specification (1) only includes 'naive' and 'dynamic' diversification. In contrast, specification (2) solely contains the three variables of 'systematic' diversification. In specification (3) I examine all five dimensions together. Moreover, I run a fourth regression, which incorporates year fixed effects as control variables. The F-tests on joint significance of all parameters are significant at the 1% level for all specifications. Moreover, the regressions explain between 19.7% and 48.0% of the variance across sample funds' rate of return.

In all regressions the number of portfolio companies has a positive effect on the rate of return of PE funds. An increase in number of portfolio companies from 25 to 35 increases IRR by 5.6 percentage points, MIRR by 1.6 percentage points, and PME by 0.35, holding all other variables constant (Tables 6.6, 6.7, 6.8, columns (4)). The coefficient is statistically significant for all regressions except for column (3) of Table 6.6. Its direction and magnitude is stable across all specifications. A possible explanation for the positive sign is the fact that holding fund size constant, a larger number of portfolio companies is equal to a lower average investment per portfolio company. Controlling also for fund types the lower average investment per portfolio company might be associated with lower prices paid for portfolio companies, explaining the positive effect.

According to hypothesis 1a, the rate of return of a PE fund declines with diversification across financing stages. The effect is statistically significant at least at the 10% level when all dimensions of diversification and year fixed effects are included in the regressions. Moreover, it is negative in all regressions. The costs of diversification across financing stages appear to

[71] The higher the VIF for a variable is, the higher the estimated variance of the corresponding coefficient, and hence, the greater the chance that serious multi-collinearity issues are present (Neter et al. 1990). However, no theory provides a threshold value for VIF to judge for serious multi-collinearity. Neter et al. state 10 to be a useful threshold.

[72] Tables D.6, D.7, and D.8 in the appendix display the results of the alternative regressions with IRR, MIRR, and PME as dependent variables.

be quite high. An increase in diversification across financing stages by one standard deviation around its mean is connected with a decline of IRR by 6.5 percentage points, of MIRR by 1.9 percentage points, and of PME by 0.36, all else equal (Tables 6.6, 6.7, 6.8, columns (4)).

Table 6.6: OLS regression for log(1+IRR)

Subsample 2 consists of 100 PE funds. The dependent variable is the logarithm of (1+IRR). Independent variables include number of portfolio companies, diversification across time, diversification across financing stages, diversification across industries, diversification across countries, rate of return of the MSCI World Index in vintage year, new funds raised in vintage year, fund size, and firm experience. Additionally, the regressions contain dummy variables indicating funds managed by PE firms with headquarters in Europe and VC funds, as well as a constant. The table reports marginal effects and robust standard errors.

	Dependent variable: log(1+IRR)			
	(1)	(2)	(3)	(4)
Number of portfolio companies	0.002*		0.003	0.004**
	(0.001)		(0.002)	(0.002)
Div. across time (months)	-0.005*		-0.005*	-0.005
	(0.003)		(0.003)	(0.004)
Div. across financing stages		-0.085	-0.143	-0.202*
		(0.099)	(0.111)	(0.107)
Div. across industries		0.185*	0.140	0.132
		(0.106)	(0.115)	(0.114)
Div. across. countries		-0.002	-0.034	-0.112
		(0.074)	(0.089)	(0.109)
Return msci in vy	-0.490***	-0.408***	-0.516***	-0.451**
	(0.171)	(0.141)	(0.167)	(0.175)
Funds raised in vy (log bil. USD 2000)	0.063***	0.078***	0.072***	0.044
	(0.020)	(0.022)	(0.020)	(0.065)
Fund size (log mil. USD 2000)	-0.064***	-0.054***	-0.073***	-0.063***
	(0.015)	(0.016)	(0.016)	(0.019)
Firm experience	0.035	0.020	0.027	0.012
	(0.022)	(0.024)	(0.023)	(0.025)
European headquarter (0/1)	-0.077	-0.110*	-0.092	-0.077
	(0.050)	(0.061)	(0.063)	(0.069)
VC fund (0/1)	-0.115**	-0.084*	-0.128**	-0.128*
	(0.055)	(0.049)	(0.056)	(0.065)
Constant	0.622***	0.390**	0.615***	0.733**
	(0.159)	(0.151)	(0.171)	(0.350)
Year F.E.	No	No	No	Yes
F-statistic	9.3	12.3	9.6	18.5
p-value of F-test	0.000	0.000	0.000	0.000
R^2	0.197	0.184	0.227	0.309
R^2-adjusted	0.126	0.103	0.131	0.155
Number of observations	100	100	100	100

Standard errors are in parentheses and are adjusted for serial correlation, heteroscedasticity and dependence between observations of one PE firm.
* significant at 10%; *** significant at 5%; *** significant at 1%

The estimated coefficients for diversification across industries are positive in all regressions. For IRR and MIRR the relationship is statistically significant in specifications (2) at the 10% level when number of portfolio companies and diversification across time is not included. For PME the coefficient is statistically significant in all specifications at the 5% level. A rise in diversification across industries by one standard deviation around its mean is linked to an increase of MIRR by 0.7 percentage points and of PME by 0.27 (Tables 6.6, 6.7, 6.8, columns

Table 6.7: OLS regression for log(1+MIRR)

Subsample 2 consists of 100 PE funds. The dependent variable is the logarithm of (1+MIRR). Independent variables include number of portfolio companies, diversification across time, diversification across financing stages, diversification across industries, diversification across countries, rate of return of the MSCI World Index in vintage year, new funds raised in vintage year, fund size, and firm experience. Additionally, the regressions contain dummy variables indicating funds managed by PE firms with headquarters in Europe and VC funds, as well as a constant. The table reports marginal effects and robust standard errors.

	Dependent variable: log(1+MIRR)			
	(1)	(2)	(3)	(4)
Number of portfolio companies	0.001**		0.001*	0.001**
	(0.000)		(0.000)	(0.001)
Div. across time (months)	-0.001		-0.001	-0.001
	(0.001)		(0.001)	(0.001)
Div. across financing stages		-0.030	-0.050	-0.071**
		(0.029)	(0.030)	(0.029)
Div. across industries		0.053*	0.033	0.034
		(0.027)	(0.030)	(0.029)
Div. across. countries		0.036	0.020	-0.011
		(0.025)	(0.024)	(0.027)
Return msci in vy	-0.135***	-0.101**	-0.133***	-0.107**
	(0.047)	(0.039)	(0.047)	(0.043)
Funds raised in vy (log bil. USD 2000)	0.023***	0.025***	0.024***	0.015
	(0.005)	(0.005)	(0.005)	(0.018)
Fund size (log mil. USD 2000)	-0.018***	-0.018***	-0.023***	-0.020***
	(0.004)	(0.005)	(0.005)	(0.005)
Firm experience	0.014**	0.013*	0.014**	0.008
	(0.006)	(0.007)	(0.006)	(0.007)
European headquarter (0/1)	-0.035***	-0.053***	-0.045***	-0.040***
	(0.010)	(0.013)	(0.012)	(0.014)
VC fund (0/1)	-0.032***	-0.024**	-0.037***	-0.039**
	(0.011)	(0.009)	(0.011)	(0.015)
Constant	0.214***	0.179***	0.231***	0.268***
	(0.037)	(0.041)	(0.046)	(0.096)
Year F.E.	No	No	No	Yes
F-statistic	9.6	8.5	11.2	20.9
p-value of F-test	0.000	0.000	0.000	0.000
R^2	0.250	0.249	0.284	0.407
R^2-adjusted	0.184	0.174	0.195	0.275
Number of observations	100	100	100	100

Standard errors are in parentheses and are adjusted for serial correlation, heteroscedasticity and dependence between observations of one PE firm.
* significant at 10%; *** significant at 5%; *** significant at 1%

Table 6.8: OLS regression for log(PME)

Subsample 2 consists of 100 PE funds. The dependent variable is the logarithm of PME. Independent variables include number of portfolio companies, diversification across time, diversification across financing stages, diversification across industries, diversification across countries, rate of return of the MSCI World Index in vintage year, new funds raised in vintage year, fund size, and firm experience. Additionally, the regressions contain dummy variables indicating funds managed by PE firms with headquarters in Europe and VC funds, as well as a constant. The table reports marginal effects and robust standard errors.

	Dependent variable: log(PME)			
	(1)	(2)	(3)	(4)
Number of portfolio companies	0.010***		0.011***	0.013***
	(0.002)		(0.004)	(0.005)
Div. across time (months)	0.006		0.004	-0.003
	(0.006)		(0.006)	(0.009)
Div. across financing stages		-0.302	-0.566**	-0.633**
		(0.241)	(0.247)	(0.235)
Div. across industries		0.962***	0.583**	0.582**
		(0.299)	(0.270)	(0.284)
Div. across. countries		0.404*	0.058	-0.124
		(0.212)	(0.210)	(0.253)
Return msci in vy	-1.331***	-1.152**	-1.362***	-1.215***
	(0.440)	(0.459)	(0.440)	(0.407)
Funds raised in vy (log bil. USD 2000)	0.188***	0.196***	0.219***	0.075
	(0.048)	(0.056)	(0.044)	(0.161)
Fund size (log mil. USD 2000)	-0.161***	-0.214***	-0.204***	-0.196***
	(0.040)	(0.052)	(0.036)	(0.043)
Firm experience	0.112*	0.143	0.087	0.067
	(0.064)	(0.088)	(0.061)	(0.062)
European headquarter (0/1)	-0.376***	-0.647***	-0.484***	-0.492***
	(0.102)	(0.117)	(0.120)	(0.130)
VC fund (0/1)	-0.416***	-0.395***	-0.471***	-0.488***
	(0.108)	(0.093)	(0.106)	(0.124)
Constant	0.980**	1.101**	0.998**	1.705*
	(0.397)	(0.423)	(0.408)	(0.858)
Year F.E.	No	No	No	Yes
F-statistic	17.5	8.7	34.6	31.0
p-value of F-test	0.000	0.000	0.000	0.000
R^2	0.346	0.339	0.402	0.480
R^2-adjusted	0.289	0.273	0.327	0.364
Number of observations	100	100	100	100

Standard errors are in parentheses and are adjusted for serial correlation, heteroscedasticity and dependence between observations of one PE firm.
* significant at 10%; *** significant at 5%; *** significant at 1%

(4)). This result is at odds with hypothesis 1b which suggests that rate of return of a PE fund declines with diversification across industries. In contrast, according to the data PE funds are able to diversify successfully across industries. The benefit of additional investment opportunities in new industries seems to be higher than the costs of diversification.

The estimated effects for diversification across time and countries are mostly insignificant and have different directions across the various regressions. Hence, the data suggests no systematic relationship of diversification across time and countries with the rate of return of PE funds.

The regressions further display interesting results in comparison with previous studies on the performance of PE funds. Consistent with Kaserer & Diller (2004*c*), I find a strong negative link between rate of return of the MSCI World Index in vintage year and rate of return of a PE fund which is statistically significant at least at the 5% level in all regressions. A well performing global economy at the time of fund formation forces PE firms to pay high prices for their investments lowering the rate of return of their funds, all else equal. Varying the rate of return of the MSCI World Index in vintage year by one standard deviation from 4.7% to 14.7% leads to a decline of IRR of 6.6 percentage points, MIRR of 1.3 percentage points, and PME of 0.31, holding all other variables constant (Tables 6.6, 6.7, 6.8, columns (4)).

I also can approve the positive relationship between the amount of new funds raised by the global PE industry in the vintage year of a fund and its rate of return. Raising the logarithm of new funds raised in the vintage year by one standard deviation across its mean, increases IRR by 5.1 percentage points, MIRR by 0.7 percentage points, and PME by 0.15, holding all other variables constant (Tables 6.6, 6.7, 6.8, columns (3)). This result backs the argumentation that the total amount of new funds raised by the PE industry in a year is a signal for future investment opportunities (Kaserer & Diller 2004*c*, Gottschalg et al. 2004). As expected by the multi-collinearity analysis, the coefficient of new funds raised in vintage year loses its significance when year fixed effects are included. The amount of new funds raised has grown nearly constantly over the sample period according to the statistics of TVE. Only in the years 1990 and 1991, TVE quotes a decline of new funds raised compared to the previous year.

Consistent with Kaplan & Schoar (2005) and Gottschalg et al. (2004) the relationship between the experience of a PE firm at the time of fund formation and the rate of return is positive for all specifications. Yet it is only statistically significant at the 10% level for MIRR when year fixed effects are not included.[73]

Furthermore, I find a negative return difference between European and US PE funds, which is statistically significant at the 1% level for MIRR and PME, corroborating the result of Gottschalg et al. (2004). Over the sample period US PE funds achieved on average a 4.8

[73] Kaplan & Schoar (2005) report that for their sample the positive correlation between firm experience and fund's rate of return is only valid in cross section. Controlling for firm fixed effects they find a negative relationship between both variables. This suggests that the positive relation between firm experience and fund's rate of return in cross section is mainly caused by selection. Successful PE firms are able to raise follow-on funds, whereas unsuccessful PE firms are not. Because of the limited size of subsample 2, I am not able to approve this hypothesis.

percentage points higher MIRR and a 1.15 higher PME than their European equivalents, all else equal (Tables 6.7, 6.8, columns (4)).

However, contrary to the findings of Kaplan & Schoar (2005) and Gottschalg et al. (2004), I find returns to decrease linearly with the logarithm of total commitments. A growth in fund size by one standard deviation around its mean lowers IRR by 11.4 percentage points, MIRR by 2.9 percentage points, and PME by 0.62, holding all other variables constant (Tables 6.6, 6.7, 6.8, columns (4)).[74] There are two possible explanations for this result. On the one hand, if one has a closer look at the results reported by Kaplan & Schoar (2005), the IRR maximizing fund size for their sample is USD 90 million in 1990 purchasing power.[75] The returns of funds larger than the optimal value decline with fund size because the number of attractive companies in the economy is limited at each point in time (Kaplan & Schoar 2005). In comparison, 56 funds in subsample 2 have a fund size above USD 90 million in 1990 purchasing power. The three largest funds even have an average fund size of USD 3,618 million in 1990 purchasing power. Hence, the majority of sample funds lie far above the optimal fund size of Kaplan & Schoar (2005) which might cause the negative sign in the regressions. On the other hand, controlling for the portfolio strategy of a PE fund may induce the sign change. For instance, holding number of portfolio companies constant, a larger fund size is associated with a larger average investment per portfolio company. Simultaneously controlling for fund type, the larger average investment per portfolio company might be equal to higher prices paid for portfolio companies, which would also explain the negative effect of fund size.

VC funds in subsample 2 return less than BO funds. The difference between both groups totals up to 18.6 percentage points in IRR, 4.6 percentage points in MIRR, and 1.20 in PME, all else equal (Tables 6.6, 6.7, 6.8, columns (4)). This result is at odds with Kaplan & Schoar (2005) and Kaserer & Diller (2004*c*) and might be explained by the superior return of sample funds.[76] Whereas VC funds achieve higher rates of return than BO funds in the universe of PE funds, comparing the rate of return of both groups only for the 'top-half' of PE funds, BO funds perform better than VC funds. An alternative explanation is that the quality of BO firms to which the fund-of-funds investor had access is superior to the quality of VC firms.

6.4.3 Impact of diversification on intra-fund variation of return

In this section I analyze the impact of diversification on intra-fund variation of return in PE funds. Intra-fund variation of return is measured in terms of the standard deviation of value weighted returns of portfolio companies within a PE fund. An intra-fund variation of IRR (MIRR) of 0.05 translates into an average change of 5.0 percentage points in IRR (MIRR) if one portfolio company is taken out of the fund. Equivalently, an intra-fund variation of PME of 0.25 is equal to an average change of 0.25 in PME if one portfolio company is taken out of

[74] The inclusion of a quadratic term of fund size in an unreported regression does not change the direction of the effect.

[75] Kaplan & Schoar (2005) report in Table VIII, column two, a coefficient of log(size) of 0.18 and of $\log(\text{size})^2$ of -0.02. They measure fund size in USD million in 1990 purchasing power.

[76] Compare sample selection analysis in section 4.3.

the fund. The intra-fund variation of return can be interpreted as the average dependence of a fund's return on a single company of its portfolio and is assumed to reflect the total risk of the investment strategy of a PE firm.

The dependent variables of the regressions are the logarithm of standard deviations of Q-IRR, Q-MIRR, and Q-PME. Independent variables include number of portfolio companies, diversification across time, diversification across financing stages, diversification across industries, diversification across countries, rate of return of the MSCI World Index in vintage year, new funds raised in vintage year, fund size, and firm experience. Additionally, the regressions contain dummy variables indicating European funds and VC funds, as well as a constant.

I estimate three specifications varying across the dimensions of diversification. Specification (1) restrains the analysis to number of portfolio companies and diversification across time, while specification (2) includes the three dimensions of 'systematic' diversification, which are: diversification across financing stages, industries, and countries. In specification (3) all five variables of diversification are examined together. Additionally, I estimate a fourth specification which includes year fixed effects as control variables. Tables 6.9, 6.10, and 6.11 contain the estimated parameters, robust standard errors, and summary statistics.[77] The F-tests on joint significance of all parameters are significant at the 1% level for all specifications. The regressions explain between 33.3% and 60.3% of the variance of intra-fund variation of return across sample funds.

According to hypothesis 2e, 'naive' diversification has a negative impact on intra-fund variation of return of a PE fund. The coefficient of number of portfolio companies is significant at the 5% level in all regressions except for column (4) of Table 6.11. An increasing number of portfolio companies lowers the intra-fund variation of return. Each additional portfolio company reduces intra-fund variation of IRR by 2.2%, intra-fund variation of MIRR by 2.1%, and intra-fund variation of PME by 1.1%, holding all other variables constant (Tables 6.9, 6.10, 6.11, columns (4)).[78] The more portfolio companies a PE fund contains, the less its rate of return depends on the outcome of a single company in its portfolio. This result is in line with modern portfolio theory reporting a decrease of total risk through 'naive' diversification (Evans & Archer 1968).

An equivalent result is found for diversification across time. The coefficient for diversification across time is statistically significant at least at the 5% level for intra-fund variation of IRR and MIRR and has a comparable magnitude across all specifications. Though it is not statistically significant for intra-fund variation of PME, it is also negative. An increase in the investment period by one month is associated with a decline of intra-fund variation of IRR by 3.1% and of intra-fund variation of MIRR by 2.5% (Tables 6.9, 6.10, columns (4)). As supposed by hypothesis 2b, by investing over a long period of time a PE firm can leverage the ups and downs in capital markets, which influence rates of return of single portfolio companies. The

[77] Tables D.9, D.10, and D.11 in the appendix show the results of the alternative regression for standard deviation of Q-IRR, Q-MIRR, and Q-PME.

[78] The coefficients in this subsection are interpreted as semi-elasticities.

Table 6.9: OLS regression for log(sd(Q-IRR))

Subsample 2 consists of 100 PE funds. The dependent variable is the logarithm of the standard deviation of Q-IRR. Independent variables include number of portfolio companies, diversification across time, diversification across financing stages, diversification across industries, diversification across countries, rate of return of the MSCI World Index in vintage year, new funds raised in vintage year, fund size, and firm experience. Additionally, the regressions contain dummy variables indicating funds managed by PE firms with headquarters in Europe and VC funds, as well as a constant. The table reports marginal effects and robust standard errors.

	Dependent variable: log(sd(Q-IRR))			
	(1)	(2)	(3)	(4)
Number of portfolio companies	-0.022***		-0.021***	-0.018**
	(0.005)		(0.006)	(0.007)
Div. across time (months)	-0.033***		-0.034***	-0.031**
	(0.010)		(0.011)	(0.013)
Div. across financing stages		-0.822**	-0.320	-0.552
		(0.353)	(0.325)	(0.356)
Div. across industries		-0.615	0.264	0.289
		(0.465)	(0.431)	(0.440)
Div. across. countries		-0.908***	-0.065	-0.280
		(0.319)	(0.323)	(0.358)
Return msci in vy	-2.168**	-2.359***	-2.221**	-1.868**
	(0.908)	(0.819)	(0.899)	(0.873)
Funds raised in vy (log bil. USD 2000)	0.328***	0.437***	0.345***	0.044
	(0.086)	(0.113)	(0.091)	(0.264)
Fund size (log mil. USD 2000)	-0.253***	-0.165	-0.273***	-0.249***
	(0.063)	(0.109)	(0.074)	(0.087)
Firm experience	0.162*	-0.039	0.148	0.066
	(0.083)*	(0.168)	(0.090)	(0.115)
European headquarter (0/1)	-0.221	0.138	-0.249	-0.273
	(0.170)	(0.293)	(0.217)	(0.221)
VC fund (0/1)	-0.180	-0.238	-0.210	-0.284
	(0.244)	(0.282)	(0.258)	(0.284)
Constant	-1.600**	-2.822***	-1.582**	-0.234
	(0.701)	(0.729)	(0.777)	(1.425)
Year F.E.	No	No	No	Yes
F-statistic	30.8	11.5	21.1	34.8
p-value of F-test	0.000	0.000	0.000	0.000
R^2	0.490	0.317	0.496	0.542
R^2-adjusted	0.446	0.249	0.433	0.440
Number of observations	100	100	100	100

Standard errors are in parentheses and are adjusted for serial correlation, heteroscedasticity and dependence between observations of one PE firm.
* significant at 10%; *** significant at 5%; *** significant at 1%

Table 6.10: OLS regression for log(sd(Q-MIRR))

Subsample 2 consists of 100 PE funds. The dependent variable is the logarithm of the standard deviation of Q-MIRR. Independent variables include number of portfolio companies, diversification across time, diversification across financing stages, diversification across industries, diversification across countries, rate of return of the MSCI World Index in vintage year, new funds raised in vintage year, fund size, and firm experience. Additionally, the regressions contain dummy variables indicating funds managed by PE firms with headquarters in Europe and VC funds, as well as a constant. The table reports marginal effects and robust standard errors.

	Dependent variable: log(sd(Q-MIRR))			
	(1)	(2)	(3)	(4)
Number of portfolio companies	-0.022***		-0.023***	-0.021***
	(0.004)		(0.005)	(0.006)
Div. across time (months)	-0.027***		-0.027***	-0.025**
	(0.009)		(0.009)	(0.011)
Div. across financing stages		-0.556*	-0.016	-0.165
		(0.321)	(0.230)	(0.260)
Div. across industries		-0.860**	0.030	0.095
		(0.384)	(0.282)	(0.303)
Div. across. countries		-0.653**	0.189	0.077
		(0.295)	(0.220)	(0.207)
Return msci in vy	-1.504*	-1.677**	-1.437*	-1.220*
	(0.781)	(0.798)	(0.768)	(0.692)
Funds raised in vy (log bil. USD 2000)	0.375***	0.452***	0.370***	0.204
	(0.074)	(0.120)	(0.078)	(0.145)
Fund size (log mil. USD 2000)	-0.172**	-0.095	-0.180**	-0.176**
	(0.064)	(0.101)	(0.071)	(0.076)
Firm experience	0.215***	0.048	0.220***	0.168**
	(0.050)	(0.127)	(0.054)	(0.076)
European headquarter (0/1)	-0.282***	0.060	-0.330***	-0.368***
	(0.086)	(0.166)	(0.113)	(0.120)
VC fund (0/1)	0.043	-0.032	0.039	-0.038
	(0.172)	(0.212)	(0.179)	(0.204)
Constant	-3.936***	-4.852***	-3.886***	-3.136***
	(0.493)	(0.573)	(0.607)	(0.991)
Year F.E.	No	No	No	Yes
F-statistic	47.5	15.7	49.9	69.3
p-value of F-test	0.000	0.000	0.000	0.000
R^2	0.567	0.353	0.568	0.603
R^2-adjusted	0.529	0.288	0.514	0.514
Number of observations	100	100	100	100

Standard errors are in parentheses and are adjusted for serial correlation, heteroscedasticity and dependence between observations of one PE firm.
* significant at 10%; *** significant at 5%; *** significant at 1%

Table 6.11: OLS regression for log(sd(Q-PME))

Subsample 2 consists of 100 PE funds. The dependent variable is the logarithm of the standard deviation of Q-PME. Independent variables include number of portfolio companies, diversification across time, diversification across financing stages, diversification across industries, diversification across countries, rate of return of the MSCI World Index in vintage year, new funds raised in vintage year, fund size, and firm experience. Additionally, the regressions contain dummy variables indicating funds managed by PE firms with headquarters in Europe and VC funds, as well as a constant. The table reports marginal effects and robust standard errors.

	Dependent variable: log(sd(Q-PME))			
	(1)	(2)	(3)	(4)
Number of portfolio companies	-0.013***		-0.012**	-0.011
	(0.005)		(0.006)	(0.007)
Div. across time (months)	-0.005		-0.007	-0.018
	(0.008)		(0.009)	(0.011)
Div. across financing stages		-0.894***	-0.600*	-0.639*
		(0.316)	(0.341)	(0.354)
Div. across industries		0.232	0.666	0.723
		(0.418)	(0.441)	(0.464)
Div. across. countries		-0.255	0.145	-0.073
		(0.245)	(0.285)	(0.311)
Return msci in vy	-2.279***	-2.496***	-2.282***	-2.220***
	(0.733)	(0.628)	(0.705)	(0.688)
Funds raised in vy (log bil. USD 2000)	0.214**	0.277**	0.247**	0.119
	(0.104)	(0.115)	(0.103)	(0.223)
Fund size (log mil. USD 2000)	-0.244***	-0.275***	-0.293***	-0.291***
	(0.062)	(0.071)	(0.071)	(0.073)
Firm experience	0.237***	0.143	0.211**	0.182*
	(0.085)	(0.092)	(0.083)	(0.105)
European headquarter (0/1)	-0.646***	-0.598***	-0.786***	-0.802***
	(0.143)	(0.163)	(0.159)	(0.175)
VC fund (0/1)	-0.432**	-0.565***	-0.490**	-0.517**
	(0.181)	(0.157)	(0.184)	(0.213)
Constant	-0.391	-0.570	-0.375	0.325
	(0.568)	(0.463)	(0.665)	(1.213)
Year F.E.	No	No	No	Yes
F-statistic	11.9	9.4	10.4	8.2
p-value of F-test	0.000	0.000	0.000	0.000
R^2	0.333	0.324	0.364	0.429
R^2-adjusted	0.275	0.257	0.284	0.302
Number of observations	100	100	100	100

Standard errors are in parentheses and are adjusted for serial correlation, heteroscedasticity and dependence between observations of one PE firm.
* significant at 10%; *** significant at 5%; *** significant at 1%

leveraging of economic fluctuations makes the return of a PE fund less dependent on single portfolio companies. A complementary explanation is the opportunistic investment behavior of PE firms which has been shown in chapter 5.[79] PE firms invest very quickly in 'boom' times of the economy in order to benefit from good exit opportunities. Because of the good development of public stock markets in these periods, PE firms are also able to generate very high returns for some portfolio companies, increasing intra-fund variation of return.

The estimates of the impact of 'systematic' diversification on intra-fund variations of return are less precise. In specification (2), which does not contain number of portfolio companies, all three dimensions of 'systematic' diversification have negative coefficients except for diversification across industries in the regression for intra-fund variation of PME. For intra-fund variation of MIRR, all three effects are statistically significant at the 10% level. For intra-fund variation of IRR, diversification across financing stages and countries are statistically significant at the 5% level. For intra-fund variation of PME, only diversification across financing stages is statistically significant at the 1% level. The negative impact of 'systematic' diversification on intra-fund variation of return corroborates hypotheses 2a, 2b, and 2c. PE funds which contain companies that belong to different investment clusters have lower intra-fund variations of return than PE funds which invest in companies that belong to the same investment cluster.

However, including number of portfolio companies in specification (3) and (4) makes 'systematic' diversification lose its magnitude, so that the coefficients of diversification across financing stages, industries, and countries are no longer statistically different from zero. Only for intra-fund variation of PME, diversification across financing stages stays statistically significant at the 1% level. These results suggest that the negative influence of 'systematic' diversification on intra-fund variation of return in specification (2) is mainly caused by the positive correlation of diversification across financing stages, industries, and countries with number of portfolio companies.[80] In order to realize diversification, PE firms appear to enlarge their portfolios.

The development of the global economy and the perception of PE market conditions at the time of fund formation influence intra-fund variation of return in the same way as rate of return. The rate of return of the MSCI World Index has a negative relation, the amount of new funds raised a positive relation with intra-fund variation of return in PE funds, holding all other variables constant. Moreover, larger PE funds have lower intra-fund variations of return than smaller funds, holding all other variables constant. A doubling in fund size decreases intra-fund variation of IRR by 24.9%, intra-fund variation of MIRR by 17.6%, and intra-fund variation of PME by 29.1%, all else equal (Tables 6.9, 6.10, 6.11, columns (4)). The return of bigger PE funds is less dependent on the outcome of single portfolio companies than of small PE funds.

Somewhat astonishing is the effect of firm experience on intra-fund variation of return. It has a positive sign in all regressions except for specification (2) in Table 6.9. Additionally, it is statistically significant at the 10% level in specifications (1), (2), and (3) for intra-fund

[79] For more information see section 5.5.

[80] Compare Table D.3.

variation of MIRR and intra-fund variation of PME. A doubling in fund sequence number increases intra-fund variation of MIRR by 16.8% and intra-fund variation of PME by 18.2% (Tables 6.10, 6.11, columns (4)). PE funds with higher sequence numbers show larger intra-fund variations of return than PE funds with lower sequence numbers. At odds, one would expect that the knowledge and reputation of experienced PE firms allow them to grow their portfolio companies more equally than unexperienced PE firms. The positive relation between firm experience and intra-fund variation of MIRR and PME suggests that PE firms with a large track record are more willing to bet their funds on a few portfolio companies than PE firms with a short track record. Experienced PE firms are less risk averse because they can set off a bad performance of one fund with the results of their preceding funds. Young PE firms with very limited or no track record do not have this possibility, and thus, prefer to grow their portfolio companies more equally than experienced PE firms.

Furthermore, I find evidence that European PE funds have lower intra-fund variation of return than their US counterparts. The coefficients for European headquarters are negative in all regressions, controlling for number of portfolio companies and diversification across time and are statistically significant at the 1% level for intra-fund variation of MIRR and PME. The difference in intra-fund variation of return between European and US PE funds totals up to 36.8% for MIRR and 80.2% for PME, all else equal (Tables 6.10, 6.11, columns (4)). One possible explanation for this finding is that the better exit opportunities on public stock markets (e.g. on the technology stock market NASDAQ) in the USA allow US PE firms to achieve very high rates of return for some of their portfolio companies, raising intra-fund variation of return. This argument is consistent with the higher rate of return of US PE funds, compared to European PE funds presented in the subsection before.

Finally, a difference in intra-fund variation of PME can be found between VC and BO funds which is statistically significant at the 5% level. Intra-fund variation of PME of BO funds is 51.7% higher than that of VC funds. However, the difference between intra-fund variations of IRR and MIRR are not statistically significant.

6.4.4 Impact of diversification on shortfall probability

Another measure characterizing the performance of PE funds is shortfall probability. Shortfall probability of a PE fund is estimated as the percentage of portfolio companies which return less than a threshold. I consider probability of loss, i.e., the fraction of portfolio companies with a return of less than 0%, and probability of total loss, i.e., the fraction of portfolio companies with a rate of return of -100%.

Table 6.12 and 6.13 display the results of OLS estimation for probability of loss and probability of total loss. For both measures, I again estimate the same four specifications as in the subsections before. The F-tests on joint significance of all parameters are significant at the 1% level for all specifications. Specification (4) explains 55.0% of the variation of probability of loss and 40.5% of the variation of probability of total loss across funds in subsample 2.

Of the five dimensions of diversification, only diversification across financing stages has a clear effect on shortfall probability. Contrary to hypothesis 3a, diversification across financing stages enhances probability of loss and total loss. The effects are statistically significant at least at the 5% level and stable in magnitude across all specifications. A standard deviation change in diversification across financing stages raises the fraction of losses in a PE fund by 4.8 percentage points and the fraction of total losses by 3.1 percentage points, holding all other variables constant (Tables 6.12 and 6.13, columns (4)). PE firms investing in multiple financing stages seem either to fund a higher fraction of low quality companies or to give less management support compared to PE firms which invest in fewer financing stages.

An increasing number of portfolio companies seems to be associated with a rise in probability of loss. In contrast, diversification across time appears to lower the fraction of portfolio companies in a PE fund, returning less than their investment. However, the coefficients of both variables become insignificant when year fixed effects are introduced. Furthermore, neither diversification across industries nor diversification across countries have a significant effect on shortfall probability in any of the regressions.

A growing amount of new funds raised in the vintage year of a PE fund enhances shortfall probability. A doubling in the amount of new funds raised is associated with a 10.5 percentage points higher fraction of losses and a 5.7 percentage points higher fraction of total losses in a PE fund, all else equal (Tables 6.12 and 6.13, columns (4)). PE firms fund a disproportionately high fraction of low quality investments when a large amount of capital is available.

Finally, VC funds have a significantly higher shortfall probability than BO funds. Holding all other variables constant, a VC fund has a 13.5 percentage points higher fraction of loss and a 6.5 percentage points higher fraction of total losses than a BO fund, all else equal (Tables 6.12 and 6.13, columns (3)). VC funds invest mainly in companies which are in their early stages of development. The selection process of early stage companies is characterized by a scarcity of objective information making it difficult to judge the success and survival of these companies. In comparison, established companies, which are the focus of BO funds, have a long history of activity. The scarcity of objective information leads to a higher percentage of losses and total losses in VC funds relative to BO funds. The remaining variables do not have a significant influence on shortfall probability.

6.4.5 Influence of intra-fund variation of return and shortfall probability on rate of return

In the previous three subsections, the impact of diversification on rate of return, intra-fund variation of return, and shortfall probability was examined independently from each other. In the following, I evaluate the influence of intra-fund variation of return and shortfall probability on the rate of return of PE funds, controlling for the level of diversification and a variety of other exogenous factors.

Table 6.12: OLS regression for probability of loss

Subsample 2 consists of 100 PE funds. The dependent variable is probability of loss, i.e., the fraction of portfolio companies in a PE fund returning less than 0%. Independent variables include number of portfolio companies, diversification across time, diversification across financing stages, diversification across industries, diversification across countries, rate of return of the MSCI World Index in vintage year, new funds raised in vintage year, fund size, and firm experience. Additionally, the regressions contain dummy variables indicating funds managed by PE firms with headquarters in Europe and VC funds, as well as a constant. The table reports marginal effects and robust standard errors.

	Dependent variable: probability of loss			
	(1)	(2)	(3)	(4)
Number of portfolio companies	0.003**		0.002	0.002
	(0.001)		(0.001)	(0.001)
Div. across time (months)	-0.005*		-0.004*	-0.002
	(0.002)		(0.002)	(0.003)
Div. across financing stages		0.297***	0.248***	0.224***
		(0.069)	(0.075)	(0.078)
Div. across industries		-0.093	-0.133	-0.121
		(0.111)	(0.094)	(0.098)
Div. across. countries		0.029	0.000	0.020
		(0.080)	(0.083)	(0.085)
Return msci in vy	0.000	0.111	0.022	0.024
	(0.140)	(0.131)	(0.140)	(0.138)
Funds raised in vy (log bil. USD 2000)	0.055**	0.052***	0.048***	0.105**
	(0.022)	(0.018)	(0.016)	(0.041)
Fund size (log mil. USD 2000)	-0.015	0.016	0.001	-0.002
	(0.017)	(0.015)	(0.017)	(0.020)
Firm experience	0.006	0.007	0.012	0.017
	(0.029)	(0.025)	(0.026)	(0.030)
European headquarter (0/1)	-0.002	0.004	0.020	0.016
	(0.038)	(0.040)	(0.041)	(0.044)
VC fund (0/1)	0.124**	0.184***	0.148***	0.135**
	(0.053)	(0.043)	(0.048)	(0.050)
Constant	0.193	-0.055	0.122	-0.141
	(0.169)	(0.126)	(0.165)	(0.223)
Year F.E.	No	No	No	Yes
F-statistic	18.2	12.3	16.3	11.5
p-value of F-test	0.000	0.000	0.000	0.000
R^2	0.418	0.471	0.509	0.550
R^2-adjusted	0.367	0.418	0.447	0.450
Number of observations	100	100	100	100

Standard errors are in parentheses and are adjusted for serial correlation, heteroscedasticity and dependence between observations of one PE firm.
* significant at 10%; *** significant at 5%; *** significant at 1%

Table 6.13: OLS regression for probability of total loss

Subsample 2 consists of 100 PE funds. The dependent variable is probability of total loss, i.e., the fraction of portfolio companies in a PE fund returning nothing. Independent variables include number of portfolio companies, diversification across time, diversification across financing stages, diversification across industries, diversification across countries, rate of return of the MSCI World Index in vintage year, new funds raised in vintage year, fund size, and firm experience. Additionally, the regressions contain dummy variables indicating funds managed by PE firms with headquarters in Europe and VC funds, as well as a constant. The table reports marginal effects and robust standard errors.

	Dependent variable: prob. of total loss			
	(1)	(2)	(3)	(4)
Number of portfolio companies	0.000		-0.001	-0.001
	(0.001)		(0.001)	(0.001)
Div. across time (months)	-0.002		-0.002	0.000
	(0.002)		(0.002)	(0.002)
Div. across financing stages		0.140***	0.155***	0.144**
		(0.041)	(0.047)	(0.054)
Div. across industries		-0.078	-0.049	-0.032
		(0.097)	(0.088)	(0.090)
Div. across. countries		-0.016	0.012	0.033
		(0.054)	(0.066)	(0.066)
Return msci in vy	0.019	0.039	0.037	0.044
	(0.113)	(0.120)	(0.121)	(0.130)
Funds raised in vy (log bil. USD 2000)	0.034*	0.035**	0.032**	0.057*
	(0.018)	(0.015)	(0.015)	(0.032)
Fund size (log mil. USD 2000)	-0.004	0.011	0.006	0.002
	(0.012)	(0.012)	(0.012)	(0.012)
Firm experience	0.001	-0.005	0.003	0.004
	(0.021)	(0.020)	(0.018)	(0.019)
European headquarter (0/1)	-0.033	-0.015	-0.028	-0.038
	(0.025)	(0.023)	(0.024)	(0.026)
VC fund (0/1)	0.064	0.081**	0.079**	0.065*
	(0.040)	(0.032)	(0.035)	(0.033)
Constant	0.075	-0.044	0.015	-0.106
	(0.117)	(0.110)	(0.123)	(0.155)
Year F.E.	No	No	No	Yes
F-statistic	4.7	7.4	6.6	16.8
p-value of F-test	0.000	0.000	0.000	0.000
R^2	0.244	0.300	0.321	0.405
R^2-adjusted	0.178	0.230	0.236	0.273
Number of observations	100	100	100	100

Standard errors are in parentheses and are adjusted for serial correlation, heteroscedasticity and dependence between observations of one PE firm.
* significant at 10%; *** significant at 5%; *** significant at 1%

Table 6.14, 6.15, and 6.16 summarize the results of the OLS regressions. For each return variable I estimate four regressions. Specification (1) serves as reference and regresses the rate of return on the level of diversification and the exogenous variables. In specification (2), I add intra-fund variation of return to the set of independent variables. In exchange, specification (3) contains probability of loss as an additional variable. Specification (4) unifies (2) and (3), embodying both intra-fund variation of return and probability of loss of a PE fund. The F-tests on joint significance of all parameters are significant at the 1% level for all specifications.

The coefficients for intra-fund variation of return are large and positive in specifications (2) and (4). An increase in intra-fund variation of IRR by one standard variation around its mean increases IRR by 31.1 percentage points, holding all other variables constant (Table 6.14, column (4)). An increase in intra-fund variation of MIRR by one standard variation around its mean is associated with a growth in MIRR by 3.9 percentage points, all else equal (Table 6.15, column (4)). An increase in intra-fund variation of IRR by one standard variation around its mean is linked to an increase of PME by 1.45, holding all other variables constant (Table 6.16, column (4)). The positive relationship backs the interpretation of intra-fund variation of return as a proxy for the total risk of a PE firm's investment strategy. According to hypothesis 4, a higher total risk of a PE fund is rewarded by a higher rate of return. This result is in line with Jones & Rhodes-Kropf (2003), who report a positive relationship between idiosyncratic risk and IRR of a PE fund, and Gottschalg et al. (2004), who find a positive correlation between the systematic risk and the rate of return of PE funds.

In contrast, probability of loss in a PE fund has a negative impact on the rate of return of a PE fund. The larger the fraction of portfolio companies that are returning less than their investment, the lower is the rate of return of a PE fund. A decline in probability of loss by one standard deviation around its mean decreases IRR by 11.8 percentage points, MIRR by 3.3 percentage points, and PME by 0.43, all else equal (Tables 6.14, 6.15, 6.16, columns (4)). The large and negative relations suggest that the fraction of losses is not a meaningful measure for the total risk of a PE fund. It rather describes an additional characteristic of a PE fund's performance. This view is encouraged by the fact that intra-fund variation of return and probability of loss explain different parts of the return across sample funds. The coefficients of both variables do not differ significantly whether they are included in the regression analysis individually (specifications (2) and (3)) or jointly (specification (4)).

Additionally, the inclusion of intra-fund variation of return and shortfall probability in the set of independent variables substantially changes the magnitude and significance of the remaining coefficients. The effect of number of portfolio companies in a PE fund nearly doubles and becomes significant at the 1% level if intra-fund variation of return and probability of loss are included in the regressions. Holding intra-fund variation of return, shortfall probability, and fund size constant, PE funds earn a higher rate of return with each additional portfolio company.

Furthermore, the difference in rate of return between VC and BO funds can be explained through the higher fraction of losses in VC funds. Including probability of loss in the regressions,

Table 6.14: OLS regression of log(1+IRR) on intra-fund variation of IRR and shortfall probability

Subsample 2 consists of 100 PE funds. The dependent variable is the logarithm of (1+IRR). Independent variables include logarithm of sd(Q-IRR), probability of loss, number of portfolio companies, diversification across time, diversification across financing stages, diversification across industries, diversification across countries, rate of return of the MSCI World Index in vintage year, new funds raised in vintage year, fund size, and firm experience. Additionally, the regressions contain dummy variables indicating funds managed by PE firms with headquarters in Europe and VC funds, as well as a constant. The table reports marginal effects and robust standard errors.

	Dependent variable: log(1+IRR)			
	(1)	(2)	(3)	(4)
log(sd(Q-IRR))		0.172***		0.175***
		(0.032)		(0.033)
Probability of loss			-0.443***	-0.479***
			(0.142)	(0.075)
Number of portfolio companies	0.004**	0.007***	0.005**	0.008***
	(0.002)	(0.002)	(0.002)	(0.001)
Div. across time (months)	-0.005	-0.000	-0.006*	-0.001
	(0.004)	(0.003)	(0.004)	(0.003)
Div. across financing stages	-0.202*	-0.107	-0.103	0.002
	(0.107)	(0.074)	(0.104)	(0.072)
Div. across industries	0.132	0.083	0.079	0.024
	(0.114)	(0.067)	(0.121)	(0.075)
Div. across. countries	-0.112	-0.063	-0.103	-0.053
	(0.109)	(0.066)	(0.098)	(0.059)
Return msci in vy	-0.451**	-0.129	-0.441**	-0.112
	(0.175)	(0.127)	(0.165)	(0.120)
Funds raised in vy (log bil. USD 2000)	0.044	0.037	0.091	0.087*
	(0.065)	(0.041)	(0.069)	(0.044)
Fund size (log mil. USD 2000)	-0.063***	-0.020	-0.064***	-0.020
	(0.019)	(0.014)	(0.019)	(0.014)
Firm experience	0.012	0.001	0.020	0.009
	(0.025)	(0.017)	(0.026)	(0.015)
European headquarter (0/1)	-0.077	-0.030	-0.070	-0.021
	(0.069)	(0.042)	(0.064)	(0.035)
VC fund (0/1)	-0.128*	-0.079**	-0.068	-0.014
	(0.065)	(0.036)	(0.079)	(0.041)
Constant	0.733**	0.774***	0.671*	0.707***
	(0.350)	(0.225)	(0.348)	(0.241)
Year F.E.	Yes	Yes	Yes	Yes
F-statistic	18.5	36.4	20.2	100.4
p-value of F-test	0.000	0.000	0.000	0.000
R^2	0.309	0.642	0.373	0.717
R^2-adjusted	0.155	0.557	0.224	0.646
Number of observations	100	100	100	100

Standard errors are in parentheses and are adjusted for serial correlation, heteroscedasticity and dependence between observations of one PE firm.
* significant at 10%; *** significant at 5%; *** significant at 1%

Table 6.15: OLS regression of log(1+MIRR) on intra-fund variation of MIRR and shortfall probability

Subsample 1 consists of 100 PE funds. The dependent variable is the logarithm of (1+MIRR). Independent variables include logarithm of sd(Q-MIRR), probability of loss, number of portfolio companies, diversification across time, diversification across financing stages, diversification across industries, diversification across countries, rate of return of the MSCI World Index in vintage year, new funds raised in vintage year, fund size, and firm experience. Additionally, the regressions contain dummy variables indicating funds managed by PE firms with headquarters in Europe and VC funds, as well as a constant. The table reports marginal effects and robust standard errors.

	Dependent variable: log(1+MIRR)			
	(1)	(2)	(3)	(4)
log(sd(Q-MIRR))		0.039***		0.041***
		(0.014)		(0.015)
Probability of loss			-0.151***	-0.165***
			(0.033)	(0.032)
Number of portfolio companies	0.001**	0.002***	0.002***	0.003***
	(0.001)	(0.001)	(0.001)	(0.001)
Div. across time (months)	-0.001	-0.000	-0.002	-0.001
	(0.001)	(0.001)	(0.001)	(0.001)
Div. across financing stages	-0.071**	-0.065**	-0.038	-0.028
	(0.029)	(0.026)	(0.031)	(0.026)
Div. across industries	0.034	0.030	0.016	0.010
	(0.029)	(0.024)	(0.024)	(0.020)
Div. across. countries	-0.011	-0.014	-0.008	-0.011
	(0.027)	(0.025)	(0.024)	(0.022)
Return msci in vy	-0.107**	-0.060	-0.104**	-0.053
	(0.043)	(0.039)	(0.040)	(0.033)
Funds raised in vy (log bil. USD 2000)	0.015	0.007	0.031*	0.024
	(0.018)	(0.016)	(0.018)	(0.016)
Fund size (log mil. USD 2000)	-0.020***	-0.013**	-0.020***	-0.013**
	(0.005)	(0.005)	(0.005)	(0.005)
Firm experience	0.008	0.002	0.011	0.004
	(0.007)	(0.007)	(0.006)	(0.006)
European headquarter (0/1)	-0.040***	-0.026*	-0.038***	-0.022**
	(0.014)	(0.014)	(0.012)	(0.011)
VC fund (0/1)	-0.039**	-0.037***	-0.018	-0.015
	(0.015)	(0.012)	(0.020)	(0.015)
Constant	0.268***	0.389***	0.247**	0.374***
	(0.096)	(0.085)	(0.094)	(0.094)
Year F.E.	Yes	Yes	Yes	Yes
F-statistic	20.9	20.9	14.7	45.2
p-value of F-test	0.000	0.000	0.000	0.000
R^2	0.407	0.527	0.490	0.626
R^2-adjusted	0.275	0.415	0.369	0.532
Number of observations	100	100	100	100

Standard errors are in parentheses and are adjusted for serial correlation, heteroscedasticity and dependence between observations of one PE firm.
* significant at 10%; *** significant at 5%; *** significant at 1%

Table 6.16: OLS regression of log(PME) on intra-fund variation of PME and shortfall probability

Subsample 1 consists of 100 PE funds. The dependent variable is the logarithm of (PME). Independent variables include logarithm of sd(Q-PME), probability of loss, number of portfolio companies, diversification across time, diversification across financing stages, diversification across industries, diversification across countries, rate of return of the MSCI World Index in vintage year, new funds raised in vintage year, fund size, and firm experience. Additionally, the regressions contain dummy variables indicating funds managed by PE firms with headquarters in Europe and VC funds, as well as a constant. The table reports marginal effects and robust standard errors.

	Dependent variable: log(PME)			
	(1)	(2)	(3)	(4)
log(sd(Q-PME))		0.489***		0.449***
		(0.085)		(0.085)
Probability of loss			-1.582***	-1.002***
			(0.295)	(0.208)
Number of portfolio companies	0.013***	0.019***	0.017***	0.020***
	(0.005)	(0.003)	(0.004)	(0.003)
Div. across time (months)	-0.003	0.006	-0.006	0.003
	(0.009)	(0.005)	(0.008)	(0.005)
Div. across financing stages	-0.633**	-0.321**	-0.279	-0.122
	(0.235)	(0.140)	(0.240)	(0.121)
Div. across industries	0.582**	0.228	0.390	0.136
	(0.284)	(0.167)	(0.241)	(0.144)
Div. across. countries	-0.124	-0.088	-0.092	-0.071
	(0.253)	(0.133)	(0.204)	(0.121)
Return msci in vy	-1.215***	-0.128	-1.177***	-0.195
	(0.407)	(0.287)	(0.353)	(0.254)
Funds raised in vy (log bil. USD 2000)	0.075	0.017	0.241	0.127
	(0.161)	(0.087)	(0.160)	(0.092)
Fund size (log mil. USD 2000)	-0.196***	-0.054	-0.199***	-0.067
	(0.043)	(0.043)	(0.040)	(0.042)
Firm experience	0.067	-0.022	0.094	0.002
	(0.062)	(0.049)	(0.060)	(0.048)
European headquarter (0/1)	-0.492***	-0.099	-0.467***	-0.116
	(0.130)	(0.091)	(0.113)	(0.074)
VC fund (0/1)	-0.488***	-0.236***	-0.274	-0.121
	(0.124)	(0.078)	(0.179)	(0.097)
Constant	1.705*	1.546***	1.482*	1.418**
	(0.858)	(0.551)	(0.835)	(0.567)
Year F.E.	Yes	Yes	Yes	Yes
F-statistic	31.0	206.1	49.5	221.3
p-value of F-test	0.000	0.000	0.000	0.000
R^2	0.480	0.776	0.577	0.813
R^2-adjusted	0.364	0.723	0.477	0.766
Number of observations	100	100	100	100

Standard errors are in parentheses and are adjusted for serial correlation, heteroscedasticity and dependence between observations of one PE firm.

* significant at 10%; *** significant at 5%; *** significant at 1%

the coefficient of the VC dummy is not statistically different from zero (specifications (3) and (4)). The same is true for the effect of diversification across financing stages. Diversification across financing stages significantly increases the probability of loss and, consequently, lowers the rate of return of a PE fund.[81] Thus, the inclusion of probability of loss in specification (3) and (4) leads to an insignificant coefficient of diversification across financing stages.

The effects of the remaining variables on the rate of return of a PE also lose some of their size and become mostly insignificant. Hence, intra-fund variation of return and probability of loss explain most of the variation in rate of return across sample funds. This is corroborated by the high values of R^2 of 0.72 for log(1+IRR), 0.63 for log(1+MIRR), and 0.81% for log(PME).

The regression analysis presented in this section might suffer from endogeneity. Intra-fund variation of return and probability of loss might be endogenous, because they are simultaneously determined with rate of return over the lifetime of a PE fund. The statistically correct treatment would be to use instrumental variables and apply two stage least square estimations (Baltagi 1998, Wooldridge 2002). Regrettably, I lack instrumental variables satisfying the order and rank conditions for the identification of single equations in a simultaneous equation model.

6.5 Summary: two basic strategies to increase rate of return

The aim of this chapter was twofold: to analyze the impact of diversification on PE funds' performance and to evaluate the influence of intra-fund variation of return and shortfall probability on the rate of return of PE funds.

While the return of PE financing has received a tremendous amount of attention from academic researchers, the role of diversification in PE funds has received little systematic consideration. Contrary to the model presented in chapter 3, I only find weak evidence for the hypothesis that the rate of return of PE funds decline with 'systematic' diversification. According to hypothesis 1a, the rate of return of sample funds decreases with diversification across financing stages. However, in contrast to hypothesis 2a, the rate of return of sample funds increases with diversification across industries. The benefits of additional investment opportunities in various industries appear to be higher than the costs of diversification across industries. No impact of diversification across countries on rate of return of PE funds is found. The same is true for diversification across time. Additionally, I find rate of return of PE funds to enhance with number of portfolio companies. PE funds with a larger number of portfolio companies have a higher rate of return compared to PE funds with fewer portfolio companies at the same fund size and equivalent characteristics.

Furthermore, chapter 3 supposes that the total risk of PE funds decreases with diversification. Presuming intra-fund variation of return and shortfall probability as proxies for the total risk of PE funds, the hypothesis is only partially confirmed. On the one hand, in line

[81] Compare Table 6.12

with hypothesis 2a and 2b intra-fund variation of return declines significantly with the number of portfolio companies in a PE fund and diversification across time. The more portfolio companies a PE fund contains and the slower it invests its capital, the less its rate of return depends on the outcome of a single portfolio company. However, intra-fund variation of return only decreases with 'systematic' diversification across financing stages, industries, and countries when the number of portfolio companies is not included in the regressions. The reduction in intra-fund variation of return seems to be caused by the higher number of portfolio companies which is positively correlated with a higher level of diversification across financing stages, industries, and countries. On the other hand, probabilities of loss do not decrease significantly with diversification. In contrast to hypothesis 3a, I even find a positive relation between diversification across financing stages and the probabilities of loss. PE firms investing in multiple financing stages have higher percentages of losses and total losses in their portfolios than PE funds focused on fewer financing stages.

Despite the large amount of academic research on the rate of return of PE funds, there is still ambiguity on the relationship between return and risk of PE funds. Assuming the intra-fund variation of return to be a proxy for the total risk of an investment strategy, I find strong evidence for the hypothesis that return and total risk of PE funds are positively correlated. The higher the intra-fund variation of return in a PE fund, the larger is its rate of return, and vice versa. In contrast, the rate of return of a PE fund decreases with probability of loss, that is, the fraction of portfolio companies returning less than 0%.

The results discourage the theoretical model presented in chapter 3. The concept of set-up costs seems to be insufficient to describe the impact of diversification on the return and risk of PE funds. Although PE firms appear to bear substantial set-up costs for diversification across financing stages, the costs for diversification across industries or countries are very low. Moreover, the positive relation between diversification across industries and the rate of return of PE funds suggests that in some cases PE firms can generate benefits rather than costs through diversification. To conclude, more effort in the modeling of PE funds is needed to understand the effects of diversification in PE funds.

Nevertheless, the empirical findings have several implications for the management of PE funds. First, there seems to be rather limited influence of diversification on the performance of PE funds. Despite prevailing opinion, the results suggest no return premium of funds specialized on certain industries or countries compared to diversified funds. However, through diversification across number of portfolio companies and time, PE firms are able to lower the intra-fund variation of return of their funds.

Secondly, the analysis reveals two basic strategies for PE firms to enhance the return of their funds. The return distribution of portfolio companies in a PE fund is usually right skewed. The left side of the distribution is characterized by a substantial fraction of portfolio companies returning less than their investment or even nothing at all. On the right side of the distribution there are a small number of portfolio companies considerably multiplying their investment. As a consequence, PE firms can either select portfolio companies with low risk and put their effort to the part of portfolio companies, which are expected to be on the left side of the distribution, in order to reduce the fraction of losses in their portfolio. Alternatively, they can select portfolio companies with a large upside potential as well as large downside risk and appoint their resources to the part of portfolio companies, which are expected to be on the right side of the distribution, in order to increase intra-fund variation of return. The empirical results show that both strategies can raise the rate of return of a PE fund, when successfully applied. However, it might be difficult and risky to strive for both strategies at the same time.[82] Assuming an equal effort in order to change both measures by one standard deviation, the data suggest an increase in intra-fund variation of return to be more effective than a reduction of probability of loss. All else equal, a standard deviation increase in intra-fund variation of return rises IRR by 31.1 percentage points, MIRR by 3.9 percentage points, and PME by 1.45, while a standard deviation decrease in probability of loss enhances IRR by 11.8 percentage points, MIRR by 3.3 percentage points, and PME by 0.43 (Tables 6.14, 6.15, 6.16, columns (4)).

There are some caveats to consider. First of all, the data set used in this chapter is limited in size and biased towards larger, older, and superior performing funds in comparison to the universe of PE funds. As a consequence, some of the results reported in this chapter might be specific for the 'top-half' of PE funds, but not valid for the 'bottom-half' of PE funds. Therefore, future research should repeat the analysis undertaken in this chapter with a larger and less biased data set. Secondly, some results might be caused by unobserved differences between the PE firms rather than the studied variables. Yet, the size and structure of the data set inhibit the ability to control for firm fixed effects. Thirdly, intra-fund variation of return and shortfall probability are utilized as proxies for the total risk of PE firms' investment strategies. They are not based on value-variation over time as standard risk measures usually applied in financial analysis. Moreover, they do not enable to distinguish between systematic and unsystematic risk. Hence, it is another task of future research to study the impact of diversification on alternative risk measures for PE funds. In particular, it would be interesting to examine the influence of diversification on the variation of quarterly returns which are based on the capital invested, realized amounts, and NAV reported over the lifetime of a PE fund. Regrettably, this data is not available for the sample used in this thesis. Finally, the measures of 'systematic' diversification are not capturing all aspects of diversification. The literature on the impact of diversification in big sized public companies find quantitative diversification measures to explain less of financial success than qualitative diversification measures (Hall & John 1994). However, applying qualitative diversification measures similar to the relation-ratios of Rumelt on a sample of portfolio companies appears to be an unpractical task (Rumelt 1974, Rumelt 1982). For instance, for subsample 2 the relation of the businesses of 2,892 portfolio companies have to be judged, demanding an unavailable amount of information and time.

Another research opportunity, which will be examined in the future is the pattern of intra-fund variation of return and probability of loss across subsequent funds of PE firms. Are there PE firms which either persistently have a higher intra-fund variation of return or constantly

[82] In an unreported regression of probability of loss on intra-fund variation of return controlling for a variety of variables, there is a positive relationship between both variables.

show a low fraction of losses in their funds? Or do the two strategies alternate across subsequent funds of PE firms?

Chapter 7

Summary

Very different portfolio strategies can be observed across PE funds. Some PE funds are highly specialized, whereas others are highly diversified. The decision determining portfolio composition plays a crucial role in the formation of a PE fund. It is a long term strategic decision that is difficult to change. The objective of this thesis was to examine the economics underlying the different portfolio strategies applied by PE funds. In order to do so, three steps were accomplished: (1) the relationship between diversification and performance of PE funds was evaluated in a theoretical model, (2) the determinants driving the choice of portfolio strategies by PE firms were analyzed in multivariate regressions, and (3) the impact of different portfolio strategies on the performance of PE funds was studied. A portfolio strategy of a PE fund was defined as its level of diversification across the number of portfolio companies, time, financing stages, industries, and countries. In the following, the main results are summarized.

In *chapter 3*, the trade-off between specialization and diversification in PE funds is modeled based on modern portfolio theory. The global investment scope of potential portfolio companies is divided into investment clusters of financing stages, industries, and countries. It is assumed that companies which belong to different investment clusters are more likely to have lower co-movements than companies which belong to the same investment cluster. Acting in an investment cluster is costly for a PE firm. For each investment cluster a PE firm has to pay set-up costs in order to overcome the informational asymmetries and agency problems inherent in the investment in private companies (e.g. investments in cluster specific human capital and network ties). Maximizing the utility of a risk averse PE firm leads to an optimal number of investment clusters, that is, the optimal level of diversification in a PE fund. Comparative statics reveal the following hypotheses: The better the expected return-risk characteristics of potential portfolio companies are, the smaller the optimal number of investments clusters. In contrast, the more risk averse a PE firm is, the higher the optimal number of investment clusters. In addition, an increase in set-up costs decreases the optimal number of investment clusters. Finally, with an increasing number of investment clusters, the rate of return diminishes as well as the total risk of a PE fund.

Chapter 4 describes the data set and variables used in the empirical part of the thesis. The entire data set contains information about 6,758 investments made by 227 PE funds started between 1997 and 2003 from 51 PE firms. The sample can be divided into 54 seed/early VC funds, 54 other VC funds, 61 BO funds, and 58 generalist funds. The data distinguishes itself from other data sets through its high level of detail. For the first time it is possible to measure the level of diversification in a PE fund along the five dimensions: number of portfolio companies, financing stages, industries, countries, and time. Moreover, the availability of the entire gross cash flow records between portfolio companies and their funds enables the calculation of three performance measures: (1) rate of return, (2) intra-fund variation of return, and (3) shortfall probability. Intra-fund variation of return measures the variation of value-weighted returns across portfolio companies within a PE fund. Shortfall probability is defined as the fraction of portfolio companies in a PE fund returning less than a threshold. However, the data set is biased towards bigger funds with a higher sequence number and a superior performance relative to the average PE fund reported by Thomson Venture Economics.

The choice of portfolio strategies by PE firms is analyzed in *chapter 5*. Each measure for diversification is regressed on a variety of potential determinants. The results show that diversification across time is predominantly an opportunistic reaction to market conditions. Diversification across time declines with an increase in the rate of return of the MSCI World index in the vintage year, the annual rate of return of the MSCI World Index during investment period, and the amount of new funds raised in the vintage year of a PE fund. In times of a well performing economy, PE firms invest very quickly in order to benefit from the open exit window. In contrast, different levels of 'naive' and 'systematic' diversification of PE funds can be explained by different characteristics of PE funds and firms. According to expectations, diversification across number of portfolio companies, financing stages, industries and countries grows with firm internationalization, firm experience, and fund size. European PE funds show a higher level of diversification across industries and countries than their US counterparts. The relatively small economies of the European countries, compared to the US economy, force European PE firms to spread their funds more across industries and countries than their US counterparts. Moreover, fund types differ significantly with respect to their level of diversification. Seed/early VC funds are most diversified, followed by other VC funds, generalist funds, and BO funds according to the number of portfolio companies, industries and countries. Hence, PE firms predominantly involved in early stage financing diversify the higher risk of their portfolio companies through diversification, compared to PE firms focused on later stage financing. The only exception to this order is the level of diversification across industries of seed/early VC funds. Across industries, seed/early VC funds are more specialized than the other fund types. Because of the high technical uncertainties of seed and early stage projects, seed/early VC firms have to invest significantly in specialized knowledge in very few industries in order to be able to select successful projects.

The impact of diversification on PE funds' performance is the driving question in *chapter 6*. Contrary to the results in chapter 3, there is only weak evidence that the rate of return of PE funds is declining with the level of 'systematic' diversification. Although the rate of return of sample funds is declining with diversification across financing stages, it is increasing with diversification across industries. Diversification across countries has no significant influence on the rate of return of PE funds. Equivalently, the hypothesis that PE funds' intra-fund variations of return decline with their level of diversification can only be partially confirmed. Intra-fund variations of return of sample funds decrease with number of portfolio companies and diversification across time. The more portfolio companies a PE fund contains and the slower it spends its capital, the less dependent is its rate of return on the outcome of a single portfolio company. However, the effect of 'systematic' diversification on the intra-fund variation of return is only significant when the number of portfolio companies is not included in the regression. Hence, the reduction in intra-fund variation of return, caused by 'systematic' diversification, is related to the larger number of portfolio companies in PE funds with a high level of 'systematic' diversification. Finally, diversification has limited influence on the shortfall probabilities of PE funds. An increase in diversification across financing stages enhances probabilities of loss and total of PE funds. In summary, these results suggest that the model presented in chapter 3 is insufficient to explain the impact of diversification on the return and risk of PE funds. More effort in the modeling of PE investing is needed to understand the effects of diversification in PE funds.

Chapter 6 also evaluates the relationship between PE funds' rates of return, intra-fund variations of return and shortfall probabilities. Assuming that intra-fund variation is a proxy for the total risk of a PE fund's portfolio strategy, there is strong evidence that the rate of return is positively linked to the total risk of a PE fund. PE funds with high intra-fund variations of return achieve high rates of return, and vice versa. In contrast, shortfall probability is negatively correlated with the rate of return of PE funds. The larger the fraction of portfolio companies in a PE fund that return less than their investment, the lower is the fund's rate of return. This result suggests that shortfall probability is an inappropriate measure of a PE fund's portfolio strategy.

The results have several implications for investors and PE firms. Chapter 5 allows investors to predict more accurately the choice of portfolio strategies of PE funds they intend to invest in. The information assists investors in allocating their capital according to their own investment strategy. The findings in chapter 6 have consequences mainly for PE firms. On the one hand, the results demonstrate the rather limited influence of diversification on the performance of PE funds. Despite prevailing opinion, no return premium of funds specialized in certain industries or countries compared to diversified funds can be observed. However, through diversification across number of portfolio companies and time, PE firms are able to lower the intra-fund variation of return of their funds. On the other hand, the relations between PE funds' rates of return, intra-fund variations of return and probabilities of loss point out two basic strategies to raise the rate of return of a PE fund: PE firms can either concentrate their efforts to reduce the fraction of losses in their portfolios or appoint their resources to the potential winners in their funds, in order to increase intra-fund variation of return. The empirical results show that both strategies can raise the rate of return of a PE fund when successfully applied.

To conclude, despite its importance, portfolio strategies applied by PE firms have received little attention from the research community so far. This thesis is the first systematic analysis of determinants underlying the choice of portfolio strategies by PE firms and the impact of these choices on the PE funds' performance. It contributes to the growing amount of literature analyzing the investment behavior and performance of PE firms. The unique data set allowed for the first time to measure exactly the diversification of PE funds across various dimensions and to evaluate the relationship between these dimensions and the performance of sample funds. The results should prove to be important for both the research community as well as practitioners. The findings highlight the need for future research that aims at understanding the investment behavior and performance of PE firms.

Bibliography

Admati, A. R. & Pfleiderer, P. (1994), 'Robust financial contracting and the role of venture capitalists', *The Journal of Finance* **49**(2), 371–402.

AltAssets (2005), 'Glossary of private equity and venture capital terminology'. http://www.altassets.com/hm_glossary.php, December 14, 2005.

Amit, R., Brander, J. & Zott, C. (1998), 'Why do venture capital firms exist? theory and canadian evidence', *Journal of Business Venturing* **13**, 443–466.

Ayayi, A. (2002), 'Good news, bad news: Ten years' lessons from the canadian labour-sponsored venture capital corporations', Working paper, CESifo Conference Centre, Munich, November 22-23, 2002.

Baltagi, B. H. (1998), *Econometrics*, Springer, New York.

Bernile, G. & Lyandres, E. (2003), 'Optimal structure of venture capitalist's portfolio', The Bradley Policy Research Center, Financial Reserach and Policy Working Paper No. FR 03-17. June 2003, http://ssrn.com/abstract=419200.

Birley, S., Muzyka, D. & Hay, M. (1999), 'Management buyout: Perception of opportunity - a research note', *Journal of Management Studies* **36**(1), 109–122.

Born, B. (2004), The risk profile of venture capital fund-of-funds, Diploma thesis, Chair of Banking of Finance, Johann Wolfgang Goethe-University, Frankfurt/Main, Germany.

Box, G. & Cox, D. (1964), 'An analysis of transformation', *Journal of the Royal Statistical Society, Series B* **26**, 211–243.

Brander, J. A., Amit, R. & Antweiler, W. (2002), 'Venture-capital syndication: Improved venture selection vs. the value added hypothesis', *Journal of Economics & Management Strategy* **11**(3), 423–452.

Bygrave, W. (1987), 'Syndicated investments by venture capital firms: A networking perspective', *Journal of Business Venturing* **2**, 139–154.

Bygrave, W. (1988), 'The structure of investment networks in the venture capital industry', *Journal of Business Venturing* **3**, 137–157.

Bygrave, W. D. & Timmons, J. A. (1992), *Venture Capital at the Crossroads*, Harvard Business School Press, Boston.

Bygrave, W., Fast, N., Khoylian, R., Vincent, L. & Yue, W. (1989), 'Early rates of 131 venture capital funds started 1978-1984', *Journal of Business Venturing* **4**, 93–105.

Cameron, A. & Trivedi, P. (1986), 'Econometric models based on count data: Comparisons and applications of some estimators and tests', *Journal of Applied Econometrics* **1**, 29–53.

Center for Private Equity and Entrepreneurship (2006), 'Private equity glossary', Website. http://mba.tuck.dartmouth.edu/pecenter/resources/glossary.html, May 20, 2006.

Chan, Y.-S. (1983), 'On the positive role of financial intermediation in allocation of venture capital in a market with imperfect information', *The Journal of Finance* **38**(5), 1543–1568.

Chiampou, G. F. & Kallett, J. J. (1989), 'Risk/return profile of venture capital', *Journal of Business Venturing* **4**, 1–10.

Cochrane, J. H. (2001), 'The risk and return of venture capital', NBER Working Paper No. 8006. January 2001.

Cochrane, J. H. (2005), 'The risk and return of venture capital', *Journal of Financial Economics* **75**, 3–52.

Commission, E. (2005), Merits and possibilities of a european fund structure for venture capital funds, Technical report, European Commission, Directorate-General for Enterprise and Industry, Brussels.

Cumming, D., Flemming, G. & Schwienbacher, A. (2004), 'Liquidity risk and venture finance', SSRN Working Paper. March 2004, http://ssrn.com/abstract=553122.

Cumming, D. J. (2004), 'The determinants of venture capital portfolio size: Empirical evidence', University of Alberta Working Paper. February 2004, http://ssrn.com/abstract=261747.

Cumming, D. & Walz, U. (2004), 'Private equity returns and disclosure around the world', Working paper, Center of Private Equity Research. March 2004, http://www.cepres.de.

Dorsey, T. (2000), 'A portfolio model for venture captal performance measurement and investment selection', Unpublished working paper. January 2000, http://www.garp.com/library/Articles/Dorsey.pdf.

Evans, J. L. & Archer, S. H. (1968), 'Diversification and the reduction of dispersion: An empirical analysis', *The Journal of Finance* **23**(5), 761–767.

Fama, E. F. & French, K. R. (1997), 'Industry costs of equity', *Journal of Industrial Economics* **43**, 153–194.

Fenn, G. W., Liang, N. & Prowse, S. D. (1995), *The Economics of the Private Equity Market*, Board of Governors of the Federal Reserve System, Washington.

Golier, C., Koehl, P.-F. & Rochet, J.-C. (1995), 'Risk-taking behaviour with limited liability and risk aversion', Center for Financial Institutions Working Paper 96-13, The Wharton School, University of Pennsylvania. July 1995.

Gompers, P. (1996), 'Grandstanding in the venture capital industry', *Journal of Financial Economics* **42**, 133–156.

Gompers, P. A. (1995), 'Optimal investment, monitoring, and the staging of venture capital', *The Journal of Finance* **50**(5), 1461–1489.

Gompers, P. A. (1999), 'Ownership and control in entrepreneurial firms: An examination of convertible securities in venture capital investments', Working Paper, Harvard University.

Gompers, P. A. & Lerner, J. (2004), *The Venture Capital Cycle*, The MIT Press.

Gompers, P., Kovner, A., Lerner, J. & Scharfstein, D. (2005), 'Venture capital investment cycles: the impact of public markets', NBER Working Paper No. 11385. May 2005.

Gompers, P. & Lerner, J. (2000), 'Money chasing deals? the impact of fund inflows on private equity valuations', *Journal of Financial Economics* **55**, 281–325.

Gorman, M. & Sahlman, W. A. (1989), 'What do venture capitalists do?', *Journal of Business Venturing* **4**, 231–248.

Gottschalg, O., Phalippou, L. & Zollo, M. (2004), 'Performance of private equity funds: Another puzzle?', Working paper, INSEAD-Wharton Alliance Center for Global Research & Development. September 2004.

Green, W. H. (2003), *Econometric Analysis*, Prentice Hill, New Jersey, USA.

Gupta, A. K. & Sapienza, H. J. (1992), 'Determinants of venture capital firms' preferences regarding the industry diversity and geographic scope of their investments', *Journal of Business Venturing* **7**, 347–362.

Hall, E. H. & John, C. H. (1994), 'A methodological note on diversity measurement', *Strategic Management Journal* **15**(2), 153–168.

Hall, M. & Tidemann, N. (1967), 'Measures of concentration', *Journal of the American Statistical Association* **62**(317), 162–168.

Hege, U., Palomino, F. & Schwienbacher, A. (2003), 'Determinants of venture capital performance: Europe and the United States', Working paper, HEC School of Management. January 2003.

Herfindahl, O. (1950), Concentration in the Steel Industry, PhD thesis, Columbia University, New York, USA.

Hirschman, A. (1945), *National Power and the Structure of Foreign Trade*, University of California Press, Berkley/Los Angeles.

Ick, M. (2005), 'Performance measurement and appraisal of private equity investments relative to public equity markets', Working paper, Center of Private Equity Research. May 2005, http://www.cepres.de.

Jones, C. M. & Rhodes-Kropf, M. (2003), 'The price of diversifiable risk in venture capital and private equity', Working paper, Columbia University Graduate School of Business. May 2003.

Kanniainen, V. & Keuschnigg, C. (2003), 'The optimal portfolio of start-up firms in venture capital finance', *Journal of Corporate Finance* **9**, 521–534.

Kaplan, S. & Schoar, A. (2003), 'Private equity performance: Returns, persistence and capital flows', NBER Working Paper No. 9807. June 2003.

Kaplan, S. & Schoar, A. (2005), 'Private equity performance: Returns, persistence and capital flows', *Journal of Finance* **60**(4), 1791–1823.

Kaserer, C. & Diller, C. (2004*a*), 'Beyond irr once more', *Private Equity International* (July/August).

Kaserer, C. & Diller, C. (2004*b*), European private equity funds - a cash flow based performance analysis, *in* 'Performance Measurement and Asset Allocation for European Private Equity Funds', European Private Equity & Venture Capital Association (EVCA).

Kaserer, C. & Diller, C. (2004*c*), 'What drives cash flow based european private equity returns? - fund inflows, skilled gps, and/or risk?', Working paper, Center for Entrepreneurial and Financial Studies, Technical University Munich. November 2004.

Leibowitz, M. L. & Henrickson, R. (1989), 'Portfolio optimization with shortfall constraints: A confidence-limit approach to managing downside risk', *Financial Analysty Journal* (March/April), 34–41.

Lerner, J. (1994), 'The syndication of venture capital investments', *Financial Management* **23**, 16–27.

Lintner, J. (1965), 'Security prices, risk, and maximal gains from diversification', *The Journal of Finance* **20**(4), 587–615.

Ljungqvist, A. & Richardson, M. (2003*a*), 'The cash flow, return and risk characteristics of private equity', NBER Working Paper No. 9454. January 2003.

Ljungqvist, A. & Richardson, M. (2003*b*), 'The investment behavior of private equity fund managers', RICAFE Working Paper No. 005. October 2003.

Long, S. J. & Freese, J. (2001), *Regression Models for Categorial Dependent Variables Using Stata*, Stata Press, College Station.

Manigart, S., Lockett, A., Meuleman, M., Wright, M., Landstrom, H., Bruining, H., Desbriéres, P. & Hommel, U. (2004), 'Why do venture capital companies syndicate', Working paper, Universiteit Gent, Faculteit Economie en Bredrijfskunde. February 2004.

Markowitz, H. M. (1952), 'Portfolio selection', *The Journal of Finance* **7**(1), 77–91.

Markowitz, H. M. (1959), *Portfolio Selection, Efficient Diversification of Investments*, John Wiley & Sons, Inc., New York et al.

Markowitz, H. M. (1999), 'The early history of portfolio theory: 1600-1960', *Financial Analysts Journal* (July/August), 5–16.

Martin, R. (1995), 'Internal rate of return revisited', SSRN working paper. October 1995, http://ssrn.com/abstract=39520.

Merton, R. C. (1987), 'A simple model of capital market equilibrium with incomplete information', *The Journal of Finance* **42**(3), 483–510.

Neter, J., Wasserman, W. & Kutner, M. H. (1990), *Applied Linear Statistical Models: Regression, Analysis of Variance, and Experimental Designs*, Irwin, Homewood/Boston.

Norton, E. & Tenebaum, B. H. (1993), 'Specialization versus diversification as a venture capital investment strategy', *Journal of Business Venturing* **8**, 431–442.

Pratt, S. E. (1988), Overview and introduction to the venture capital industry, *in* S. E. Pratt & J. K. Morris, eds, 'Pratt's Guide to Venture Capital Sources', Venture Economics, Inc., Wellesly Hills, pp. 7–10.

Pratt, S. E. & Morris, J. K., eds (1987), *Pratt's Guide to Venture Capital Sources*, Venture Economics, Inc., Wellesly Hills.

Reyes, J. E. (1990), 'Industry struggling to forge tools for measuring risk', *Venture Capital Journal* (September), 23–27.

Rogers, W. (1993), 'Regression standard errors in clustered samples', *Stata Technical Bulletin Reprints* **3**, 88–94.

Roy, A. (1965), 'Safety-first and holding of assets', *Econometrica* **52**, 591–611.

Rumelt, R. P. (1974), *Strategy, Structure, and Economic Performance*, Harvard University Press, Boston.

Rumelt, R. P. (1982), 'Diversification strategy and profitability', *Strategic Management Journal* **3**, 359–369.

Sahlman, W. A. (1990), 'The structure and governance of venture-capital organizations', *Journal of Financial Economics* **27**, 473–524.

Schmidt, D. (2004), 'Private equity-, stock- and mixed asset-portfolios: A bootstrap approach to determine performance characteristics, diversification benefits and optimal portfolio allocations', Working paper, Center of Private Equity Research. December 2004, http://www.cepres.de.

Schmidt, K. M. (2003), 'Convertible securities and venture capital finance', *The Journal of Finance* **58**(3), 1139–1166.

Schneeweiss, H. (1967), *Entscheidungskriterien bei Risiko*, Berlin et al.

Schoar, A. (2002), 'The effect of diversification on firm productivity', *The Journal of Finance* **62**(6), 2379–2403.

Sharpe, W. F. (1964), 'Capital asset prices: a theory of market equilibrium under conditions of risk', *The Journal of Finance* **19**(3), 425–442.

Sorenson, O. & Stuart, T. E. (2001), 'Syndication networks and the spatial distribution of venture capital investments', *American Journal of Sociology* **106**, 1546–1588.

Thomson Venture Economics (2005), 'Glossary', Website. http://www.ventureeconomics.com/vec/glossary.html, December 14, 2005.

Tobin, J. (1958), 'Liquidity preference as behaviour towards risk', *The Review of Economic Studies* **25**(2), 65–86.

Tyebjee, B. & Bruno, A. (1984), 'A model of venture capitalist investment activity', *Management Science* **30**(9), 1051–1066.

Weidig, T. & Mathonet, P.-Y. (2004), 'The risk profiles of private equity', EIF Working paper. January 2004.

White, H. (1980), 'A heteroskedasticity-consistent covariance matrix estimator and a direct test for heteroskedasticity', *Econometrica* **48**(4), 817–830.

Wooldridge, J. M. (2002), *Econometric Analysis of Cross Section and Panel Data*, The MIT Press, Cambridge.

Wright, M., Hoskisson, R. E., Busenitz, L. W. & Dial, J. (2001), 'Finance and management buyouts: agency versus entrepreneurial perspectives', *Venture Capital: An International Journal of Entrepreneurial Finance* **3**(3), 239–261.

Wright, M. & Robbie, K. (1998), 'Venture capital and private equity: A review and synthesis', *Journal of Business Finance & Accounting* **25**(June/July), 521–570.

Zimmerman, H., Bilo, S., Christiophers, H. & Degosciu, M. (2005), 'Risk, returns, and biases of listed private equity portfolios', University of Basel, WWZ, Department of Finance, WWZ Working Paper No.1-05. April 2005.

Appendix A

Appendix chapter 3

A.1 Expected rate of return and risk of an investment cluster

The expected rate of return of an investment cluster is given by:

$$\mu_k = E(R_k) = E\left(\frac{W_t/K - W_0/K}{W_0/K}\right) = \frac{E(W_t)/K - W_0/K}{W_0/K} \tag{A.1}$$

The expected terminal wealth of an investment cluster is:

$$E(W_t)/K = \sum_{i=1}^{I_k} (X_{ki}(W_0/K)\mu_{ki} + X_{ki}(W_0/K)) \tag{A.2}$$

Using the information given in (3.5) and (3.11) one obtains:

$$E(W_t)/K = \left(1 - \frac{C}{W_0/K}\right)\mu(W_0/K) + \left(1 - \frac{C}{W_0/K}\right)(W_0/K) \tag{A.3}$$

From (A.1) and (A.3), finally follows t:

$$\begin{aligned}
\mu_k = E(R_k) &= \frac{\left(1 - \frac{C}{W_0/K}\right)\mu(W_0/K) + \left(1 - \frac{C}{W_0/K}\right)(W_0/K)}{W_0/K} - 1 \\
&= \mu - \mu\frac{C}{W_0/K} - \frac{C}{W_0/K} \\
&= \mu - (1+\mu)\frac{C}{W_0/K}
\end{aligned} \tag{A.4}$$

The same result is achieved by interpreting an investment cluster as a portfolio consisting of a subportfolio which contains companies $i = 1, 2, \ldots, I_k$ and the set-up costs. The subportfolio of companies has the expected rate of return μ, and its fraction of the investment cluster's budget is $1 - \frac{C}{W_0/K}$. The set-up costs correspond to a riskless asset with a rate of return of -1. Its fraction of an investment cluster's budget is $\frac{C}{W_0/K}$. As a result, the expected rate of return of an investment cluster is calculated by:

$$\begin{aligned} \mu_k &= \left(1 - \frac{C}{W_0/K}\right)\mu - \frac{C}{W_0/K} \\ &= \mu - (1+\mu)\frac{C}{W_0/K} \end{aligned} \tag{A.5}$$

and is identical to (A.4). The same interpretation is used calculating the risk of an investment cluster. The subportfolio of companies has the risk σ. The set-up costs are assumed to be given exogenous. They have a variance of 0. Its correlation with the subportfolio of companies is 0. Thus, the variance of an investment cluster's return is:

$$\begin{aligned} \sigma_k^2 &= \left(1 - \frac{C}{W_0/K}\right)^2 \sigma^2 + \left(\frac{C}{W_0/K}\right)^2 0 + 2\left(1 - \frac{C}{W_0/K}\right)\left(\frac{C}{W_0/K}\right)0 \\ &= \left(1 - \frac{C}{W_0/K}\right)^2 \sigma^2 \end{aligned} \tag{A.6}$$

By finding the square root one obtains the risk of an investment cluster:

$$\sigma_k = \left(1 - \frac{C}{W_0/K}\right)\sigma \tag{A.7}$$

A.2 Risk of a fund

To calculate the risk of a fund one needs variance of the investment clusters (see equation (A.7)) and the covariance between investment clusters. As stated before, an investment cluster consists of a subportfolio of companies with equal return distributions and a riskless asset with a rate of return of -1, the set-up costs. As a result, the correlation between investment clusters is equal to the correlation between companies' rates of return which belong to different investment clusters:

$$r_{kl}^b = r_{ij}^b = 0 \tag{A.8}$$

Consequently, the covariance between investment clusters is given by:

$$\sigma_{kl}^b = \sigma_k \sigma_l r_{ij}^b = 0 \tag{A.9}$$

The variance of a fund's return is calculated as follows:

$$\sigma_F^2 = V(R_F) = \sum_{k=1}^{K} \left(\frac{1}{K}\right)^2 \sigma_k^2 + \sum_{k=1}^{K} \sum_{\substack{l=1 \\ k \neq l}}^{K} \left(\frac{1}{K}\right)\left(\frac{1}{K}\right) \sigma_{kl}^b \tag{A.10}$$

Using (A.7) and (A.9) one obtains:

$$\sigma_F^2 = \left(1 - \frac{C}{W_0/K}\right)^2 \frac{1}{K}\sigma^2 \tag{A.11}$$

Finding the square root results in a standard deviation of:

$$\sigma_F = \left(1 - \frac{C}{W_0/K}\right) \sqrt{\frac{1}{K}}\sigma \tag{A.12}$$

The first derivative of σ_F with respect to the number of investment clusters K is negative:

$$\frac{\partial \sigma_F}{\partial K} = -\frac{1}{2} \frac{W_0 + CK}{W_0 K^2 \sqrt{\frac{1}{K}}} \sigma < 0 \tag{A.13}$$

The second derivative of σ_F with respect to the number K of investment clusters is positive:

$$\frac{\partial^2 \sigma_F}{\partial K^2} = \frac{1}{4} \frac{3W_0 + CK}{W_0 K^3 \sqrt{\frac{1}{K}}} \sigma > 0 \tag{A.14}$$

A.3 Optimal number of investment clusters

The optimal number of investment clusters is calculated by maximizing the PE firm's utility with respect to K:

$$\max_K u = \mu_F - \frac{\alpha}{2}\sigma_F^2 \tag{A.15}$$

Replacing μ_F and σ_F by equations (3.14) and (3.15) leads to the following maximization problem:

$$\max_K u(\mu_F, \sigma_F) = \mu - K(1+\mu)\frac{C}{W_0} - \frac{\alpha}{2}\left(1 - \frac{C}{W_0/K}\right)^2 \frac{1}{K}\sigma^2 \tag{A.16}$$

The first derivative with respect to K is:

$$\frac{\partial U}{\partial K} = -\frac{1}{2}\frac{2CW_0K^2 + 2\mu CWK^2 - \alpha\sigma^2 W_0^2 + \alpha\sigma^2 K^2 C^2}{W_0^2 K^2} \tag{A.17}$$

To find the optimal number of investment clusters K^* the numerator of (A.17) has to be equal to zero:

$$2CW_0K^2 + 2\mu CWK^2 - \alpha\sigma^2 W_0^2 + \alpha\sigma^2 K^2 C^2 = 0 \tag{A.18}$$

Equation (A.18) is a quadratic function with respect to K. Solving the equality leads to two solution:

$$K_1^* = \frac{\sqrt{(\alpha C\left(\alpha\sigma^2 C + 2W_0 + 2\mu W_0\right))}\sigma W_0}{2CW_0 + 2\mu CW + \alpha\sigma^2 C^2} \tag{A.19}$$

$$K_2^* = -\frac{\sqrt{(\alpha C\left(\alpha\sigma^2 C + 2W_0 + 2\mu W_0\right))}\sigma W_0}{2CW_0 + 2\mu CW + \alpha\sigma^2 C^2} \tag{A.20}$$

Since K_2^* is negative, it is of no interest for this analysis. K_1^* is the valid solution for the considered problem and named K^* in chapter 3.

A.4 Comparative statics

The first derivative of the optimal number of investment clusters K^* with respect to the set-up costs C is negative, at least for all $\mu \geq 0$:

$$\frac{\partial K^*}{\partial C} = -\frac{(\sigma W_0 \alpha)\left(\alpha\sigma^2 C + W_0 + \mu W_0\right)}{C\sqrt{(\alpha C\left(\alpha\sigma^2 C + 2W_0 + 2\mu W_0\right))}\left(\alpha\sigma^2 C + 2W_0 + 2\mu W_0\right)} < 0 \tag{A.21}$$

The first derivative of the optimal number of investment clusters K^* with respect to the fund size W_0 is positive, at least for all $\mu \geq 0$:

$$\frac{\partial K^*}{\partial W_0} = \frac{\alpha\sigma\left(\alpha\sigma^2 C + W_0 + \mu W_0\right)}{\left(\alpha\sigma^2 C + 2W_0 + 2\mu W_0\right)\sqrt{(\alpha C\left(\alpha\sigma^2 C + 2W_0 + 2\mu W_0\right))}} > 0 \tag{A.22}$$

The first derivative of the optimal number of investment clusters K^* with respect to the level of risk aversion α is positive, at least for all $\mu \geq 0$:

$$\frac{\partial K^*}{\partial \alpha} = \frac{(1+\mu)\,\sigma W_0^2}{\left(\alpha\sigma^2 C + 2W_0 + 2\mu W_0\right)\sqrt{(\alpha C\left(\alpha\sigma^2 C + 2W_0 + 2\mu W_0\right))}} > 0 \tag{A.23}$$

The first derivative of the optimal number of investment clusters K^* with respect to the expected rate of return of portfolio companies μ is negative, at least for all $\mu \geq 0$:

$$\frac{\partial K^*}{\partial \mu} = -\frac{\alpha \sigma W_0^2}{\left(\alpha \sigma^2 C + 2W_0 + 2\mu W_0\right) \sqrt{\left(\alpha C \left(\alpha \sigma^2 C + 2W_0 + 2\mu W_0\right)\right)}} < 0 \tag{A.24}$$

The first derivative of the optimal number of investment clusters K^* with respect to the risk of portfolio companies σ is positive, at least for all $\mu \geq 0$:

$$\frac{\partial K^*}{\partial \sigma} = \frac{2\left(1+\mu\right) \alpha \sigma W_0^2}{\left(\alpha \sigma^2 C + 2W_0 + 2\mu W_0\right) \sqrt{\left(\alpha C \left(\alpha \sigma^2 C + 2W_0 + 2\mu W_0\right)\right)}} > 0 \tag{A.25}$$

Appendix B

Appendix chapter 4

Table B.1: Classification of portfolio companies

Each portfolio company was assigned to a financing state, an industry, and a country. The table displays the distribution of portfolio companies across the three classifications.

Panel A: Financing stages

	Number of portfolio companies	%
Seed / early stage VC	2,928	43.45
Second, expansion and later stage VC	2,066	30.66
Buyout capital	1,611	23.91
Listed securities	73	1.8
Other financing stage	61	0.91
All portfolio companies	6,739	100.00

Panel B: Industries

	Number of portfolio companies	%
Internet and Computers	2,104	32.92
Communications and Electronics	1,200	18.78
Business and Industrial	420	6.57
Consumer	554	8.67
Energy and Utilities	88	1.38
Biotechnology and Healthcare	1,402	21.94
Financial Services	265	4.15
Business Services	335	5.24
Other	23	0.36
All portfolio companies	6,391	100.00

continued

Table B.1 – *Continued*

Panel C: Countries

Country	Number of portfolio companies	%
Argentina	3	0.04
Australia	6	0.09
Austria	13	0.19
Belgium	12	0.18
Bermuda	6	0.09
Brazil	15	0.22
Canada	64	0.95
China	27	0.40
Czech Republic	3	0.04
Denmark	12	0.18
Finland	4	0.06
France	310	4.59
Germany	236	3.49
Greece	2	0.03
Hong Kong	22	0.33
Hungary	2	0.03
Iceland	2	0.03
India	38	0.56
Indonesia	5	0.07
Republic of Ireland	22	0.33
Israel	67	0.99
Italy	94	1.39
Japan	12	0.18
Luxembourg	5	0.07
Malaysia	2	0.03
Mexico	2	0.03
Netherlands	38	0.56
New Zealand	3	0.04
Norway	4	0.06
Philippines	6	0.09
Poland	6	0.09
Portugal	5	0.07
Romania	1	0.01
Russia	2	0.03
Singapore	9	0.13
South Africa	1	0.01
South Korea	9	0.13
Spain	64	0.95
Sweden	33	0.49
Switzerland	28	0.41
Taiwan	10	0.15
Thailand	1	0.01
United Kingdom	585	8.66
United States of America	4,967	73.50
All portfolio companies	6,758	100.00

Appendix C

Appendix chapter 5

Figure C.1: Distribution of subsample 1 across vintage years

The figure shows the distribution of the observations across vintage years. Subsample 1 contains 174 PE funds with vintage years between 1977 and 2000. PE funds are divided into liquidated and active funds. Active funds have a NAV larger than zero. Liquidated funds have no NAV any more. Vintage year is defined as the year of the first investment of a fund.

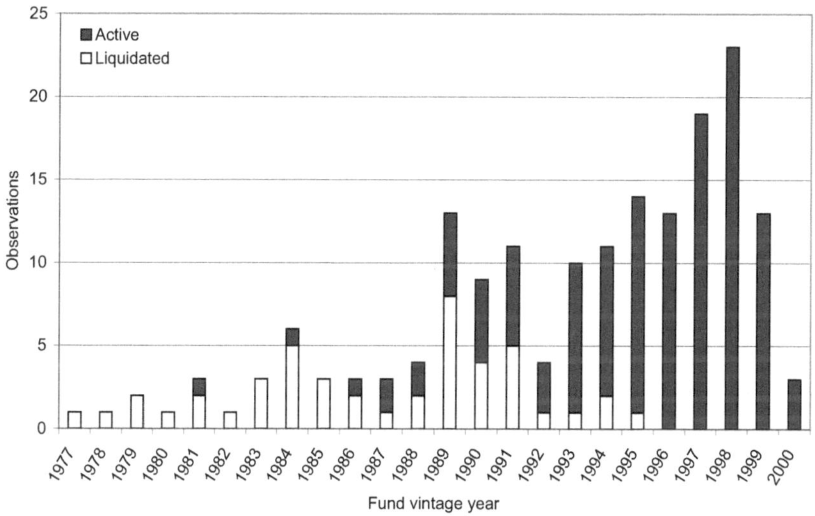

Table C.1: Correlation analysis of independent variables chapter 5

The table shows Pearson product-moment correlation between interval scaled independent variables of the regression analysis conducted in chapter 5. All correlations are based on 174 observations

		Pearson product-moment correlation					
		(1)	(2)	(3)	(4)	(5)	(6)
(1)	Return msci in vy	1.0					
(2)	Return msci invest period (p.a.)	-0.171**	1.0				
		(0.025)					
(3)	Funds raised in vy (log bil. USD 2000)	0.292***	-0.265***	1.0			
		(0.000)	(0.000)				
(4)	Firm internationalization	0.046	0.013	-0.018	1.0		
		(0.551)	(0.861)	(0.818)			
(5)	Firm experience	0.193**	-0.101	0.276***	0.144*	1.0	
		(0.011)	(0.184)	(0.002)	(0.059)		
(6)	Fund size (log mil. USD 2000)	0.234***	-0.140*	0.303***	0.236***	0.537***	1.0
		(0.002)	(0.066)	(0.000)	(0.002)	(0.000)	
(7)	Time trend (1977 = 1)	0.150**	-0.181**	0.932***	0.019	0.275***	0.227***
		(0.049)	(0.017)	(0.000)	(0.805)	(0.000)	(0.003)

p-values are in parentheses.
* significant at 10%; ** significant at 5%; *** significant at 1%

Table C.2: Variance inflation factors chapter 5

Subsample 1 contains 174 PE funds. The table shows variance inflation factors for the independent variables of the regression analysis conducted in chapter 5.

	Variance inflation factor (VIF)		
	(1)	(2)	(3)
Return msci in vy	1.15	1.30	1.35
Return msci invest period (p.a.)	1.09	1.13	1.56
Funds raised in vy (log bil. USD 2000)	1.45	11.02	14.05
Firm internationalization	1.64	1.65	1.71
Firm experience	1.56	3.23	1.66
Fund size (log mil. USD 2000)	2.07	2.16	2.36
European headquarters (0/1)	1.63	1.66	1.74
Seed/early VC fund (0/1)	1.81	1.86	1.89
Other VC fund (0/1)	1.67	1.72	1.74
Buyout fund (0/1)	1.75	1.78	1.85
Time trend (1977 = 1)		9.84	
First-time fund (0/1)		2.44	
Year F.E.	No	No	Yes

Figure C.2: New funds raised across vintage years

The figure shows the amount of new funds raised by the PE industry worldwide in USD billion of 2000 purchasing power across vintage years. Source: Thomson Venture Economics, June 30, 2005.

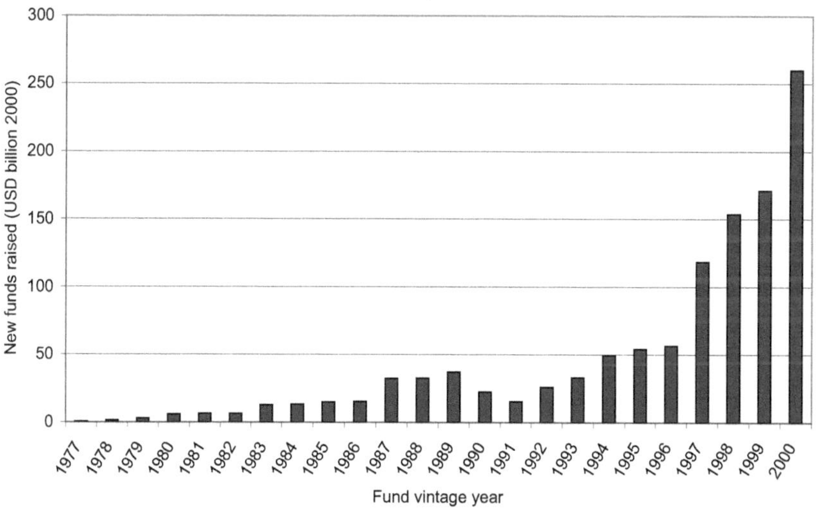

Table C.3: Regression coefficients for number of portfolio companies

Subsample 1 consists of 174 PE funds. The dependent variable is number of portfolio companies. Independent variables include rate of return of the MSCI World Index in vintage year, annual rate of return of the MSCI World Index during investment period, new funds raised in vintage year, firm internationalization, firm experience, and fund size. Additionally, the regressions contain dummy variables indicating funds managed by PE firms with headquarters in Europe, seed/early VC funds, other VC funds, and BO funds, as well as a constant. The table reports coefficients of the NBRM and robust standard errors.

	Dependent variable: Number of portfolio companies		
	(1)	(2)	(3)
Return msci in vy	0.067	-0.235	-0.307
	(0.295)	(0.209)	(0.288)
Return msci invest period (p.a.)	-1.072***	-0.871*	- 0.575
	(0.408)	(0.456)	(0.557)
Funds raised in vy (log bil. USD 2000)	-0.120	0.130*	0.108
	(0.075)	(0.077)	(0.114)
Firm internationalization	0.044*	0.046**	0.450**
	(0.024)	(0.023)	(0.022)
Firm experience	0.167*	0.166	0.167*
	(0.100)	(0.135)	(0.091)
Fund size (log mil. USD 2000)	0.174**	0.161*	0.179**
	(0.086)	(0.083)	(0.077)
European headquarter (0/1)	-0.094	-0.061	0.680
	(0.124)	(0.117)	(0.112)
Seed/early VC fund (0/1)	0.312*	0.303*	0.324**
	(0.165)	(0.157)	(0.162)
Other VC fund (0/1)	0.235**	0.255***	0.254***
	(0.097)	(0.095)	(0.098)
Buyout fund (0/1)	-0.784***	-0.778***	- 0.791***
	(0.195)	(0.193)	(0.197)
Time trend (1977 = 1)		-0.050**	
		(0.018)	
First-time fund (0/1)		-0.076	
		(0.134)	
Constant	2.737***	2.695***	2.384***
	(0.210)	(0.274)	(0.271)
Year F.E.	No	No	Yes
Log pseudo-likelihood	-670.2	-666.5	-663.9
χ^2-statistic	131.9	221.3	1241.8
p-value of χ^2-test	0.000	0.000	0.000
Number of observations	174	174	174

Standard errors are in parentheses and are adjusted for serial correlation, heteroscedasticity and dependence between observations from one PE firm.
* significant at 10%; *** significant at 5%; *** significant at 1%

Table C.4: Regression coefficients for diversification across financing stages

Subsample 1 consists of 174 PE funds. The dependent variable is diversification across financing stages. Independent variables include rate of return of the MSCI World Index in vintage year, annual rate of return of the MSCI World Index during investment period, new funds raised in vintage year, firm internationalization, firm experience, and fund size. Additionally, the regressions contain dummy variables indicating funds managed by PE firms with headquarters in Europe, seed/early VC funds, other VC funds, and BO funds, as well as a constant. The table reports coefficients of the Tobit regression and robust standard errors.

	Dependent variable: Diversification across financing stages			
	(1)	(2)	(3)	(4)
Return msci in vy	-0.184	-0.168	-0.116	0.019
	(0.164)	(0.151)	(0.176)	(0.111)
Return msci invest period (p.a.)	-0.210	-0.216	-0.068	-0.110
	(0.180)	(0.189)	(0.208)	(0.153)
Funds raised in vy (log bil. USD 2000)	0.021	0.007	0.048	0.013
	(0.030)	(0.032)	(0.058)	(0.026)
Firm internationalization	0.041***	0.041***	0.043***	0.014***
	(0.011)	(0.011)	(0.011)	(0.005)
Firm experience	0.057**	0.061*	0.067**	0.008
	(0.028)	(0.034)	(0.030)	(0.022)
Fund size (log mil. USD 2000)	-0.055**	-0.054**	-0.059**	-0.004
	(0.028)	(0.027)	(0.027)	(0.013)
European headquarter (0/1)	-0.175**	-0.177**	-0.181**	-0.058
	(0.088)	(0.087)	(0.086)	(0.040)
Seed/early VC fund (0/1)				-0.262***
				(0.031)
Other VC fund (0/1)				-0.093***
				(0.025)
Buyout fund (0/1)				-0.441***
				(0.044)
Time trend (1977 = 1)		0.003		
		(0.007)		
First-time fund (0/1)		0.013		
		(0.050)		
Constant	0.478***	0.473***	0.654***	0.669***
	(0.098)	(0.110)	(0.093)	(0.060)
Year F.E.	No	No	Yes	Yes
Log likelihood	7.15	7.21	11.15	96.84
χ^2-statistic	27.22	31.51	85.64	580.89
p-value of χ^2-test	0.000	0.000	0.000	0.000
Number of left-censored observations	18	18	18	18
Number of observations	174	174	174	174

Standard errors are in parentheses and are adjusted for serial correlation, heteroscedasticity and dependence between observations of one PE firm.
* significant at 10%; *** significant at 5%; *** significant at 1%

Table C.5: Regression coefficients for diversification across industries

Subsample 1 consists of 174 PE funds. The dependent variable is diversification across industries. Independent variables include rate of return of the MSCI World Index in vintage year, annual rate of return of the MSCI World Index during investment period, new funds raised in vintage year, firm internationalization, firm experience, and fund size. Additionally, the regressions contain dummy variables indicating funds managed by PE firms with headquarters in Europe, seed/early VC funds, other VC funds, and BO funds, as well as a constant. The table reports coefficients of the Tobit regression and robust standard errors.

	Dependent variable: Diversification across industries		
	(1)	(2)	(3)
Return msci in vy	0.064	-0.039	-0.010
	(0.109)	(0.099)	(0.110)
Return msci invest period (p.a.)	-0.115	-0.046	-0.149
	(0.150)	(0.149)	(0.181)
Funds raised in vy (log bil. USD 2000)	-0.035	0.038	0.036*
	(0.026)	(0.035)	(0.046)
Firm internationalization	0.010	0.011*	0.009
	(0.007)	(0.007)	(0.007)
Firm experience	0.042	0.069*	0.046
	(0.034)	(0.041)	(0.034)
Fund size (log mil. USD 2000)	0.024	0.018	0.025
	(0.017)	(0.017)	(0.017)
European headquarter (0/1)	0.085*	0.095**	0.105**
	(0.046)	(0.046)	(0.046)
Seed/early VC fund (0/1)	-0.050	-0.046	-0.047
	(0.064)	(0.063)	(0.060)
Other VC fund (0/1)	0.036	0.048	0.047
	(0.052)	(0.052)	(0.053)
Buyout fund (0/1)	-0.019	-0.010	-0.023
	(0.049)	(0.050)	(0.050)
Time trend (1977 = 1)		-0.014***	
		(0.005)	
First-time fund (0/1)		0.044	
		(0.036)	
Constant	0.543***	0.494***	0.411***
	(0.103)	(0.099)	(0.141)
Year F.E.	No	No	Yes
Log likelihood	66.65	69.23	70.83
χ^2-statistic	40.43	45.41	103.98
p-value of χ^2-test	0.000	0.000	0.000
Number of left-censored observations	3	3	3
Number of observations	174	174	174

Standard errors are in parentheses and are adjusted for serial correlation, heteroscedasticity and dependence between observations of one PE firm.
* significant at 10%; *** significant at 5%; *** significant at 1%

Table C.6: Regression coefficients for diversification across countries

Subsample 1 consists of 174 PE funds. The dependent variable is diversification across countries. Independent variables include rate of return of the MSCI World Index in vintage year, annual rate of return of the MSCI World Index during investment period, new funds raised in vintage year, firm internationalization, firm experience, and fund size. Additionally, the regressions contain dummy variables indicating funds managed by PE firms with headquarters in Europe, seed/early VC funds, other VC funds, and BO funds, as well as a constant. The table reports coefficients of the Tobit regression and robust standard errors.

	Dependent variable: Diversification across countries		
	(1)	(2)	(3)
Return msci in vy	-0.478***	-0.437***	-0.446***
	(0.186)	(0.167)	(0.172)
Return msci invest period (p.a.)	-0.076	-0.103	0.165
	(0.246)	(0.25)	(0.339)
Funds raised in vy (log bil. USD 2000)	0.058**	0.022	0.069
	(0.029)	(0.065)	(0.069)
Firm internationalization	0.047***	0.046***	0.049***
	(0.0156)	(0.0152)	(0.014)
Firm experience	0.013	0.006	0.012
	(0.049)	(0.072)	(0.045)
Fund size (log mil. USD 2000)	0.064*	0.067*	0.062*
	(0.034)	(0.035)	(0.033)
European headquarter (0/1)	0.190**	0.185**	0.171**
	(0.085)	(0.088)	(0.086)
Seed/early VC fund (0/1)	0.149**	0.149**	0.148**
	(0.076)	(0.076)	(0.072)
Other VC fund (0/1)	0.072	0.068	0.087
	(0.076)	(0.071)	(0.074)
Buyout fund (0/1)	-0.056	-0.060	-0.040
	(0.056)	(0.055)	(0.058)
Time trend (1977 = 1)		0.007	
		(0.015)	
First-time fund (0/1)		-0.008	
		(0.082)	
Constant	-0.637***	-0.621***	-0.678*
	(0.177)	(0.172)	(0.400)
Year F.E.	No	No	Yes
Log likelihood	-39.8	-39.6	-36.8
χ^2-statistic	68.7	92.4	437.2
p-value of χ^2-test	0.000	0.000	0.000
Number of left-censored observations	71	71	71
Number of observations	174	174	174

Standard errors are in parentheses and are adjusted for serial correlation, heteroscedasticity and dependence between observations of one PE firm.
* significant at 10%; *** significant at 5%; *** significant at 1%

Appendix D

Appendix chapter 6

Figure D.1: Distribution of subsample 2 across vintage years
The figure shows the distribution of observations across vintage years. Subsample 2 contains 100 PE funds with vintage years between 1979 and 1998. PE funds are divided into liquidated and active funds. Active funds have a NAV larger than zero. Liquidated funds have no NAV any more. Vintage year is defined as the year of the first investment of a fund.

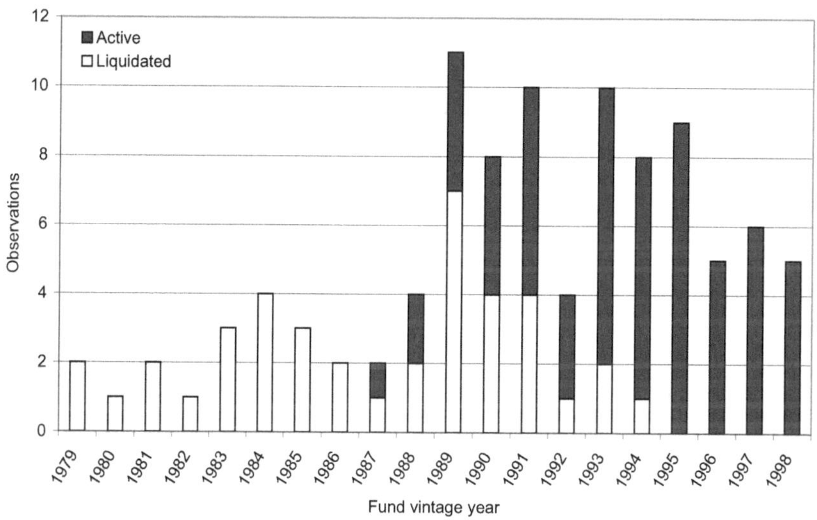

Figure D.2: Histograms of performance measures

The figure shows histograms of the performance measures. Panel A includes histograms of IRR, MIRR, and PME. Panel B displays histograms of intra-fund variation of IRR, intra-fund variation of MIRR, and intra-fund variation of PME. Panel C shows histograms of probability of loss and probability of total loss. The y-axis is scaled so that the sum of the bars' areas equals one. Subsample 2 contains 100 PE funds.

Panel A: Rate of return

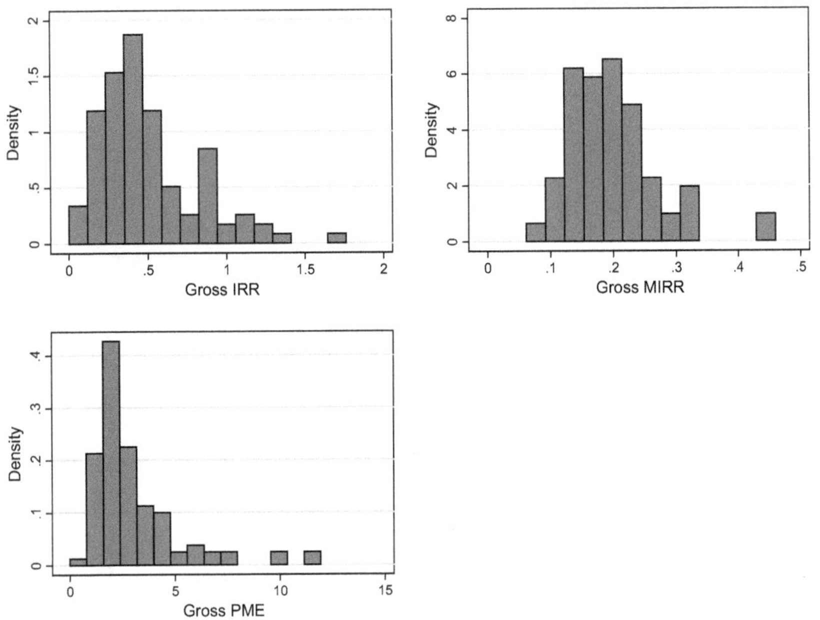

continued

Figure D.2 – *Continued*

Panel B: Intra-fund variation of return

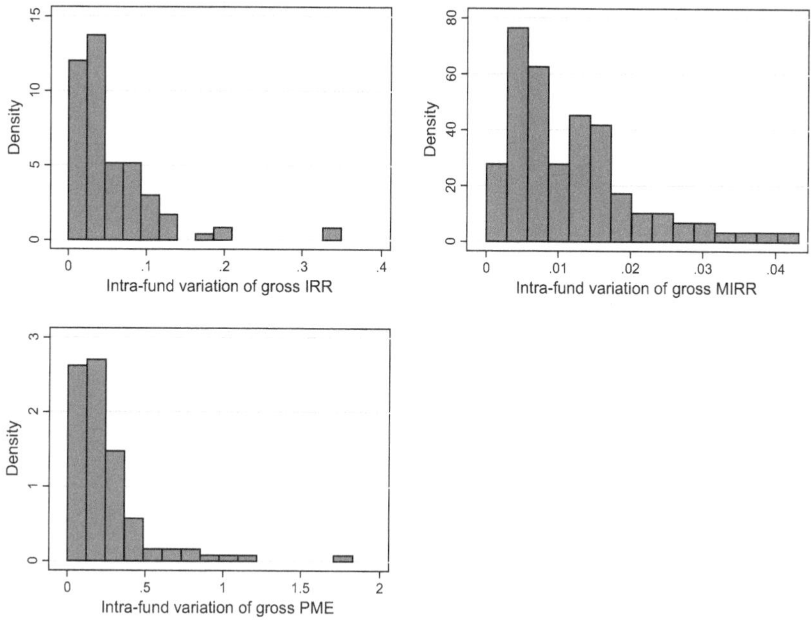

Panel C: Shortfall probability

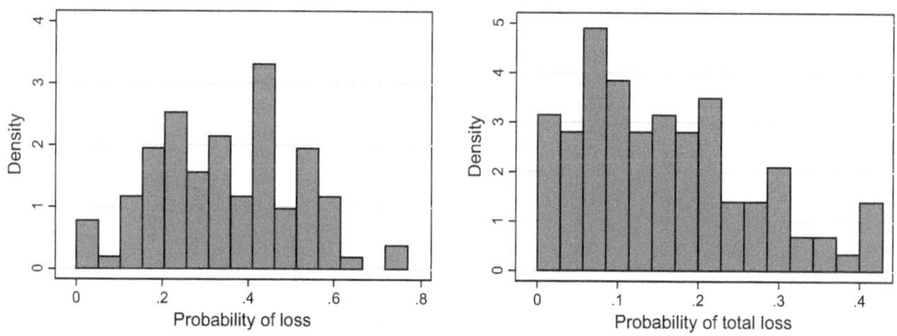

Table D.1: Correlation analysis within performance measures

The table displays Pearson product-moment correlations between rates of return, intra-fund variations of return, and shortfall probabilities. All correlations are based on 100 observations.

		Pearson product-moment correlation						
		(1)	(2)	(3)	(4)	(5)	(6)	(7)
(1)	IRR	1.0						
(2)	MIRR	0.849***	1.0					
		(0.000)						
(3)	PME	0.746***	0.857***	1.0				
		(0.000)	(0.000)					
(4)	Sd(Q-IRR)	0.665***	0.407***	0.240**	1.0			
		(0.000)	(0.000)	(0.016)				
(5)	Sd(Q-MIRR)	0.435***	0.474***	0.217**	0.659***	1.0		
		(0.000)	(0.000)	(0.030)	(0.000)			
(6)	Sd(Q-PME)	0.742***	0.768***	0.743***	0.617***	0.669***	1.0	
		(0.000)	(0.000)	(0.000)	(0.000)	(0.000)		
(7)	Prob(loss)	-0.145	-0.147	-0.220**	-0.077	0.175**	-0.181**	
		(0.151)	(0.145)	(0.028)	(0.449)	(0.083)	(0.072)	
(8)	Prob(tot. loss)	-0.051	-0.077	-0.188*	0.021	0.213**	-0.101	0.749***
		(0.617)	(0.445)	(0.061)	(0.837)	(0.033)	(0.320)	(0.000)

p-values are in parenthesis.

* significant at 10%; ** significant at 5%; *** significant at 1%

Table D.2: Box-Cox transformations

The table contains the results of Box-Cox regressions. λ is the estimated parameter of the Box-Cox transformation of the dependent variable: $y^{(\lambda)} = \frac{y^{\lambda}-1}{\lambda}$. λ equal 1 is equivalent to a linear functional form of the dependent variable. λ equal to 0 is consistent with a logarithmic transformation of the dependent variable. Column (1) displays the different dependent variables. Column (2) shows the estimates of λ. Column (3) to (6) contain the test statistics and p-values of likelihood-ratio tests for $\lambda = 1$ and $\lambda = 0$.

Dependent variable	Box-Cox parameter	H_0: $\lambda = 1$		H_0: $\lambda = 0$	
	$\widehat{\lambda}$	χ^2-statistic	p-value	χ^2-statistic	p-value
(1)	(2)	(3)	(4)	(5)	(6)
IRR	0.269	35.79	0.000	6.30	0.012
MIRR	0.037	24.04	0.000	0.04	0.849
PME	-0.215	84.50	0.000	2.58	0.108
Sd(Q-IRR)	0.073	130.81	0.000	1.25	0.263
Sd(Q-MIRR)	0.236	62.83	0.000	10.55	0.001
Sd(Q-PME)	-0.034	136.86	0.000	0.21	0.649

Table D.3: Correlation analysis of independent variables chapter 6

The table shows Pearson product-moment correlation between independent variables. All correlations are based on 100 observations.

		Pearson product-moment correlation							
		(1)	(2)	(3)	(4)	(5)	(6)	(7)	(8)
(1)	Number of portfolio companies	1.0							
(2)	Diversification across time (months)	0.317***	1.0						
		(0.001)							
(3)	Diversification across financing stages	0.440***	0.150	1.0					
		(0.000)	(0.137)						
(4)	Diversification across industries	0.381***	0.190*	0.160	1.0				
		(0.000)	(0.058)	(0.112)					
(5)	Diversification across countries	0.241**	0.076	0.094	0.171*	1.0			
		(0.016)	(0.454)	(0.353)	(0.090)				
(6)	Return msci in vy	0.122	-0.131	0.032	0.055	-0.113	1.0		
		(0.228)	(0.193)	(0.750)	(0.588)	(0.263)			
(7)	Funds raised in vy (log bil. USD 2000)	-0.139	-0.217**	-0.113	-0.203**	0.152	0.147	1.0	
		(0.169)	(0.030)	(0.265)	(0.043)	(0.132)	(0.144)		
(8)	Fund size (log mil. USD 2000)	0.074	-0.228**	-0.166*	0.164	0.157	0.089	0.142	1.0
		(0.465)	(0.022)	(0.099)	(0.103)	(0.118)	(0.382)	(0.158)	
(9)	Firm experience	0.233**	0.152	0.049	0.295***	0.050	0.147	0.208**	0.436***
		(0.020)	(0.132)	(0.630)	(0.003)	(0.621)	(0.144)	(0.038)	(0.000)

p-values are in parenthesis.
* significant at 10%; ** significant at 5%; *** significant at 1%

Table D.4: Variance inflation factors chapter 6, part 1

The table shows variance inflation factors (VIF) for the regressions conducted in chapter 6. The third row contains the number of the tables, for which VIFs are valid.

	Variance inflation factor (VIF)				
	Tables 6.6, 6.7, 6.8, 6.9, 6.10, 6.11, 6.12, 6.13, D.6, D.7, D.8, D.9, D.10, D.11				Tables 6.14, 6.15, 6.16 D.12, D.13, D.14
	(1)	(2)	(3)	(4)	(5)
Number of portfolio companies	1.50		2.49	2.80	2.90
Div. across time (months)	1.50		1.53	2.57	2.60
Div. across financing stages		1.14	1.37	1.52	1.71
Div. across industries		1.43	1.67	1.69	1.73
Div. across. countries		1.37	1.63	1.77	1.77
Return msci in vy	1.10	1.07	1.16	1.29	1.29
Funds raised in vy (log bil. USD 2000)	1.22	1.34	1.38	8.28	8.87
Fund size (log mil. USD 2000)	1.73	1.62	1.98	2.08	2.08
Firm experience	1.56	1.54	1.67	1.87	1.88
European headquarter (0/1)	1.24	1.72	2.01	2.14	2.15
VC fund (0/1)	1.79	1.54	1.85	1.98	2.33
Probability of loss					2.22
Year F.E.	No	No	No	Yes	Yes

Table D.5: Variance inflation factors chapter 6, part 2

The table shows variance inflation factors (VIF) for the regressions conducted in chapter 6. The third row contains the number of the tables, for which VIFs are valid.

	Variance inflation factor (VIF)											
	Table D.12		Table D.13		Table D.14		Table 6.14		Table 6.15		Table 6.16	
	(1)	(2)	(3)	(4)	(5)	(6)	(7)	(8)	(9)	(10)	(9)	(10)
Number of portfolio companies	2.81	2.91	3.07	3.18	2.84	2.92	3.00	3.11	3.26	3.40	2.88	2.95
Div. across time (months)	2.79	2.83	2.69	2.71	2.58	2.62	2.76	2.78	2.76	2.78	2.64	2.69
Div. across financing stages	1.56	1.74	1.52	1.72	1.53	1.71	1.56	1.73	1.53	1.72	1.57	1.73
Div. across industries	1.70	1.73	1.69	1.73	1.74	1.76	1.70	1.75	1.69	1.73	1.73	1.75
Div. across. countries	1.79	1.79	1.77	1.77	1.78	1.78	1.78	1.78	1.77	1.77	1.77	1.77
Return msci in vy	1.30	1.30	1.32	1.32	1.31	1.31	1.37	1.37	1.34	1.34	1.41	1.42
Funds raised in vy (log bil. USD 2000)	8.28	8.87	8.60	9.15	8.31	8.99	8.28	8.87	8.38	8.93	8.30	8.98
Fund size (log mil. USD 2000)	2.29	2.29	2.25	2.25	2.19	2.20	2.30	2.30	2.25	2.25	2.40	2.43
Firm experience	1.87	1.88	1.97	1.98	1.88	1.90	1.87	1.88	1.93	1.94	1.91	1.94
European headquarter (0/1)	2.15	2.15	2.22	2.22	2.29	2.29	2.18	2.18	2.24	2.25	2.47	2.48
VC fund (0/1)	2.01	2.35	2.02	2.36	2.00	2.33	2.03	2.39	1.98	2.34	2.14	2.40
Probability of loss		2.23		2.23		2.32		2.23		2.23		2.35
Sd(Q-IRR)	1.47	1.48										
Sd(Q-MIRR)			2.02	2.03								
Sd(Q-PME)					1.26	1.32						
Log(sd(Q-IRR)							2.18	2.18				
Log(sd(Q-MIRR))									2.52	2.53		
Log(sd(Q-PME))											1.75	1.85
Year F.E.	Yes	Yes	Yes	Yes	Yes	Yes	Yes	Yes	Yes	Yes	Yes	Yes

Table D.6: OLS regression for IRR

Subsample 2 consists of 100 PE funds. The dependent variable is IRR scaled as percentages. Independent variables include number of portfolio companies, diversification across time, diversification across financing stages, diversification across industries, diversification across countries, rate of return of the MSCI World Index in vintage year, new funds raised in vintage year, fund size, and firm experience. Additionally, the regressions contain dummy variables indicating funds managed by PE firms with headquarters in Europe and VC funds, as well as a constant. The table reports marginal effects and robust standard errors.

	Dependent variable: IRR			
	(1)	(2)	(3)	(4)
Number of portfolio companies	0.285		0.368	0.566*
	(0.191)		(0.281)	(0.311)
Div. across time (months)	-0.754		-0.808	-0.854
	(0.489)		(0.518)	(0.662)
Div. across financing stages		-10.987	-19.396	-28.489
		(15.767)	(17.979)	(17.120)
Div. across industries		29.942*	23.860	22.742
		(17.197)	(18.701)	(18.999)
Div. across. countries		-4.390	-8.460	-20.525
		(11.739)	(13.829)	(17.771)
Return msci in vy	-73.453***	-61.969***	-78.390***	-68.343**
	(25.945)	(21.155)	(25.213)	(26.331)
Funds raised in vy	9.752***	12.435***	11.43***	7.710
(log bil. USD 2000)	(3.178)	(3.648)	(3.313)	(11.051)
Fund size (log mil. USD 2000)	-9.824***	-8.007***	-10.962***	-9.449***
	(2.358)	(2.623)	(2.774)	(3.209)
Firm experience	5.909*	3.205	4.476	2.297
	(3.401)	(3.788)	(3.558)	(3.986)
European headquarter (0/1)	-11.811	-16.083	-13.745	-11.149
	(7.999)	(9.654)	(10.007)	(10.839)
VC fund (0/1)	-16.751*	-11.817	-18.489*	-18.461
	(9.695)	(8.018)	(10.089)	(11.467)
Constant	86.019***	45.567*	81.165**	96.172
	(27.106)	(24.884)	(30.592)	(62.452)
Year F.E.	No	No	No	Yes
F-statistic	10.5	12.9	10.2	17.9
p-value of F-test	0.000	0.000	0.000	0.000
R^2	0.177	0.165	0.204	0.276
R^2-adjusted	0.104	0.081	0.104	0.115
Number of observations	100	100	100	100

Standard errors are in parentheses and are adjusted for serial correlation, heteroscedasticity and dependence between observations of one PE firm.
* significant at 10%; *** significant at 5%; *** significant at 1%

Table D.7: OLS regression for MIRR

Subsample 2 consists of 100 PE funds. The dependent variable is MIRR scaled as percentages. Independent variables include number of portfolio companies, diversification across time, diversification across financing stages, diversification across industries, diversification across countries, rate of return of the MSCI World Index in vintage year, new funds raised in vintage year, fund size, and firm experience. Additionally, the regressions contain dummy variables indicating funds managed by PE firms with headquarters in Europe and VC funds, as well as a constant. The table reports marginal effects and robust standard errors.

	Dependent variable: MIRR			
	(1)	(2)	(3)	(4)
Number of portfolio companies	0.094**		0.108*	0.166**
	(0.036)		(0.058)	(0.070)
Div. across time (months)	-0.118		-0.138	-0.168
	(0.096)		(0.102)	(0.129)
Div. across financing stages		-3.483	-5.990	-8.606**
		(3.623)	(3.795)	(3.619)
Div. across industries		6.585*	4.127	4.282
		(3.340)	(3.594)	(3.541)
Div. across. countries		4.258	2.294	-1.512
		(3.172)	(3.104)	(3.439)
Return msci in vy	-16.335***	-12.193**	-16.035***	-12.925**
	(5.605)	(4.633)	(5.595)	(5.158)
Funds raised in vy	2.789***	3.043***	2.934***	1.922
(log bil. USD 2000)	(0.618)	(0.675)	(0.605)	(2.342)
Fund size (log mil. USD 2000)	-2.262***	-2.223***	-2.749***	-2.391***
	(0.522)	(0.622)	(0.583)	(0.661)
Firm experience	1.804**	1.654**	1.705**	1.064
	(0.730)	(0.808)	(0.749)	(0.900)
European headquarter (0/1)	-4.258***	-6.457***	-5.450***	-4.902***
	(1.242)	(1.602)	(1.518)	(1.682)
VC fund (0/1)	-3.762**	-2.833**	-4.359***	-4.581**
	(1.381)	(1.116)	(1.470)	(1.894)
Constant	24.016***	19.500***	25.902***	29.974**
	(4.585)	(5.118)	(5.827)	(12.172)
Year F.E.	No	No	No	Yes
F-statistic	9.3	8.1	10.1	19.8
p-value of F-test	0.000	0.000	0.000	0.000
R^2	0.245	0.243	0.277	0.396
R^2-adjusted	0.178	0.167	0.186	0.262
Number of observations	100	100	100	100

Standard errors are in parentheses and are adjusted for serial correlation, heteroscedasticity and dependence between observations of one PE firm.
* significant at 10%; *** significant at 5%; *** significant at 1%

Table D.8: OLS regression for PME

Subsample 2 consists of 100 PE funds. The dependent variable is PME. Independent variables include number of portfolio companies, diversification across time, diversification across financing stages, diversification across industries, diversification across countries, rate of return of the MSCI World Index in vintage year, new funds raised in vintage year, fund size, and firm experience. Additionally, the regressions contain dummy variables indicating funds managed by PE firms with headquarters in Europe and VC funds, as well as a constant. The table reports marginal effects and robust standard errors.

	Dependent variable: PME			
	(1)	(2)	(3)	(4)
Number of portfolio companies	0.036***		0.041**	0.050**
	(0.012)		(0.016)	(0.021)
Div. across time (months)	0.021		0.017	-0.002
	(0.027)		(0.029)	(0.039)
Div. across financing stages		-0.402	-1.376	-1.681**
		(0.897)	(0.905)	(0.777)
Div. across industries		3.347***	1.946**	1.997*
		(1.088)	(0.900)	(0.999)
Div. across. countries		0.736	-0.547	-1.200
		(0.796)	(0.754)	(1.047)
Return msci in vy	-4.546***	-4.116***	-4.879***	-4.257***
	(1.459)	(1.371)	(1.544)	(1.369)
Funds raised in vy (log bil. USD 2000)	0.558***	0.603**	0.692***	0.355
	(0.178)	(0.234)	(0.195)	(0.680)
Fund size (log mil. USD 2000)	-0.635***	-0.762***	-0.721***	-0.691***
	(0.130)	(0.207)	(0.141)	(0.168)
Firm experience	0.612***	0.706*	0.499**	0.431
	(0.215)	(0.354)	(0.209)	(0.270)
European headquarter (0/1)	-1.372***	-2.166***	-1.561***	-1.589***
	(0.365)	(0.442)	(0.404)	(0.423)
VC fund (0/1)	-1.356**	-1.207***	-1.479***	-1.564**
	(0.498)	(0.365)	(0.538)	(0.610)
Constant	3.550**	3.504*	3.075*	4.620
	(1.449)	(1.808)	(1.727)	(3.945)
Year F.E.	No	No	No	Yes
F-statistic	16.3	6.3	29.6	25.5
p-value of F-test	0.000	0.000	0.000	0.000
R^2	0.340	0.313	0.373	0.417
R^2-adjusted	0.282	0.245	0.295	0.287
Number of observations	100	100	100	100

Standard errors are in parentheses and are adjusted for serial correlation, heteroscedasticity and dependence between observations of one PE firm.
* significant at 10%; *** significant at 5%; *** significant at 1%

Table D.9: OLS regression for sd(Q-IRR)

Subsample 2 consists of 100 PE funds. The dependent variable is the standard deviation of Q-IRR scaled as percentages. Independent variables include number of portfolio companies, diversification across time, diversification across financing stages, diversification across industries, diversification across countries, rate of return of the MSCI World Index in vintage year, new funds raised in vintage year, fund size, and firm experience. Additionally, the regressions contain dummy variables indicating funds managed by PE firms with headquarters in Europe and VC funds, as well as a constant. The table reports marginal effects and robust standard errors.

	Dependent variable: sd(Q-IRR)			
	(1)	(2)	(3)	(4)
Number of portfolio companies	-0.077**		-0.044	-0.036
	(0.029)		(0.047)	(0.054)
Div. across time (months)	-0.207**		-0.220**	-0.243
	(0.091)		(0.103)	(0.145)
Div. across financing stages		-5.596	-4.500	-4.484
		(3.326)	(3.817)	(3.618)
Div. across industries		-0.518	2.324	2.069
		(2.941)	(2.820)	(2.947)
Div. across. countries		-5.135*	-2.219	-2.792
		(2.535)	(2.581)	(3.391)
Return msci in vy	-5.940	-5.950	-7.154*	-6.222
	(4.217)	(3.709)	(4.022)	(4.365)
Funds raised in vy (log bil. USD 2000)	1.017	1.683***	1.211*	0.266
	(0.722)	(0.575)	(0.661)	(1.928)
Fund size (log mil. USD 2000)	-1.584***	-1.057*	-1.800**	-1.749**
	(0.539)	(0.608)	(0.718)	(0.718)
Firm experience	0.357	-0.694	0.183	0.141
	(0.759)	(1.047)	(0.796)	(0.829)
European headquarter (0/1)	-0.662	0.750	-0.538	-0.515
	(1.459)	(1.838)	(1.839)	(1.708)
VC fund (0/1)	-1.369	-1.180	-1.781	-1.715
	(1.912)	(1.869)	(2.198)	(2.148)
Constant	17.968**	9.892	18.619**	22.546
	(7.630)	(6.257)	(8.862)	(13.341)
Year F.E.	No	No	No	Yes
F-statistic	8.7	4.2	5.7	5.1
p-value of F-test	0.000	0.000	0.000	0.000
R^2	0.281	0.197	0.310	0.320
R^2-adjusted	0.217	0.116	0.224	0.169
Number of observations	100	100	100	100

Standard errors are in parentheses and are adjusted for serial correlation, heteroscedasticity and dependence between observations of one PE firm.
* significant at 10%; *** significant at 5%; *** significant at 1%

Table D.10: OLS regression for sd(Q-MIRR)

Subsample 2 consists of 100 PE funds. The dependent variable is the standard deviation of Q-MIRR scaled as percentages. Independent variables include number of portfolio companies, diversification across time, diversification across financing stages, diversification across industries, diversification across countries, rate of return of the MSCI World Index in vintage year, new funds raised in vintage year, fund size, and firm experience. Additionally, the regressions contain dummy variables indicating funds managed by PE firms with headquarters in Europe and VC funds, as well as a constant. The table reports marginal effects and robust standard errors.

	Dependent variable: sd(Q-MIRR)			
	(1)	(2)	(3)	(4)
Number of portfolio companies	-0.019***		-0.019***	-0.019**
	(0.005)		(0.006)	(0.007)
Div. across time (months)	-0.027**		-0.027**	-0.023*
	(0.010)		(0.012)	(0.013)
Div. across financing stages		-0.545	-0.095	-0.151
		(0.419)	(0.410)	(0.423)
Div. across industries		-0.637	0.129	0.192
		(0.401)	(0.370)	(0.407)
Div. across. countries		-0.707	0.025	0.012
		(0.440)	(0.350)	(0.348)
Return msci in vy	-1.101*	-1.260**	-1.101*	-1.049
	(0.613)	(0.607)	(0.595)	(0.642)
Funds raised in vy (log bil. USD 2000)	0.387***	0.470***	0.394***	0.428**
	(0.067)	(0.102)	(0.075)	(0.193)
Fund size (log mil. USD 2000)	-0.184**	-0.108	-0.192*	-0.204*
	(0.077)	(0.114)	(0.099)	(0.106)
Firm experience	0.270***	0.108	0.265***	0.255**
	(0.093)	(0.158)	(0.095)	(0.109)
European headquarter (0/1)	-0.354**	-0.044	-0.381**	-0.374**
	(0.131)	(0.218)	(0.183)	(0.179)
VC fund (0/1)	0.293	0.243	0.284	0.242
	(0.228)	(0.236)	(0.251)	(0.255)
Constant	1.719**	0.737	1.709*	1.499
	(0.679)	(0.721)	(0.946)	(1.192)
Year F.E.	No	No	No	Yes
F-statistic	21.5	7.5	19.0	14.8
p-value of F-test	0.000	0.000	0.000	0.000
R^2	0.492	0.337	0.493	0.505
R^2-adjusted	0.447	0.271	0.429	0.395
Number of observations	100	100	100	100

Standard errors are in parentheses and are adjusted for serial correlation, heteroscedasticity and dependence between observations of one PE firm.
* significant at 10%; *** significant at 5%; *** significant at 1%

Table D.11: OLS regression for sd(Q-PME)

Subsample 2 consists of 100 PE funds. The dependent variable is the standard deviation of Q-PME. Independent variables include number of portfolio companies, diversification across time, diversification across financing stages, diversification across industries, diversification across countries, rate of return of the MSCI World Index in vintage year, new funds raised in vintage year, fund size, and firm experience. Additionally, the regressions contain dummy variables indicating funds managed by PE firms with headquarters in Europe and VC funds, as well as a constant. The table reports marginal effects and robust standard errors.

	Dependent variable: sd(Q-PME)			
	(1)	(2)	(3)	(4)
Number of portfolio companies	-0.003		-0.004	-0.003
	(0.002)		(0.003)	(0.003)
Div. across time (months)	-0.001		-0.001	-0.002
	(0.004)		(0.005)	(0.006)
Div. across financing stages		-0.158	-0.073	-0.088
		(0.115)	(0.145)	(0.129)
Div. across industries		0.159	0.276**	0.288*
		(0.119)	(0.130)	(0.146)
Div. across. countries		-0.117	-0.010	-0.071
		(0.096)	(0.098)	(0.117)
Return msci in vy	-0.363**	-0.450***	-0.375**	-0.354**
	(0.159)	(0.145)	(0.163)	(0.167)
Funds raised in vy (log bil. USD 2000)	0.038	0.061*	0.055*	0.055
	(0.029)	(0.031)	(0.032)	(0.092)
Fund size (log mil. USD 2000)	-0.059***	-0.065***	-0.066**	-0.064**
	(0.020)	(0.023)	(0.028)	(0.029)
Firm experience	0.054*	0.024	0.040	0.035
	(0.032)	(0.038)	(0.030)	(0.036)
European headquarter (0/1)	-0.168***	-0.159***	-0.210***	-0.197***
	(0.048)	(0.054)	(0.055)	(0.056)
VC fund (0/1)	-0.053	-0.086	-0.059	-0.058
	(0.090)	(0.069)	(0.100)	(0.106)
Constant	0.573**	0.448**	0.453	0.442
	(0.248)	(0.181)	(0.334)	(0.599)
Year F.E.	No	No	No	Yes
F-statistic	4.6	4.6	3.8	5.8
p-value of F-test	0.001	0.001	0.001	0.000
R^2	0.157	0.155	0.181	0.209
R^2-adjusted	0.083	0.070	0.079	0.033
Number of observations	100	100	100	100

Standard errors are in parentheses and are adjusted for serial correlation, heteroscedasticity and dependence between observations of one PE firm.
* significant at 10%; *** significant at 5%; *** significant at 1%

Table D.12: OLS regression of IRR on intra-fund variation of IRR and shortfall probability

Subsample 2 consists of 100 PE funds. The dependent variable is IRR scaled as percentages. Independent variables include sd(Q-IRR), probability of loss, number of portfolio companies, diversification across time, diversification across financing stages, diversification across industries, diversification across countries, rate of return of the MSCI World Index in vintage year, new funds raised in vintage year, fund size, and firm experience. Additionally, the regressions contain dummy variables indicating funds managed by PE firms with headquarters in Europe and VC funds, as well as a constant. The table reports marginal effects and robust standard errors.

	Dependent variable: IRR			
	(1)	(2)	(3)	(4)
sd(Q-IRR)		4.146***		4.059***
		(0.676)		(0.718)
Probability of loss			-66.516***	-54.835***
			(23.030)	(15.577)
Number of portfolio companies	0.566*	0.717***	0.708**	0.831***
	(0.311)	(0.213)	(0.311)	(0.209)
Div. across time (months)	-0.854	0.155	-0.991	0.020
	(0.662)	(0.447)	(0.686)	(0.439)
Div. across financing stages	-28.489	-9.895	-13.595	1.991
	(17.120)	(12.002)	(16.856)	(12.757)
Div. across industries	22.742	14.163	14.673	7.692
	(18.999)	(12.808)	(20.005)	(13.618)
Div. across. countries	-20.525	-8.949	-19.203	-8.104
	(17.771)	(11.727)	(15.981)	(10.843)
Return msci in vy	-68.343**	-42.545**	-66.748**	-41.774**
	(26.331)	(19.124)	(25.143)	(16.640)
Funds raised in vy	7.710	6.608	14.692	12.387
(log bil. USD 2000)	(11.051)	(7.290)	(11.660)	(8.048)
Fund size (log mil. USD 2000)	-9.449***	-2.196	-9.577***	-2.454
	(3.209)	(2.715)	(3.157)	(2.781)
Firm experience	2.297	1.711	3.444	2.668
	(3.986)	(2.858)	(4.330)	(2.585)
European headquarter (0/1)	-11.149	-9.015	-10.115	-8.208
	(10.839)	(6.163)	(10.339)	(6.073)
VC fund (0/1)	-18.461	-11.350*	-9.450	-4.071
	(11.467)	(6.013)	(13.626)	(8.360)
Constant	96.172	2.688	86.781	-3.085
	(62.452)	(47.794)	(61.884)	(50.999)
Year F.E.	Yes	Yes	Yes	Yes
F-statistic	17.9	38.1	14.9	25.6
p-value of F-test	0.000	0.000	0.000	0.000
R^2	0.276	0.661	0.330	0.698
R^2-adjusted	0.115	0.580	0.171	0.621
Number of observations	100	100	100	100

Standard errors are in parentheses and are adjusted for serial correlation, heteroscedasticity and dependence between observations of one PE firm.
* significant at 10%; *** significant at 5%; *** significant at 1%

Table D.13: OLS regression of MIRR on intra-fund variation of MIRR and shortfall probability

Subsample 2 consists of 100 PE funds. The dependent variable is MIRR scaled as percentages. Independent variables include sd(Q-MIRR), probability of loss, number of portfolio companies, diversification across time, diversification across financing stages, diversification across industries, diversification across countries, rate of return of the MSCI World Index in vintage year, new funds raised in vintage year, fund size, and firm experience. Additionally, the regressions contain dummy variables indicating funds managed by PE firms with headquarters in Europe and VC funds, as well as a constant. The table reports marginal effects and robust standard errors.

	Dependent variable: MIRR			
	(1)	(2)	(3)	(4)
sd(Q-MIRR)		5.311***		5.458***
		(1.232)		(1.301)
Probability of loss			-17.989***	-19.247***
			(4.014)	(3.643)
Number of portfolio companies	0.166**	0.266***	0.204***	0.310***
	(0.070)	(0.062)	(0.065)	(0.056)
Div. across time (months)	-0.168	-0.046	-0.205	-0.083
	(0.129)	(0.115)	(0.131)	(0.102)
Div. across financing stages	-8.606**	-7.801**	-4.578	-3.469
	(3.619)	(3.080)	(3.954)	(2.863)
Div. across industries	4.282	3.262	2.099	0.899
	(3.541)	(2.765)	(2.969)	(2.664)
Div. across. countries	-1.512	-1.577	-1.155	-1.196
	(3.439)	(3.115)	(3.076)	(2.759)
Return msci in vy	-12.925**	-7.356	-12.494**	-6.741*
	(5.158)	(4.508)	(4.787)	(3.605)
Funds raised in vy	1.922	-0.350	3.810	1.607
(log bil. USD 2000)	(2.342)	(1.788)	(2.301)	(1.806)
Fund size (log mil. USD 2000)	-2.391***	-1.309*	-2.426***	-1.316**
	(0.661)	(0.711)	(0.684)	(0.637)
Firm experience	1.064	-0.289	1.375	0.006
	(0.900)	(0.983)	(0.827)	(0.690)
European headquarter (0/1)	-4.902***	-2.917	-4.623***	-2.563*
	(1.682)	(1.725)	(1.472)	(1.409)
VC fund (0/1)	-4.581**	-5.868***	-2.144	-3.296*
	(1.894)	(1.501)	(2.489)	(1.829)
Constant	29.974**	22.011**	27.434**	19.073*
	(12.172)	(10.289)	(11.993)	(10.385)
Year F.E.	Yes	Yes	Yes	Yes
F-statistic	19.8	20.5	13.0	76.2
p-value of F-test	0.000	0.000	0.000	0.000
R^2	0.396	0.599	0.473	0.687
R^2-adjusted	0.262	0.504	0.348	0.608
Number of observations	100	100	100	100

Standard errors are in parentheses and are adjusted for serial correlation, heteroscedasticity and dependence between observations of one PE firm.
* significant at 10%; *** significant at 5%; *** significant at 1%

Table D.14: OLS regression of PME on intra-fund variation of PME and shortfall probability

Subsample 2 consists of 100 PE funds. The dependent variable is PME. Independent variables include sd(Q-PME), probability of loss, number of portfolio companies, diversification across time, diversification across financing stages, diversification across industries, diversification across countries, rate of return of the MSCI World Index in vintage year, new funds raised in vintage year, fund size, and firm experience. Additionally, the regressions contain dummy variables indicating funds managed by PE firms with headquarters in Europe and VC funds, as well as a constant. The table reports marginal effects and robust standard errors.

	Dependent variable: PME			
	(1)	(2)	(3)	(4)
sd(Q-PME)		5.984***		5.713***
		(0.556)		(0.585)
Probability of loss			-5.241***	-2.794***
			(0.936)	(0.623)
Number of portfolio companies	0.050**	0.068***	0.061***	0.073***
	(0.021)	(0.011)	(0.019)	(0.009)
Div. across time (months)	-0.002	0.012	-0.013	0.006
	(0.039)	(0.015)	(0.038)	(0.013)
Div. across financing stages	-1.681**	-1.152**	-0.508	-0.551
	(0.777)	(0.478)	(0.865)	(0.390)
Div. across industries	1.997*	0.276	1.361	0.015
	(0.999)	(0.604)	(0.838)	(0.570)
Div. across. countries	-1.200	-0.773	-1.095	-0.737
	(1.047)	(0.562)	(0.813)	(0.482)
Return msci in vy	-4.257***	-2.141*	-4.131***	-2.170*
	(1.369)	(1.190)	(1.281)	(1.141)
Funds raised in vy (log bil. USD 2000)	0.355	0.025	0.905	0.333
	(0.680)	(0.285)	(0.650)	(0.293)
Fund size (log mil. USD 2000)	-0.691***	-0.308**	-0.702***	-0.331***
	(0.168)	(0.134)	(0.147)	(0.116)
Firm experience	0.431	0.223	0.521**	0.280*
	(0.270)	(0.190)	(0.240)	(0.152)
European headquarter (0/1)	-1.589***	-0.413	-1.508***	-0.422**
	(0.423)	(0.250)	(0.410)	(0.194)
VC fund (0/1)	-1.564**	-1.217***	-0.854	-0.854**
	(0.610)	(0.336)	(0.753)	(0.320)
Constant	4.620	1.975	3.880	1.700
	(3.945)	(1.774)	(3.823)	(1.879)
Year F.E.	Yes	Yes	Yes	Yes
F-statistic	25.5	64.2	80.3	117.9
p-value of F-test	0.000	0.000	0.000	0.000
R^2	0.417	0.844	0.491	0.864
R^2-adjusted	0.287	0.807	0.370	0.830
Number of observations	100	100	100	100

Standard errors are in parentheses and are adjusted for serial correlation, heteroscedasticity and dependence between observations of one PE firm.
* significant at 10%; *** significant at 5%; *** significant at 1%

FSC
www.fsc.org
MIX
Papier | Fördert gute Waldnutzung
FSC® C083411

Kolibri 360 GmbH
Ferdinand-Jühlke-Straße 7
99095 Erfurt, Deutschland
produktsicherheit@kolibri360.de